Introduction to
PUBLIC RELATIONS

Introduction to
PUBLIC RELATIONS

Edited by
Sue Wolstenholme

PEARSON

Harlow, England • London • New York • Boston • San Francisco • Toronto • Sydney • Auckland • Singapore • Hong Kong
Tokyo • Seoul • Taipei • New Delhi • Cape Town • São Paulo • Mexico City • Madrid • Amsterdam • Munich • Paris • Milan

PEARSON EDUCATION LIMITED
Edinburgh Gate
Harlow CM20 2JE
Tel: +44 (0)1279 623623
Website: www.pearson.com/uk

First published 2013 (print and electronic)

ISBN: 978-0-273-75098-7 (print)
         978-0-273-75099-4 (PDF)
         978-0-273-78114-1 (eText)

British Library Cataloguing-in-Publication Data
A catalogue record for the print edition is available from the British Library

Library of Congress Cataloging-in-Publication Data
Wolstenholme, Sue.
 Introduction to public relations / Sue Wolstenholme.
  p. cm.
 Includes bibliographical references and index.
 ISBN 978-0-273-75098-7 (print) — ISBN 978-0-273-75099-4
 (PDF) — ISBN 978-0-273-78114-1 (eText) 1. Public relations. I. Title.
 HD59.W557 2013
 659.2 — dc23

                               2012044296

10 9 8 7 6 5 4 3 2 1
16 15 14 13 12

Print edition typeset in 9/12 ITC Giovanni Std by 73
Printed and bound by L.E.G.O. S.p.A., Italy

NOTE THAT ANY PAGE CROSS-REFERENCES REFER TO THE PRINT EDITION

To Scarlett Eliza Abel

The mosaic in Hyde Park was chosen for the cover of this book because it represents a history of people trying to change things to improve their lives. Where public relations is practised there will almost certainly be changes made as a result. Where public relations is practised *professionally* the changes resulting will be better.

The words around the mosaic read:

This mosaic has been designed to commemorate 'reformers tree'. A venerable tree which was burnt down during the reform league riots in 1866. The remaining stump became a notice board for political demonstration and a gathering point for reform league meetings. A new oak tree was planted by the then Prime Minister James Callahan on 7 November 1977 on the spot where 'reformers tree' was thought to have stood.

Contents

Lecturer Resources

For password-protected online resources tailored to support the use of this textbook in teaching, please visit **www.pearsoned.co.uk/Wolstenholme**

Introduction

Where public relations is practised there will almost certainly be changes made as a result. Where public relations is practised *professionally* the changes resulting will be for the better.

This sounds like a sweeping statement and, in that it does not account for accidents and mistakes, it is.

This book has been written to introduce you to public relations as a subject for study and a profession in which to base a rewarding career, almost anywhere in the world.

There are a lot of questions within the book, to challenge you to think about what you have read as well as what you already know and are experiencing in life. It is intentionally done this way to prepare you for a profession which is extremely challenging and where you will have to be in the habit of questioning almost everything you see and hear.

Public relations is an international profession and there are several instances throughout this book, which indicate that the questions that need asking will often be the same in every country. But regardless as to how often they are asked, they always demand and deserve careful attention because the answers can be different in barely noticeable but vitally important ways. However academic the theories or straightforward the practical elements are, the authors of all the chapters have illustrated their ideas with examples from almost every century and a great many countries.

The first chapter defines the basic terms and sets the scene for the rest, with some history, some international comparisons, some differences from other communication disciplines and some theories, which are always needed to make sense of the practice. There is also a challenge to remind us that public relations is a powerful tool and it can be used for harm as well as for good. The chapter concludes with some extracts from Professor Noam Chomsky's work, in which he is highly critical of public relations practitioners.

In a Croatian and wider context and entirely relevant to the public relations world, the second chapter looks at the practice and the people doing it. Adding detail to the outlines in Chapter 1, the theories are set against the realities in diaries written by five different practitioners. The diaries will show you that the days are rarely alike and as there is so much that needs to be done, they are usually full and interesting. They will also make it clear that professional PR practitioners are working at a number of levels in a variety of settings to achieve often similar objectives.

Relationships are what public relations is really about. Chapter 3 examines why they need to be built and how they should be built to last, putting the term 'publics' forward as the key to understanding how these relationships differ from others in the communication world. The chapter explains how defining and knowing specific publics well forms the basis for issues management and corporate social responsibility.

Being professional is about knowing what you are doing and why you are likely to succeed and it is also, most importantly, about knowing how and why it matters to be ethical. Chapter 4 looks at how morals are formed and examines three Western and two Eastern philosophical schools. The way in which ethical theory can guide the public relations professional to improve their work and be more effective in relationships is explained.

Building on an introduction to it in Chapter 1, working internationally is considered in more detail in Chapter 5. Time, distance and culture are big challenges presented to the international practitioner and we are given a few theoretical foundations upon which to support a range of practical solutions.

The sixth chapter is about writing. The practitioners surveyed in the first chapter were unanimous about the prime importance of skilled writing and here the particular requirements of the news and social media are explained meticulously. The examples and exercises given will test and improve the diligent student.

Chapter 7 moves us to South Africa to present the meat and drink of public relations practice: the well-planned and carefully executed campaign. The importance of clearly defined objectives is illustrated through theoretical approaches to communication and stimulating practical examples.

In Chapter 8, crisis management is discussed as the threat and opportunity that it poses to reputation. The theories behind the threats and opportunities inform the need for careful planning and case studies illustrate its value.

Chapter 9 draws on research done for the Swedish Public Relations Association, to look ahead to developments to improve public relations practice and consider new approaches to the profession. This work on value networks was part of the inspiration for the worldwide research that became the Stockholm Accords, which are discussed in this final chapter. Creating a platform from which to promote the value of professionally practised public relations, the Global Alliance have started a piece of work which they hope will be augmented by the readers of this book.

Reading this book might be part of a career development for you or the beginning of a new adventure, but if you are setting forth into the public relations profession it should definitely not be the last book you read. You might be studying for a CIPR award or already involved in an undergraduate degree programme at university. Either way, this is the first step on a tall and exciting ladder that can take you to the top, as a professional practitioner, to Chartered status or as an academic to a PhD, or both and beyond!

About the authors

Sven Hamrefors

Sven is professor in innovation, communication and business creation at Mälardalen University, Sweden. He is also director of various executive education programmes, such as Communication Executives Program. For the last 20 years Sven has been a frequent lecturer in Business Intelligence, Communication, Innovation and Corporate Entrepreneurship at various conferences and seminars. He has also been working with information services, communication, business creation and business intelligence in various organisations for more than 30 years.

Kristina Laco

Kristina is the CEO of Digitel Komunikacije, which is the leading and largest group in integrated market communications in Croatia, employing more than 200 highly experienced and qualified professionals. The group provides strategic consulting and full operative support in all communications areas. Before taking the reins at the top of the group Kristina was the general manager of one of its subsidiaries, Premisa.

Premisa is Croatia's largest company specialising in public relations, in terms of its turnover and team size. From its inception, the agency has been working for numerous leading domestic and international companies, providing them with a full range of PR services. Kristina has the CIPR Diploma and teaching qualification and she led the establishment of Croatia's professional development centre, offering the full range of the CIPR's qualifications.

Eva Maclaine

Eva is the Principal at Maclaine Communications where she develops and implements strategic communications programmes, designed not simply to inform but to communicate and/or change behaviour.

She has worked in a large variety of industries and her experience includes advice to blue-chip UK clients such as Transport for London, London Underground, Pilkington, Shanks & McEwan, the London Borough of Newham, Haringey Primary Care Trust and LondonWaste.

Overseas assignments encompass work for Ogilvy & Mather, the Polish State Forests and the Samoan Water Authority; she has worked at senior government level on a number of EU projects.

Eva is skilled at incorporating complex issues – sometimes at extremely short notice – and making them relevant within the broad communications campaign.

A Fellow of the Chartered Institute of Public Relations, Eva is currently helping to develop CIPR International, its international member group, and has judged the Global sector of CIPR's Excellence Awards. She has the CAM Diploma and a BA (Hons) in Russian, French and Philosophy.

Toni Muzi Falconi

Toni, Italian, is a seasoned professional public relator, as well as scholar and teacher. More recently, he has been teaching global relations and intercultural communication as well as public affairs and issue management at NYU's Master of Science in Public Relations and Corporate Communication.

He also teaches public relations at LUMSA University in Rome.

He is senior counsel of Methodos, an Italian management consultancy, and past president of Ferpi (the Italian professional association). Toni was the founding chair of the Global Alliance (GA) and more recently the coordinator of the GA's Stockholm Accords achievement.

Paul Noble

Paul is an independent public relations trainer, consultant, academic, mentor and speaker/facilitator. He is a CIPR-approved trainer and an e-learning specialist and provides management support to growing PR consultancies, as well as mentoring young professionals. He has more than 30 years' experience in senior consultancy, in-house and academic environments.

Paul is Chief Examiner of the CIPR's Advanced Certificate and one of the examiners of the Diploma. He is a Fellow of both the CIPR and AMEC, and is a CIPR Chartered Practitioner – as well as an assessor for the scheme. Paul is co-author of *Evaluating Public Relations* (3rd edition to be published in 2013).

Ronél Rensburg, D. Litt. et Phil., CPRP

Ronél is a professor in the Communication Management Division and a founding member of the Centre for Communication and Reputation Management at the University of Pretoria. She had been the Head of the Department of Marketing and Communication Management at the University of Pretoria from 2000 to 2008 and Acting Dean of the Faculty of Economic and Management Sciences and the Chairperson of the School of Management Sciences in the Faculty of Economic and Management Sciences between 2003 and 2007. She is a member of Euprera (the European Public Relations Education and Research Association), immediate Past-President of PRISA (Public Relations Institute of Southern Africa), and a board member of the Global Alliance for Associations of Public Relations and Communication Management. She is also a member of the International Communication Association (ICA), and a member of the Eurasian Communication Association (ECA). Her current areas of research are the role of reputation management, managing country reputation, and the role of sustainable communication. She has a specific interest in serving the SADC region of Africa where public relations theory, research and practice are concerned. Ronél Rensburg provides social commentary for business and the financial media on current issues pertaining to reputation.

Sue Wolstenholme

Sue is a Chartered Public Relations Practitioner and runs a full service consultancy, Ashley Public Relations, with an event management subsidiary, which is led by Simon Abel. She has an MSc in Public Relations and has supervised PhDs on the subject for the University of Exeter.

Sue has worked as a public relations consultant for Amnesty International (relaunching the Secret Policeman's Ball and running a campaign to highlight injustice), Survival International (national membership campaign), the Rural Development Commission, the Child Accident Prevention Trust and British Telecom (reviewing their sponsorship strategy). She worked as the director of communication for the Royal Cornwall Hospitals NHS Trust for nine years and was retained by the South West Peninsula Health Authority to devise and lead their communication strategy. She was appointed to be an Associate of the Post Office nationally to advise on corporate social responsibility issues for six years.

From 1994 to 2010, Sue led the European Public Relations Research and Education Association's (Euprera) juries to find the best thesis and practical project on the subject in Europe. She was elected to be President for 2008 and 2009, of Euprera, which now has members from 35 countries, including New Zealand, the USA, South Africa, Australia, Canada, UAE and Syria.

In 2005 Sue worked with the public relations research institute of the Islamic Republic of Iran to define the role of public opinion in a democracy. The outcome of the work became the Tehran Declaration.

Recently she has been working to raise professional standards for senior PR practitioners in China, Kenya, Armenia, Qatar, Kazakhstan, the UAE, Syria, Switzerland, Egypt, Serbia, Romania and the UK. She has also been commissioned to present papers at a number of conferences for practitioners including at national events in Ukraine, Nigeria, Sweden, Norway and Denmark.

She devised and leads a course for chief executives called the Certificate of Leadership for Reputation, which has been running successfully for principals with the Association of Colleges and the CIPR for over five years. Sue has a number of publi cations in her name and was made a fellow of the Chartered Institute of Public Relations in 1998 for services towards developing the profession. She has also established the Cornish Crisp Company Ltd, which is promoted using public relations principles.

Sue is the chair of the Hall for Cornwall board of trustees and a member of the board of the Syrian International Academy. She was recently made a Fellow of the Nigerian Institute of Public Relations and elected to become the President of the CIPR, in the UK, in 2013.

Acknowledgements

We are grateful to the following for permission to reproduce copyright material:

Figures

Three figures on page 23, two figures on page 24 and figure on page 25 from www.internetworldstats.com, Copyright © 2000–2012, Miniwatts Marketing Group. All rights reserved; Figure 1.1 adapted from *Communication Models for the Study of Mass Communications*, 2nd ed., McQuail, D. and Windhal, S., Pearson Education Limited © Pearson Education Limited 1993 and with kind permission of Denis McQuail and Sven Windhal; Figure 1.2 adapted from 'Mass communication and the social system' by Riley, J.W Jr. and Riley, M. in, *Sociology Today: Problems and Prospects*, pp. 569–578 (Merton, R.K. (ed.) 1959), New York: Basic Books, Copyright © 1959 Richard K. Merton. Reprinted by permission of Basic Books, a member of the Perseus Book Group; Figure 1.3 adapted from *Communication Models for the Study of Mass Communications*, 2nd ed., McQuail, D. and Windhal, S., Pearson Education Limited © Pearson Education LImited 1993 and with kind permission of Denis McQuail and Sven Windhal; Figure 1.4 adapted with the permission of Free Press, a Division of Simon & Schuster, Inc., from COMMUNICATION NETWORKS: Toward a New Paradigm for Research by Everett M. Rogers and D. Lawrence Kincaid. Copyright © 1981 by The Free Press. All rights reserved; Figure 1.5 from DIALOGUE AND THE ART OF THINKING TOGETHER by William Isaacs, copyright © 1999 by William Isaacs. Used by permission of Doubleday, a division of Random House, Inc.; Figure 4.2 adapted from *Companies in Community: Getting the Community Investment Measure*, The London Benchmarking Group (Logan, D. 1997) p. 6, Corporate Citizen International, www.lbg-online.net; Figure 4.4 from *Ethical Consumerism Research*, Ipsos MORI, http://www.ipsos-mori.com/researchpublications/researcharchive/1496/Ethical-Consumerism-Research.aspx; Figure 4.5 from WHO (2012). *Tobacco*. Geneva, World Health Organization (Fact Sheet no. 339; www.who.int/mediacentre/factsheets/fs339/en/, accessed 2 September 2012); Figure 5.3 reproduced from *PRWeek* magazine with the permission of the copyright owner, Haymarket Business Publications Limited; Figure 5.5 from Geert Hofstede, Gert Jan Hofstede, Michael Minkov, "Cultures and Organizations, Software of the Mind", Third Revised Edition, McGrawHill 2010, ISBN 0-07-166418-1. © Geert Hofstede B.V. quoted with permission; Figure 6.4 from http://www.shiftcomm.com/downloads/smr_v1.5.pdf; Figures 8.1, 8.2, and 8.3 from *Annual ICM Crisis Report* Vol. 21 No.1, May, pp. 2–3 (Institute for Crisis Management 2011).

Logos

Logo on page 83 from The First International Symposium on Research and Public Opinion Studies in Public Relations, 2005, Arman Public Relations Institute (translated from Farsi by Amir Rastegar, Director of International Affairs); Logo on page 96 from http://www.thecornishcrisp.co.uk/

Tables

Table 1.2 adapted from *Exploring Public Relations*, Tench, R. and Yeomans, L., p. 568, Pearson Education Limited, © Pearson Education Limited 2009; Table 1.3 adapted from *Managing Public Relations*, Holt, Rinehart and Winston (Grunig, J. and Hunt, T. 1984) p. 22; Table 1.5 from www.internetworldstats.com, Copyright © 2001–2012, Miniwatts Marketing Group. All rights reserved; Table on page 40 from *The Public Relations Handbook*, Routledge (Theaker, A. 2004) p. 7 (Chapter: What is Public Relations by J. Fawkes); Table 4.2 after www.lbg-online.net, Corporate Citizen International; Table 4.3 from WHO (2008). *Tobacco Industry Interference with Tobacco Control*, Geneva, World Health Organization (Table 2: Tobacco industry tactics for resisting effective tobacco control, pp. 12–13, ISBN 978 924 159734 0, http://www.who.int/tobacco/resources/publications/Tobacco%20Industry%20Interference-FINAL.pdf; accessed 5 November 2012); Table on p. 119 REPRINTED from Annual Corruption Perceptions Index 2011, http://cpi.transparency.org/cpi2011/results. Copyright 2011 Transparency International: the global coalition against corruption. Used with permission. For more information, visit http://www.transparency.org. Table 8.1 from *Annual ICM Crisis Report* Vol. 21 No.1, May, p. 2 (Institute for Crisis Management 2011)

Text

Extracts on pp. 25–28 Noam Chomsky, excerpts from Media Control: The Spectacular Achievements of Propaganda, Second Edition. Copyright © 1991, 1997, 2002 by Noam Chomsky. Reprinted with permission of The Permissions Company, Inc., on behalf of Seven Stories Press, www.sevenstories.com; Case Study on pages 33–7 from Marina Dijaković. Director of Corporate Identity and Communications, Zagrebačka Banka d.d; Case Study on pp. 43–5 from Ben Verinder; Case Study on pages 45–6 from Ahmad Odeh, General Manager, Turjuman Consultancy; Case Study on pages 46–9 from Frank Tamuno-Koko, PR Consultant; Extract on page 69 from *Supply Chain Social Responsibility: Our supply chain principles* (IBM) Introduction, http://www-03.ibm.com/procurement/proWeb.nsf/ContentDocsByTitle/United+States~Supply+chain+social+responsibility, Reprint Courtesy of International Business Machines Corporation, © International Business Machines Corporation; Extract on pages 75–6 from Chartered Institute of Public Relations Code of Conduct, http://www.cipr.co.uk/sites/default/files/CIPR%20Code%20of%20Conduct%2029-06-2011.pdf; Extract on pages 83–4 from The First International Symposium on Research and Public Opinion Studies in Public Relations, 2005, Arman Public Relations Institute (translated from Farsi by Amir Rastegar, Director of International Affairs); Case Study on pages 94–5 from *Ethical Consumerism Research*, Ipsos MORI, http://www.ipsos-mori.com/researchpublications/researcharchive/1496/Ethical-Consumerism-Research.aspx; Extract on pages 98–9 from *A Question of Ethics* (Adrian Wheeler, Chair of the CIPR's Professional Practices Committee), http://www.cipr.co.uk/content/news-opinion/features/industry-issues/4949/a-question-of-ethics; Case Study on pages 105–6 from Kateryna Zasoukha, Head of Communications, JTI Company Ukraine; Case Study on pages 106–8 from Katarzyna Gontarczyk; Case Study on pages 130–1 from Christopher Flores, Senior Communication Consultant, Brussels, Belgium; Case Study on page 135 from 'Marks & Spencer announces details of Chairman role', http://corporate.marksandspencer.com/media/press_releases/marks_and_spencer_announced_details_of_chairman_role; Case Study on page 137 from 'Major breakthrough in investment casting optimises the manufacturing of high performance parts', Oct 21, 2009, http://www.morgantechnicalceramics.com/news_events/news/major-breakthrough-in-investment-casting-optimises-the-manufacturing-of-high-performance-parts/, Copyright of Morgan Technical Ceramics Ltd; Case Study on page 150 adapted from observations made by Neal Butterworth in conversation with the author; Extracts on pages 159–72 from *Public Relations: African Perspectives*, 2nd ed., Heinemann Publishers (Pty) Ltd, 2009 (Rensburg, R.S. and Kant, M.C. 2009) pp. 196–205, 207, 208–210, 0796223521/9780796223524; Case Study on pages 172–4 from *Evolution of Public Relations; Case Studies of Countries in Transition*, 2nd ed., Institute for Public Relations (Odedele, S. 2008); Case Study on page 186 from http://www.london-fire.gov.uk/news/959D0744117C4DDC9D4FCD43F25A9849_PR2931.asp, Strictly the quietest Bonfire Night on record, say firefighters, 26 December 2011, London Fire Brigade.

Photographs

(Key: b-bottom; c-centre; l-left; r-right; t-top)
Alamy Images: Chris Harris 197, Photofusion Picture Library 60; Corbis: John Van Hasselt 25; Corporate Citizenship: 90; Fotolia.com: cool chap 147, jhamlon 63; Getty Images: 146, AFP / © 2010 Tunisia Presidency 66, Bryn Colton 188; John Foxx Images: 61; Mary Evans Picture Library: 100; Press Association Images: Rob Pinney / Demotix 3; Reuters: Brendan McDermid 187; Rex Features: David Hartley 199, London News Pictures 196; Sozaijiten: 68; TopFoto: Chris Wood / Fast News Pix 185; Sue Wolstenholme: 180

In some instances we have been unable to trace the owners of copyright material, and we would appreciate any information that would enable us to do so.

Part 1
What is public relations?

Chapter 1
What public relations is and what it is not

Sue Wolstenholme

Learning outcomes

By the end of this chapter you should be able to:

- Explain what public relations is and how it differs from other communication disciplines
- Understand some of the skills and attributes needed by a public relations practitioner
- Know some basic communication theories, based upon models
- Know how to recognise a professional practitioner
- Understand some of the issues you need to consider when working internationally
- Understand how public relations can be used against the public interest

Introduction

PR should not be seen to be done – so how can it be recognised?

As this is an introductory book there will be some definitions as well as a consideration of the roles played by public relations people. (The roles are covered in detail in Chapter 2 and explored further for the future in Chapter 9.) A short quiz will help you to see what public relations is often mistaken for and a discussion about who is best suited to the profession will show you what skills and knowledge you might need. This is reinforced by reflections on PR education and professional development within the practice. Some theories about communication and dialogue are explained along with thoughts on women.

As public relations is widely practised it can be referred to as a trade or an industry and in this chapter it is explored to consider if it can be thought of as a profession. When it is practised in other countries these are a number of questions given here, which need to be asked.

The chapter ends with some words by Noam Chomsky, with his kind permission. As an often harsh critic of public relations, Professor Chomsky illustrates ways in which it has been used to further the ends of a few, regardless of the needs of the many. This theme will appear in other parts of the book, especially in the chapter on ethics.

Change is at the heart of most public relations objectives. They exist to change behaviour, ideas, perceptions and fortunes and to raise awareness of the need for change. Knowing how to carry out the necessary plans of action requires a lot of theoretical knowledge and practical skills.

Mini case study

Are you a troublemaker?
Source: Rob Pinney/Demotix/PA Photos

When interviewing would-be students for the BA honours in public relations, awarded by Exeter University and taught at the College of St Mark and St John in Plymouth, the author used to ask them if they were troublemakers. They always denied it, wanting to appear to be well behaved, of course, but when probed further and asked if they'd never complained about anything in writing or taken goods back to a shop because they were faulty, gone on a protest march or mounted a small campaign against some perceived injustice, or gone that bit further than others in support of something, some of them smiled knowingly. One girl quietly confessed to having led all the newspaper boys and girls in Manchester out on strike because they had asked for reflective armbands to keep them safer in the dark early mornings and had been refused. She was offered an unconditional place on the course because she was already in the right mind for the subject. If a person always walks past or just doesn't see something that needs to be dealt with, they will probably not be well suited to working in public relations. That girl was prepared to make a stand for change and it is fairly certain that whatever she is doing now she will be making a difference.

When it is often your boss or client that you need to stand up against for the sake of his or her reputation, you will need to be sure of the need for change.

DEFINITIONS

Public relations is often confused with other communication-based disciplines, such as marketing, advertising, publicity and propaganda, and it is also often misunderstood and misused. As well as being a powerful force for positive change, the opposite can also be true and the term PR can, sometimes justifiably, be used to describe actions that have been carried out to manipulate or mislead. It is the tools and the skills to use them that make it powerful. The way that the tools and skills are employed and the purpose to which they are put, or the ends to their means, indicates whether their use is ethical or otherwise. There will be further references to ethics throughout this book and in Chapter 4 because having the inclination to analyse the morality of the motives as well as the methods to meet them, will make the difference between professional public relations practice and what is far too often referred to as 'PR exercise'.

In looking for definitions, the clue is clearly in the name. The practice of public relations is about building relationships with publics. Organisations and individuals are dependent upon healthy working relationships to allow them to exist and to enable them to function properly. Within relationships, whether formal or informal, mutual understanding can be built, and only thereafter does trust develop. It is only upon a foundation of trust that a good reputation can flourish and be maintained to last through the good times as well as those that might present difficulties or challenges.

There are, most probably, as many definitions of public relations as there are people purporting to be doing it and as many again for those who encounter or write about those doing it. So rather than add to the pile this chapter will examine some of those in common use as well as some of the other names given to the practice.

The founder of the *Public Relations Journal* in the US in 1945, Dr Rex Harlow, was much later commissioned to research definitions and crystallise them into one. He found 472 definitions, which he summarised in 'Building a public relations definition' for the 1976 winter issue of *Public Relations Review* as follows:

> Public Relations is a distinctive management function, which helps establish and maintain mutual lines of communication, understanding, acceptance and cooperation between an organization and its publics; involves the management of problems or issues; helps management to keep informed on and responsive to public opinion; defines and emphasizes the responsibility of management to serve the public interest; helps management keep abreast of and effectively utilize change, serving as an early warning system to help anticipate trends; and uses research and sound ethical communication as its principal tools (Harlow in Black 1989: 4).

While this might cover most aspects of the role it is not succinct. James Grunig chose to summarise by saying that all public relations activities are part of 'the management of communication between an organization and its publics' (Grunig and Hunt 1984: 6). This editing is too severe to explain well enough what the profession is about. Many practitioners work under the job title of communication director, manager or officer but they are called upon to do a lot more than their title might suggest. (In fact, in most cases they are known as communications people, which implies that they are responsible for the telephone and IT systems as well, which can be confusing.) It is also likely that their titles and the often preferred name of communication science, for the study which encompasses public relations, have come about because public relations has become associated with the more negative uses of the skills and knowledge and therefore people feel more comfortable with the 'safer' term of communication or even communications. It is strange as the term 'communication' does not communicate all that public relations is about! Meaning needs to be understood for communication to succeed.

Red flags do not always mean danger. Here they mean lobster pots!
Source: picture by Rowan Abel

As John Peters said in his study on communication, *Speaking into the Air*, 'Too often, "communication" misleads us from the task of building worlds together. It invites us into a world of unions without politics, understandings without language and souls without bodies, only to make politics, language and bodies reappear as obstacles' (Peters 1999: 30)

To emphasise the part which Grunig's short definition omits, Inger Jensen (1997) advises us that relating means understanding what is happening when people are not necessarily in communication.

The Institute of Public Relations (now the Chartered Institute of Public Relations or CIPR) was established in Britain in 1948 and since then it has evolved its definition of the practice from

> Public relations practice is the planned and sustained effort to establish and maintain goodwill and mutual understanding between an organisation and its publics.

to

> Public relations is the discipline which looks after reputation, with the aim of earning understanding and support and influencing opinion and behaviour. It is the planned and sustained effort to establish and maintain goodwill and mutual understanding between and organisation and its publics.

And for the sake of brevity (and maybe for use on T-shirts) it is shortened to:

> Public relations is about reputation: the result of what you do, what you say and what others say about you.

This last one does not define so much as outline but at least it does include far more possibilities than Grunig's reduction. Grunig's concentration upon communication is limiting and his use of the word 'management' also constrains the function. Until recently the CIPR defined the practice as managing reputation, rather than the new version, which describes it as 'looking after'. This subtle word change moves the emphasis from one of control to a more nurturing role, which alters the perspective of the practitioner considerably.

Research by Dejan Verčič in 2000 showed that reputation is definitely affected by bad behaviour and low morale amongst staff but that it is little or not at all affected by business-as-usual or good-news stories, which many people in public relations spend a great deal of their time writing. His work showed that the role should encompass a number of functions including advising those within organisations whose behaviour could affect their reputation, leading internal communication and working closely with human resources managers to guide issues affecting staff morale and understanding the relationships most needed to influence the success of the organisation.

As reputation is built upon good working relationships it is salutary to note that this research found most relationships are built and developed with those who have little or no consequence. Building relationships with those who already like you is far easier than taking the time and considerably extra effort to develop an understanding for a relationship with a pressure group, which is always attacking your organisation or a tweeter or blogger who has nothing but derision to pour upon your name. However, if some mutual ground can be built between you and your enemies the peace can lead to positive consequences.

Looking closely at what public relations does in 1994, Cutlip could be summarised as defining the practice as one which strives to turn ignorance into knowledge and prejudice into understanding, which requires the taking of well-planned steps into enemy or opposition territory to listen carefully to their point of view, as that is the basis of mutual understanding.

That sounds highly laudable and if things were always done in accordance with worldwide PR associations' codes of conduct it would fit well. (Please see Chapter 4 as well as Chapter 9 on the Stockholm Accords). However, as Heath (2001) described so clearly, public relations can be 'truth seeking and engaging in the refinement of knowledge' at one end and 'manipulative and facile impression management' at the other with 'easily imagined descriptions of misleading and downright dishonesty to take the continuum even further into the darkness'.

Public relations exists because organisations, whether commercial, public or charitable, can only survive if they are acceptable to the public, and public acceptance can only survive if it is informed: in other words, there must be communication.

As a percentage of practitioners internationally, only a tiny handful belong to professional bodies and are thereby required to adhere to a formal code of conduct. It is an exception to the rule for a country to require professional body membership to be allowed to practise legally, as in Nigeria, where the government sees professional PR as a way to overcome corruption. Elsewhere, it could be that the many are getting a bad name for the few, but as the saying goes, 'the shoemaker's children run barefoot', so, all too often, do public relations practitioners not practise what they are encouraged to preach. (This metaphor is used again in Chapter 9 for a much earlier connection for PR with cobblers.)

ROLES

With organisations being regarded increasingly, both in society and in law, as individuals with all the attendant responsibilities, there are a number of frequently used and hotly disputed terms to describe the public relations function which is carried out on their behalf or at their behest. (See Chapter 2 for more detail about what practitioners do and Chapter 9 for thoughts on what they should be evolving to do.)

Some of the terms are:

Advocate – in the court of public opinion everyone deserves representation

Gatekeeper – only those views should be allowed out or those enquiries allowed in which cannot harm reputation

Tailor or even beautician – it is always necessary to be shown to look one's best regardless of how one feels or behaves

Conscience – publics deserve to be well treated and relationships will endure far more deeply when they are looked after openly and honestly

Question

Think about the above roles in relation to the definitions given and your own perception of public relations practice. Which one fits best and why, and which one would you prefer to be responsible for undertaking?

It is sometimes easier to understand what something is by being clearer about what it is not – here is a quiz that might help with that approach.

Quiz

What is being practised when the following are occurring?

1. Space is paid for, in print, on billboards, on television, on the internet or on radio, to present a persuasive message.
2. Messages are designed and delivered to engender particular beliefs, which can be religious, political or otherwise, to persuade an unquestioning following of those beliefs.
3. A campaign is designed and presented, following research of the target audience, to win favour or sales for an idea or product.
4. Items are engendered in the news media, which serve to enhance the status of either an individual or an organisation with a particular audience, such as 'A politician visited a hospital for sick children today' or 'A famous celebrity was asked to leave a restaurant in London last night, for refusing to wear a tie'.
5. A commercial organisation's name is displayed in public because it has given help, financial or in kind, to something that has nothing to do directly with the execution of its business.
6. Elected representatives in local, national or European government are asked, on behalf of an organisation or individual, to present a case or a set of facts to influence the outcome of a debate that could lead to legislation.
7. A campaign is launched to persuade young people that they should not start smoking cigarettes.
8. An organisation consults its employees, customers, suppliers, neighbours and shareholders about the best way forward for all concerned.

Answers are at the end of the chapter.

Task

Find an example for each of the above in a range of print, broadcast and online media. Are they exclusive to one approach or do they use a combination of disciplines?

The most commonly confused communication-based disciplines are probably marketing and public relations. Inger Jensen (2001) said of marketing, as compared with public relations, that there are 'No collective or social solutions in marketing only individual action'.

Another way of differentiating between the practices mentioned in the quiz could be to consider those with whom they are communicating or the receivers and the specific terms used to describe them and how are they communicated with (see Table 1.1).

TABLE 1.1 Defining the practices, purposes and styles

Practice	Receivers	How	Why
Advertising	Target audience	One-way	Generate sales or specific actions
Propaganda	Target audience	One-way	Generate beliefs, following of or adherence to ideas
Marketing	Target audience	One-way	Generate sales or specific actions
Publicity	Target audience	One-way	Raise awareness and/or favourability for issues, celebrities, etc.
Sponsorship	Target audience	One-way	Build a bond or favourability through association
Lobbying	Decision or law makers	One-way	Generate political support for funding or a cause, encourage the passing of a law or prevent one from being passed
Social marketing	Target audience	One-way	Generate attention to change behaviour
Public relations	Publics	Two-way	Build mutual understanding for relationships, trust and reputation

SOCIAL MARKETING

It is important to consider social marketing further as it has some similarities to parts of public relations and it might be thought to be more attractive as it is not, as yet, linked to some of the negative issues with which PR has been associated. It could be that it also does not have the power and therefore is less of a threat.

If you consider the MacFadyen et al.'s 1999 definition, there is little difference in the approach, in that they both involve the building of relationships. They say that consumer orientation is probably the key element and that the consumer is assumed to be an active participant in the change process. The social marketer, like the PR practitioner, seeks to build a relationship with target consumers over time.

However, Andraeson more closely shows the way that the fairly new discipline has grown out of marketing: 'social marketing is the application of commercial marketing techniques to the analysis, planning, execution and evaluation of programs designed to influence the voluntary behavior of target audiences in order to improve their personal welfare and that of society' (1995: 7).

This definition sounds quite controlling or even coercive and could equally be applied to propaganda. It is very different from the ambition for mutuality that can be a central feature of public relations but it is close to the manipulative aspects of PR as described by Heath above and by Chomsky below.

This approach is also very much at the heart of the even newer concept of nudge – the book of the same name (Thaler and Sunstein 2008) is subtitled 'the gentle power of choice architecture' and it is described as improving decisions about health, wealth and happiness. Using 'nudges' instead of notices or instructions, the authors describe how large numbers of people can be coerced into choosing to change their behaviours. One of the examples given is of the men's toilets at Amsterdam airport, where, instead of signs requesting that the men take care when using the urinals a fly has been painted on the inside of the bowl. It seems that, rather than not concentrating and thereby making a mess, the men aim at the fly and all is well, as they have been nudged so to do (Kirk 2010).

TABLE 1.2 Examples showing the different applications of commercial and social marketing

Commercial marketing	Social marketing	Example of social marketing
Targets most accessible part of the market (e.g. people with high disposable incomes)	Often targets hard-to-reach segments or publics	Young people 'at risk' of drug abuse
Competitive environment	Environment is less competitive (sometimes only one service provider)	Public library service provided by local council
Service or products are paid for	Services or products are often free	New state benefit
Seeks to meet consumer needs and wants	Powerful interest groups are often challenged	Advertising industry (e.g. in targeting young children with fast-food advertising)
Creates demand for a service or product	Balances demand with resource availability	Encourages pharmacy visits for common ailments to reduce demands on the local GP (doctors') surgery
Product or behaviour promoted is desired or wanted by the customer	Product or service promoted is not desired by the receiver	Sticking to a low-fat diet

Source: adapted from *Exploring Public Relations*, Tench, R. and Yeomans, L., Pearson Education Limited © Pearson Education Limited 2009 p. 586

Have a look at Table 1.2 and consider whether social marketing offers anything more, by using marketing techniques, which public relations cannot improve upon by using the relationship building approach.

The following saying has been used in a number of informal contexts and styles and it fits here as a description for public relations (and maybe for social marketing or nudging): 'It is not easy when dealing with publics who will believe that there are millions of stars in the universe and beyond but will touch a door with a wet paint sign beside it to check.' Public relations has to be ready to provide a number of opportunities for 'checking' to take place and every available appropriate channel has to be used, from meetings to social media, through which exchanges and discussions can be held to allow and encourage the most thorough checking.

Who should be in public relations and what knowledge and skills are needed?

(There is more in Chapters 2 and 9).

In the UK there is an informal club of Leos that was created by a number of PR practitioners who believed that, as all of them were born under the astrological sign of Leo, that it must be a good sign for the practice. Of course they are probably not serious about the astrology but they are using an excuse for building a network and coming together, as a group, once a year to keep the network alive because networking is definitely good for practitioners. As far as their characteristics are concerned, they are listed below. What do you think?

The Leo type is said to be the most dominant, spontaneously creative and extrovert of all the zodiacal characters. In grandeur of manner, splendour of bearing and magnanimity of personality, they are the monarchs among humans as the lion is king of beasts. They are ambitious, courageous, dominant, strong-willed, positive, independent and self-confident; there is no such word as 'doubt' in their vocabularies, and they are self-controlled. They are born leaders, either in support of, or in revolt against, the *status quo* (www.astrology-online.com/leo.htm).

Astrology probably is not the best way of creating networks. Relationships can be built with those needed for a particular purpose through those already known, and so networking sites such as LinkedIn, Facebook, Twitter, Myspace, Ning, Tagged, Bebo, Google+ etc. are flourishing in the internet and are much used by PR practitioners.

Lord Sieff, the one-time chairman of Marks and Spencer plc, who started his working life on the shop floor, expressed the view that every single member of his staff was in public relations because they know the company and communicate about it through all of their relationships (see Chapter 9 on value networks). With that in mind he created one of the best staff training and support systems in retail, to be sure that his team thought well and spoke informatively about the company (Sieff 1990).

Relationships and reputations exist whether or not someone is paid to build, shape or help them along. The big differences come when courageous leaders are prepared to be advised by public relations professionals, who know how to research, to listen to publics and discover the soundest way to build mutual understanding. They will not usefully change for the long term, however, when PR people are hired who are just prepared to do what they are told, to try and make the organisation look good on the surface, rather than responding to publics' needs and recommending possibly deep rooted changes, to the organisation, as necessary. These might, for example, be changes in the way they manage their waste, to help them to be more environmental, or in the way that staff are treated, so that they can be seen to be better employers.

Question

Can you think of some changes that PR people could recommend that would improve an organisation's reputation?

In the second issue of *Public Relations*, the journal of the then recently formed Institute of Public Relations (IPR) in the UK, Dick (R.S.) Forman wrote: 'PR was more professional whereas advertising was frankly, more commercial … the PRO as a professional man, would not allow his client to call the tune but would offer his professional advice on policy, which the client could accept or reject. The advertising man, on the other hand, usually accepted his clients' views and did his best to give effect to them, even if he disagreed with them' (1949: 11, quoted in L'Etang 2004: 102).

Despite the gender bias in the quote, it is certain that there were women working in PR and advertising then but perhaps not very noticeably and it must also be pointed out that an institute is bound to present its members' work to be of higher moral worth than that done by rival practices. The first issue of the journal carried an article by W. J. S. Seymour in which he stated that 'one belief we hold in common – that the proper practice of public relations is of unassessable importance to the future of the world' (1948: 1, quoted in L'Etang 2004: 68).

In 2001 a Delphi study[1] was undertaken to understand the parameters of public relations, with a particular emphasis on developing the European body of knowledge.

Across Europe, in 2003, the study asked in 29 countries for descriptions of theory and practice, and the conclusion of the study was: 'none of the professionalism theories were taken seriously.… Modern expertise theory shows that for simple problems, experience is enough, for complex problems one needs both emotional and rational intelligence.' (This study is referred to again when discussing the concepts behind PR in Chapter 3.)

It would seem that little had actually developed in the thinking of leading practitioners as far as professional development is concerned since the mid-1990s, but national and international associations are leading the way in terms of developing qualifications and the profession to increase our ability to deal with complex problems. (See Chapter 9 for details of efforts by the Global Alliance for Public Relations and Communication Management.)

In 1999, the IPR began to only admit new members with approved qualifications in public relations or over ten years' experience. This move was made to improve standards of work and

---

[1]A Delphi study is a structured process for collecting and distilling knowledge from a group of experts by way of a series of questionnaires, which are developed over a period of time with feedback.

to qualify for Chartered status. Chartered status is what is awarded to a professional body in the UK, after some years as the main group representing a profession. To qualify the group must indicate a proven commitment to professional quality, through a rigorously applied code of conduct, an established set of qualifications and a system for continuous professional development (CPD). The Royal Charter was granted to the institute in 2004 and to individual members, who pass the entry criteria, in 2009. CIPR members can now earn the right to be more highly regarded as professionals. In 2011, the membership criteria were relaxed to include practitioners from a wider range of backgrounds. As the qualifications were then well established and all members would be expected to follow CPD, it was felt that the institute needed to open its doors more widely to encourage more practitioners to work towards the development of a profession.

COMMUNICATION

While in itself it is not everything in public relations, communication is a large part of what the practitioner does. As Denis McQuail wrote in 2001, 'The most fundamental questions of society – those concerning the distribution and exercise of power, the management of problems and the processes of integration and change – all turn on communication.'

Communication is defined in the *Oxford English Dictionary* as: 'making common; imparting information'. George Gerbner (1967) referred to communication as being 'social interaction through messages'.

As has already been referred to and will be seen again later (in much more detail), there is a lot of debate in public relations about the need for two-way communication.

One of the UK's earliest professional practitioners was Tim Traverse-Healy, who set up his office in London in 1947. He used to say in speeches and lectures that for public relations to be practised three things must be present:

- Truth
- Concern for the public interest
- Dialogue

Truth is clearly an important element in the building of trust, as discussed above, and concern for the public interest will engender support from among those with whom relationships are needed. (This will be explored further in Chapter 3.)

Dialogue can be defined as being communication that is balanced equally (or symmetrically) between all sides. Communicative action, or an unequivocal agreement to do something, can be the result of dialogue.

Magda Pieczka developed this idea, also with reference to Jürgen Habermas, when she explained in 1995 that symmetry is a precondition of communicative action because understanding or mutual understanding is what makes communication possible and dialogue is the form that communication should take.

Various models have been developed to illustrate what is happening when communication flows one way, with interference (or noise) and symmetrically. Figures 1.1 to 1.4 (see McQuail

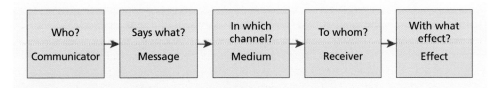

FIGURE 1.1 The Lasswell model

Source: adapted from *Communication Models for the Study of Mass Communications*, 2nd ed., McQuail, D. and Windhal, S., Pearson Education Limited © Pearson Education Limited 1993, with kind permission of Denis McQuail and Sven Windhal

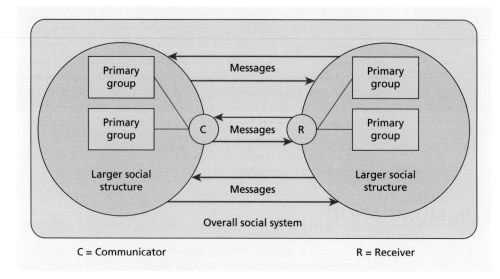

FIGURE 1.2 The Riley and Riley model
Source: based on Merton (1959)

and Windahl, 1993) show how this might look from Lasswell's early model (1948) which was devised during a period of propaganda, when communication was definitely one-way.

Then from Riley and Riley in 1959 the process of communication is portrayed as an integral part of the social system. Both the communicator and the receiver are affected by the three social

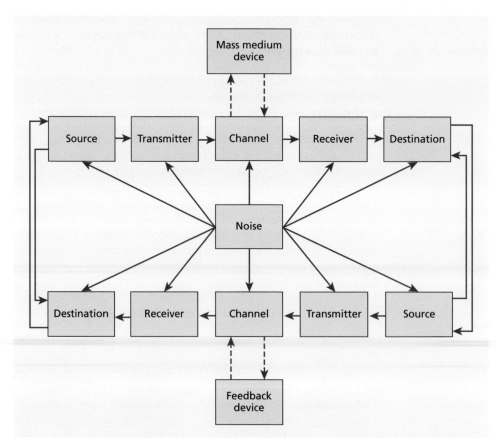

FIGURE 1.3 The De Fleur model
Source: adapted from *Communication Models for the Study of Mass Communications,* 2nd ed., McQuail, D. and Windhal, S., Pearson Education Limited © Pearson Education Limited 1993, with kind permission of Denis McQuail and Sven Windhal

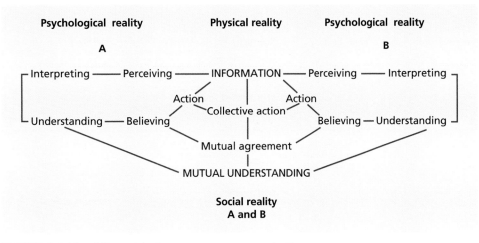

FIGURE 1.4 Kincaid's model of convergence communication
Source: E.M. Rogers and D.L. Kincaid (1981), quoted in Windahl et al. (1992: 74)

orders, being the primary group or groups of which they are members, the larger social structure, whether community, cultural, ethnic or economic (the immediate community – social, cultural, industrial – to which they belong,) and the overall social system. All these are in dynamic interaction, with messages flowing multi-directionally. Thus in Figure 1.2 the C and R are neither passive nor isolated but are related, and their messages are patterned in terms of these relationships.

De Fleur based his model (1966) on earlier work by Shannon and Weaver (1949) who, when working at the Bell Telephone Laboratories, first introduced the effect of noise into the communication flow, with a linear, one-way, sender-to-receiver model. With De Fleur two-way feedback is implicit and the communication flow is circular with the possibility of 'noise' interfering with the process at any time. The idea of noise had its physical origin in the effect of the crackling on a telephone line, which can distort what is transmitted in either direction.

Possibly most pertinent to public relations is the model by Kincaid (1979). As Figure 1.4 shows, the two people interpret and understand the messages and act upon them according to their perception and their social and economic situation (see the definition of publics in Chapter 3, which shows how the PR practitioner takes these aspects into account). In this model the communication is two-way and takes place over time. It can (but is not guaranteed to) lead to mutual understanding and so it is referred to as the convergence model.

DIALOGUE

William Isaacs has made a long-term study of dialogue and asserts that it is far from easy to achieve. He describes dialogue as being 'a conversation with a center, not sides, being employed to reach new understanding and, in doing so, to form a totally new basis from which to think and act' (1999: 19).

It is rare in everyday conversations to witness or enjoy real dialogue and much rarer still to see organisations engaging in dialogue with their publics. Figure 1.5 shows the complicated steps that Isaacs believes need to be taken for a dialogue to occur. Put simply, no party (and a dialogue can involve more than two parties) may try to lead or influence others in any way. They need to work to create a new understanding, which has not been biased by any prejudiced or former standpoint. As he shows in Figure 1.5, each party has to 'suspend' or put their egos and memories away, rather than 'defend' and try to impose their views or ideas on others.

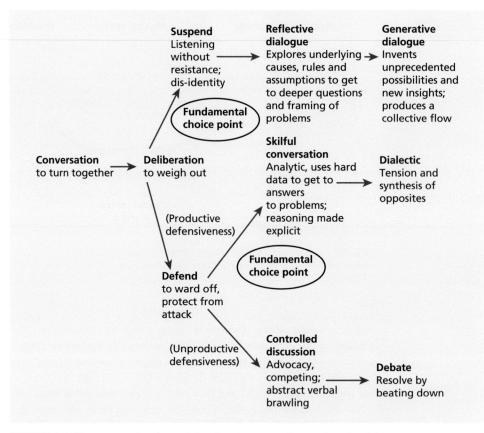

FIGURE 1.5 The progression from defending to suspending and on to dialogue
Source: from DIALOGUE AND THE ART OF THINKING TOGETHER by William Isaacs, copyright © 1999 by William Isaacs. Used by permission of Doubleday, a division of Random House, Inc.

Question

Think about yourself in a conversation. There will be a point at which you think of something to say and you cannot wait for the others to be quiet to put in your memory of an event or idea about what is being discussed, or you might worry that if you don't speak now you will forget the exciting thought. At this point, do you continue to listen to the others carefully or are you really only listening for a gap in the conversation to make your point? You will probably be nodding a lot too, which doesn't mean that you necessarily agree but that you've heard enough and want to speak. This is not therefore a dialogue. Can you think of any situation in where real dialogue occurs? (See Chapter 4 for an example of listening in business.)

At the beginning, in the UK, apart from thorough and practical introductory texts by Sam Black and Frank Jefkins, students were entirely dependent upon the US for academic references and James Grunig and Todd Hunt led the field with their 1984 book, *Managing Public Relations*.

TABLE 1.3 Based upon characteristics of four models of public relations

Characteristic	Press agentry/ publicity	Public information	Two-way asymmetric	Two-way symmetric
Purpose	Propaganda	Dissemination of information	Persuasion	Mutual understanding
Nature of communication	One-way: complete truth not essential	One-way: truth important	Two-way: imbalanced effects	Two-way: balanced effects
Communication model	Source → Receiver Lasswell	Source → Receiver	Source → Receiver Feedback ←	Group Group Riley and Riley/ Kincaid
Nature of research	Little: 'counting'	Little: readability, readership	Formative: evaluative of attitudes	Formative: evaluative of understanding
Where practiced today	Entertainment, sport, product promotion	Government, health, non-profit business	Competitive business, agencies	Regulated business, agencies

Source: adapted from Grunig and Hunt (1984: 22)

Grunig's 'four models' of PR (Table 1.3) dominated student work for many years and they are still often referred to and researched upon. An element of critical discussion has since been provided to bring some analysis into the debate to examine Grunig's earlier claims in more depth. Helping that debate to be lively and informative are some fine European researchers and authors such as Jacquie L'Etang, Inger Jensen, Dejan Verčič, Kevin Maloney, Lee Edwards, Betteke van Ruler, Ralph Tench and Liz Yeomans, all of whom and many others, deserve reference when critically examining theories, as your studies develop to higher levels.

The 'four models' have provided public relations scholars and analysts with rich material to test, prove and refute, from the linking of propaganda to all press agentry work to the estimating of organisations practicing each 'model' in 1984.

The discussion about whether communication should be asymmetric or symmetric for public relations to be well practiced (or 'excellent' as claimed by Grunig in 1992) has provided a focus for discussion and a measure for practice. L'Etang sees public relations as 'necessarily partisan and intrinsically undemocratic' (J. Grunig in Grunig et al. 2002). To her, the symmetrical model represents 'a utopian attempt to make an inherently evil practice look good'.

Mickey (2002), who analysed a range of PR case studies, is described as saying: 'Even in contexts as diverse as gardening, Aids prevention and art exhibitions, PR is inextricably linked to the interests it serves and perpetuates the environment in which those interests are most successful' (Edwards 2006: 168).

With these thoughts, there can be little chance for dialogue and it must be remembered, whether the practice is evil or for the best of intentions, it will almost always be being paid for to promote a set of ideas, practices or products, as Mickey describes. It would seem unlikely that there will be much budget given to make space for any opposing or conflicting views to be heard but they should be known and considered. (See Chapter 3 for a consideration of issues management, which tries to take all views into account.)

PUBLIC RELATIONS EDUCATION AND PROFESSIONAL DEVELOPMENT IN THE UK

Thanks in great part to Sam Black, who was one of the founders of the IPR in the UK, public relations became an academic subject at masters level in 1988, at the University of Stirling. Sam was also influential in the launch, the following year, of the bachelors programme at the College of St Mark and St John in Plymouth. However, the subject was not well received. Academic colleagues from other subject areas looked down on this interloper and even reviled its connections with the commercial world. As has been mentioned above, the PR practitioners were no more welcoming. None of them had a British university qualification in the subject and while some might have felt threatened none of them admitted it; rather they just asserted that they had managed without a PR degree and so it must not be necessary.

Despite this negativity within universities and in the working world, the subject became popular among students, which pleased university management, who welcomed the income that the large numbers of students brought in for them and so the numbers of courses grew.

Mini case study

Research was carried out in Austria in the 1990s, by Professor Benno Signitzer, to try and understand why so many more female students were drawn to the subject than males. At that time at the College of St Mark and St John in Plymouth they were outnumbering the males by 6 to 1. The surprising answer was that, in the long-running American soap *Dallas* in which money always meant power and which was not exercised with much humanity. The lead character, J.R. Ewing, who had survived many attempts by wealthy and influential men to overthrow him, was eventually brought down by a young PR woman. She destroyed his reputation and so he was finished.

Whether affected by the soap or not, there was no doubt that women wanted to become PR practitioners and the course at the College of St Mark and St John grew from 20 students in the first year, in 1989, to over 200 in all the three year groups combined, just six years later.

The critics in the universities still complained but, as the subject evolved, it became clear that it provided an excellent vehicle for undergraduate and postgraduate study. As the body of knowledge which critically reflected upon the practice from psychological, sociological, philosophical and economical standpoints, the theoretical base began to gain weight.

A search of the Universities and College Admission Services in the UK for 2011 shows that there are 257 undergraduate courses teaching public relations and 635 with communication in their title or as a subset or minor subject. There are also now 11 masters programmes in PR and a growing number of people with PhDs. Although the memory of the end of J.R. Ewing is fading and the academics in the subject have proved their worth on international conference platforms and in the several subject-specific journals, it still attracts more female students. The gender issue remains much discussed and researched, for example a major international project has recently been launched within the European Public Relations Education and Research Association, which is to be led by Serra Görpe of Istanbul University, who wrote in 2010: 'The scope of the study is not limited to women public relations professionals (consultancy and in-house) but also to women public relations academics as well. For example, in Turkey, the majority of public relations students are female and the majority of public relations academics are as well' (www.euprera.org).

WOMEN IN PUBLIC RELATIONS

According to Women In PR there are seven main reasons why there are so many women in the industry (Morris and Goldsworthy 2008: 18):

1. They are better, or natural communicators (33%)
2. They multitask and organise better than men (23%)
3. PR is a soft career suited to women – as are teaching, human resources etc. (18%)
4. They have better and more sensitive 'people skills' (18%)
5. They are better able to pay attention to detail and to look at things from different perspectives (15%)
6. They are better suited to a variety of practical administrative tasks (10%)
7. Women have greater imagination, intuition and are sensitive to nuances (8%).

The CIPR's research among its members revealed, in July 2010, that there are (of those who completed the survey) 65% female practitioners compared to 35% male. The following chart shows the differences in working levels:

Level	Men	Women
Director	18%	9%
Senior management	11%	7%
Managing director	11%	9%

Men are also twice as likely as women to be earning a salary in excess of £50,000 (www.cipr.co.uk).

There will continue to be studies into the gender issue, looking at the fact that, as Larissa Grunig saw it (Grunig et al. 2002: 183) the industry is female-intensive but male dominant as so few women hold top-level positions.

So the field and the library have grown impressively to make the subject a genuine contender for academic recognition. The practice is having to accommodate these developments too, and in the UK that is led by the Chartered Institute of Public Relations (CIPR).

The CIPR (like other national PR associations) contributes to the overall development of the PR industry by developing policies, representing its members and raising professional standards through education and training. Also, its members are required to abide by and uphold a strict code of conduct, thereby affirming their commitment to operate ethically, with integrity and transparency (see Chapter 4). As one of the strongest public relations professional associations in the world, the CIPR has been delivering education programmes since 1998 in the UK, often in partnership with leading universities.

This development has spread overseas. At the time of writing, active overseas teaching centres can be found in Armenia, Bulgaria, Croatia, Cyprus, Egypt, Greece, Kazakhstan, Kenya, Nigeria, Qatar, Romania, Serbia, Switzerland, Syria, the UAE and Ukraine. As the popularity and stature of the awards have grown, they are coming to the attention of governments. End-of-course events have been patronised by government ministers and the newly introduced CIPR qualifications have been acknowledged in their speeches, endorsing the potential influence that professional PR can have.

All accredited CIPR centres internationally become part of an international network of teachers and students, working together towards improving the profession.

SOCIAL MEDIA

With the development of social media, since the above points were made, the scene is changing and regardless of the model or the theory, many members or indeed instigators of publics (see Chapter 3) are using the new channels to make their voices heard. Symmetry is all the more possible, with the provision of open and accessible feedback opportunities. However, problems arise as so many social media channels are used to express views rather than to listen to them, and they often become more like a broadcast version of graffiti with messages squirted on to the walls of Facebook and within the open diaries of Twitter, blogs and elsewhere. Symmetry can only be achieved when all sides are paying equal attention and are listening carefully, without a preset agenda that they are trying to put across.

Question

When public relations is being practised, someone is being paid to use their skills and knowledge on behalf of another person or an organisation. How likely do you think it is that the money is handed over with the intention that no agenda of required objectives be set, no messages are devised and agreed for delivery or no behavioural change is hoped for? If you think it unlikely, what could be the place of symmetry?

These issues will continue to be argued and debated with students and practitioners needing to weigh the evidence available and critically analyse it for themselves.

IS PUBLIC RELATIONS A PROFESSION?

A profession is strictly defined as being a calling or vocation in which those working would not concern themselves with the money they make but rather be motivated by the pursuit of excellence. The term 'profession' in the UK used to be restricted to law, medicine and the church (or divinity) where high educational standards have to be attained for a person to enter and those standards must be maintained throughout their working life by continuous professional development (CPD) and upheld by adherence to a code of conduct.

The restriction is less strict nowadays, as for example lawyers are not regarded as being so vocationally driven and in fact they are often the butt of many jokes about their interest in money – such as:

How many lawyers does it take to change a light bulb?

Fifty-four. Eight to argue, one to get a continuance, one to object, one to demur, two to research precedents, one to dictate a letter, one to stipulate, five to turn in their time cards, one to depose, one to write interrogatories, two to settle, one to order a secretary to change the light bulb and twenty-eight to bill for professional services.

Medicine too has, in many countries, become associated with high earning business so that the quip that a doctor might feel your wallet before she or he feels your pulse has been coined.

However, there is no doubt that to practise in either of these fields, in many countries, there is a requirement for high educational standards and continuous professional development to be allowed to stay on the official register.

As shown above, public relations is still a long way from that situation numerically or in practice but qualifications are developing internationally, along with an adherence to a professional code of conduct, public relations is still at the very beginning of becoming likely to earn professional status.

INTERNATIONAL CONSIDERATIONS

Many types of organizations virtually and physically interact and communicate with publics and/or audiences outside their own country of origin to build a dynamic set of relationships. Trade, direct foreign investment, political coalitions, worthy global causes, information flow, and social networking, among other phenomena, are increasing the complexity of these relationships dramatically. Moreover, this complexity results in greater interdependence and interconnectivity among societies, groups of ideology-driven or cause-driven individuals, and organizations worldwide (Sharpe and Pritchard 2003). This reality parallels the evolution of public relations as a profession, practice, and field of study in every corner of the planet (Bates, quoted in Juan-Carlos Molleda 2006).

Although there is a sense abroad that public relations is a recognised and established profession, in countries like the US and the UK it is not the case. There are only Nigeria, Brazil, Panama and Peru where the work of PR practitioners is regulated nationally and in Nigeria it is also a requirement to belong to a professional association before being able to practise. The Nigerian government is fighting high levels of corruption both in business and in the public sector and regards an insistence on a professional approach to PR as a way of tackling it, as their institute will regulate dishonest claims. In most countries anyone can hang up a sign declaring that they are a public relations practitioner and few have set guidelines to help complainants argue with the quality of the service that these people provide. 'Public relations is an open profession and the level of professionalism and ethical thinking is unevenly distributed among the practitioners' (Ihlen and Rakkenes in *The Global Public Relations Handbook*, Sriramesh and Verčič 2009: 435).

The development of the profession is not only affected by the political situation and the culture in a country but also the impact of the global marketplace, bringing with it multinational companies as well as multinational PR consultancies.

The following list of questions and Table 1.4 (based on information in *The Global Public Relations Handbook*) outlines some of the questions that need to be considered when defining the position of and the possibilities for public relations in a country.

Question

Answer the questions for your country and consider what your answers might mean for public relations practice.

The infrastructure and international public relations

Political system

- What is the basic political system? Democratic, authoritarian, theocratic, totalitarian, other?
- Is there political pluralism in the society?
- Is public opinion valued? (Look for further discussions on public opinion in Chomsky's description of Laswell below and in the Tehran Declaration of Public Opinion.)
- How strong are the political institutions?
- What role do formal institutions play in political decision-making?
- Do organisations have avenues of influencing public policy-making?

Economic system and level of development

- What is the level of economic development?
- Is economic decision-making centralised in the government?

- To what extent has membership of WTO (World Trade Organization) changed the environment for private investment?

  What is the power of the private sector in determining public policy?

  What is the relationship between the private and public sectors?

- What is the level of technological development that may be relevant to public relations professionals?

Legal

- How strong and independent is the judiciary?
- What is the relationship between the judiciary and the legislative and executive branches?
- Does the country have legal codes to regulate the media?

Activism

- Historically, what role has activism played in the country (e.g. social movements)?
- What is the nature of activism prevalent in the country currently?
- Are labour unions major forces in the society?
- Currently what tools do corporations use to deal with activism?

Communication

- Is the news media free, controlled by the government or by specific business or political interests?
- Are social media widely used or mainly confined to specific ages or sections of the society or even controlled by the authorities?
- Are there other formal or informal networks operating within the society?
- What is the level of functional literacy in the country?
- What are the most trusted sources of information in the country?
- Are the news media accessible to all parts of the society or are they restricted?
- Who are the opinion formers or leaders for specific publics and what is their impact upon evolving policies?

You will also need to understand how the culture impacts upon the way the society is structured and the issues that form attitudes.

The *Handbook* shows that all countries have public relations on the university curriculum and where there is an association there is a code of conduct and a further drive towards professionalism through training and qualifications.

See Table 1.4 for some assessments of the place of professional PR in eighteen different countries.

Contributions used to create the table were from:

US: Larissa A. Grunig and James E. Grunig

China: Ni Chen and Hugh M. Culbertson

Australasia: Judy Motion, Shirley Leitch and Simon Cliffe

Japan: Takashi Inoue

Palestine: R.S. Zaharna, Ahmed Ibrahim Hammad and Jane Masri

Israel: Margalit Toledano and David McKie

Kenya: Peter Oriare Mbeke

TABLE 1.4 Statistics drawn from *The Global Public Relations Handbook* (Sriramesh and Verčič 2009)

Country	Association founded	Membership	Status	Spend
Australia	PRIA 1949 (in New South Wales)	2,856	Fast becoming a strategic function	$A250m
Brazil	ABERJE (Business communication 1967)	1,000 companies	Changes and trends have forced companies to act in a more socially responsible manner	$50m
Canada	CPRS 1956 IABC 1974	1,700 2,200	Strengths in networking and professional development but weaknesses in accreditation, regulation and advocacy	Not known
China	150 different associations	Not known	An adolescent with growing pains	$250m+
Israel	ISPRA 1961	250	Nation building and professional values	Not known
Japan	PRSJ 1980 merged from JPRIA 1964 and JPRA 1974	539	The future for public relations in Japan is very bright	Not known
Kenya	PRISK 1971	350	Nurturing professionalism	Not known
New Zealand	PRINZ 1954	653	Friendly rivalry, cultural diversity and global focus	Not known
Nigeria	NIPR 1969 (Nigerian Institute of PR) PRAN 1963 (PR Association of Nigeria)	20,000	Membership is compulsory for practitioners to obtain a licence to operate and all members must be registered for continuous professional development	Not known
Norway	NCA 1958	2,600	Norwegian practitioners are doing brisk business trading on their networks, common sense and experience	$65m
Palestine	Early days	Not known	One of the fastest growing and most exciting professions	Not known
Poland	PPRA 1994 PRF (firms 2001)	184 and 22	Practitioners in Central and Eastern Europe need to account for the influence of former systems	$100m
Romania	ARRP 1995 and CCRP (companies 2003)		Public relations education and industry are reaching early maturity	Not known
South Africa	PRISA 1957 PRCC 1977	4,000+	From rhetoric to reality – growing in importance and professionalism	Not known
Sweden	SPRA (1950s)	4,400	A strong presence, increasing in importance	6 billion SEK
UAE +	MEPRA (Middle East)	1,000+	Coming of age. Many multinationals	Not known
UK	CIPR 1948 and PRCA (for consultancies)	9,800 and Not known	A thriving PR industry aspiring to become a profession	£6.5 billion (generated)
US	PRSA 1948 plus several regional and specialist	20,000	Not there yet	Not known but it will be big

South Africa: Ronel Rensburg

UK: Jon White, Jacquie L'Etang and Danny Moss

Sweden: Bertil Flodin

Poland: Riszard Lawniczak, Waldemar Rydzak and Jack Trebecki

Romania: Adela Rogojinaru

Canada: Fraser Likely

Brazil: Juan-Carlos Molleda, Andreia Athaydes and Vivian Hirsch

Nigeria: Sue Wolstenholme

THE MEDIUM IS THE MESSAGE

As Marshall McLuhan said in 1967, 'The medium is the message', so it is today that channels and media styles affect the messages to be exchanged. It is vital that PR practitioners keep abreast at all times, of the use, by publics, of specific media.

Social media are among the channels as well as arenas where communication has to be monitored as well as instigated and joined by PR professionals. (For more on this see Chapter 6.)

There is evidence to show that the news media are monitoring social media closely themselves, as can be seen at http://blog.ouseful.info/2011/04/10/uk-journalists-on-twitter.

Marcus Messner has also studied the use of Twitter by news media in the US to explore the adoption rate of Twitter by traditional news media. He and his colleagues discovered that most tweets are still shovelware[2] and that there is little online community building and engagement.

Despite these somewhat negative findings, the fast developing area that accommodates social media needs to be constantly checked for up-to-date statistics to find the type of information Show in Table 1.5.

TABLE 1.5 World internet usage and population statistics, 31 December 2011

World regions	Population (2011 est.)	Internet users 31 Dec 2000	Internet users (latest data)	Penetration (% population)	Growth 2000–11	Users % of table
Africa	1,037,524,058	4,514,400	139,875,242	13.5%	2,988.4%	6.2%
Asia	3,879,740,877	114,304,000	1,016,799,076	26.2%	789.6%	44.8%
Europe	816,426,346	105,096,093	500,723,686	61.3%	376.4%	22.1%
Middle East	216,258,843	3,284,800	77,020,995	35.6%	2,244.8%	3.4%
North America	347,394,870	108,096,800	273,067,546	78.6%	152.6%	12.0%
Latin America/Carib.	597,283,165	18,068,919	235,819,740	39.5%	1,205.1%	10.4%
Oceania/Australia	35,426,995	7,620,480	23,927,457	67.5%	214.0%	1.1%
World total	6,930,055,154	360,985,492	2,267,233,742	32.7%	528.1%	100.0%

Notes: (1) Demographic (population) numbers are based on data from the US Census, Bureau and local census agencies. (2) Internet usage information comes from data published by Nielsen Online, by the International Telecommunications Union, by GfK, local regulators and other reliable sources. Copyright © 2001–2012, Miniwatts Marketing Group. All rights reserved worldwide.

---

[2]There are many definitions for shovelware but most indicate that it is low-grade, not well-researched, mass information that is pushed out over the internet.

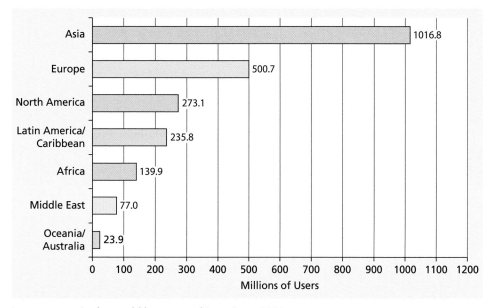

Internet users in the world by geographic regions, 2011
Source: Internet World Stats www.internetworldstats.com/stats.htm
Estimated internet users are 2,267,233,742 for 31 December 2011

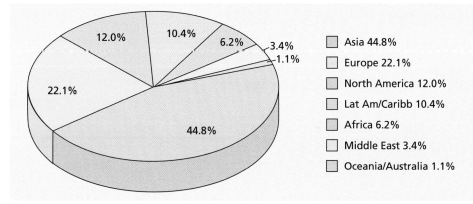

World internet users distribution by world regions, 2011
Source: Internet World Stats www.internetworldstats.com/stats.htm
2,267,233,742 internet users for 31 December 2011

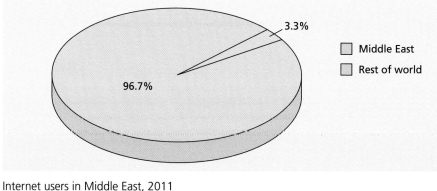

Internet users in Middle East, 2011
Source: Internet World Stats www.internetworldstats.com
Middle East had 68,553,666 estimated internet users for 31 March 2011

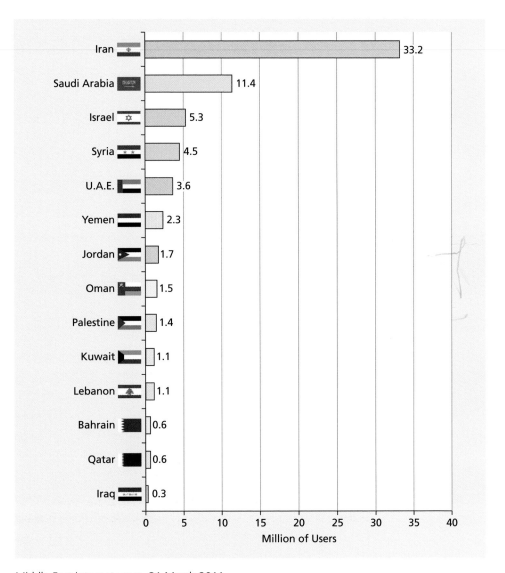

Middle East internet users, 31 March 2011
Source: Internet World Stats www.internetworldstats.com/stats5.htm
68,553,666 internet users approximately in the Middle East as of Q1 2011
Copyright © 2000–2012 Miniwatts Marketing Group. All rights reserved.

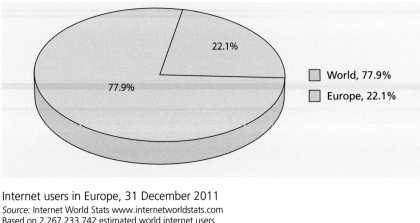

Internet users in Europe, 31 December 2011
Source: Internet World Stats www.internetworldstats.com
Based on 2,267,233,742 estimated world internet users
Copyright © 2000–2012 Miniwatts Marketing Group. All rights reserved.

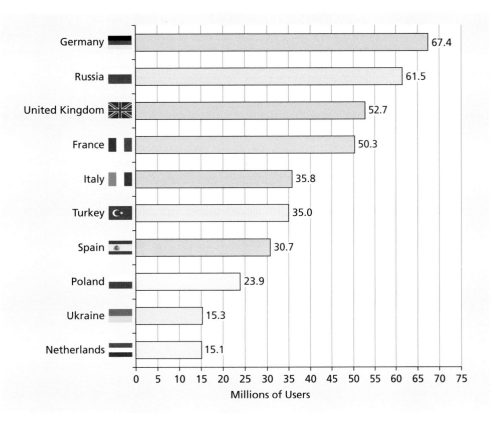

Country	Millions of Users
Germany	67.4
Russia	61.5
United Kingdom	52.7
France	50.3
Italy	35.8
Turkey	35.0
Spain	30.7
Poland	23.9
Ukraine	15.3
Netherlands	15.1

Top 10 internet countries in Europe, 31 December 2011
Source: Internet World Stats www.internetworldstats.com/stata4.htm
Basis: 500,723,686 estimated internet users in Europe for Q4 2011
Copyright © 2000–2012 Miniwatts Marketing Group. All rights reserved.

Finally, it must never be forgotten that public relations is a tool which can be used as much for harm as it can for good. The following case study, by Professor Noam Chomsky, details an approach to PR which is not to be tolerated by a professional practitioner.

Case study

Extracts from *Media Control, the Spectacular Achievements of Propaganda* by Noam Chomsky, Seven Stories Press, New York, 2002

Early history of propaganda, pp. 11–14

Let's begin with the first modern government propaganda operation. That was under the Woodrow Wilson Administration. Woodrow Wilson was elected president in 1916 on the platform 'Peace without victory'. That was right in the middle of World War I. The population was extremely pacifistic and saw no reason to become involved in a European war. The Wilson Administration was actually committed to war and had to do something about it. They established a government propaganda commission, called the Creel Commission, which succeeded, within six months, in turning a pacifist population into a hysterical, war-mongering population, which wanted to destroy everything German, tear the Germans limb from limb, go to war and save the world. That was a major achievement and it led to a further achievement. Right at that time and after the war the same techniques were used to

Source: © John Van Hasselt/Corbis

whip up a hysterical Red scare, as it was called, which succeeded pretty much in destroying unions and eliminating such dangerous problems as freedom of the press and freedom of political thought. There was very strong support from the media and from the business establishment.

Among those who participated actively and enthusiastically in Wilson's war were the progressive intellectuals, people of the John Dewey circle, who took great pride, as you can see from their own writings at the time, in having shown that what they called the 'more intelligent members of the community', namely themselves, were able to drive a reluctant population into a war by terrifying them and eliciting jingoistic fanaticism. The means that were used were extensive. For example, there was a good deal of fabrication of atrocities by the Huns, Belgian babies with their arms torn off, all sorts of awful things that you will still read in history books. Much of it was invented by the British propaganda ministry, whose own commitment at the time, as they put it in their secret deliberations, was to 'direct the thought of most of the world'. But more crucially they wanted to control the thought of the more intelligent members of the community in the United States, who would then disseminate the propaganda that they were concocting and convert the pacifist country to wartime hysteria. That worked. It worked very well. And it taught a lesson: State propaganda, when supported by the educated classes and when no deviation is permitted from it, can have a big effect. It was a lesson learned by Hitler and many others, and it has been pursued to this day.

[*Also examine the role played by PR Company Hill & Knowlton in the initiation of the Gulf War.*]

From Spectator democracy, pp. 14–15

Another group that was impressed by these successes was one of liberal democratic theorists and leading media figures, like, for example, Walter Lippmann, who was the dean of American journalists, a major foreign and domestic policy critic and also a major theorist of liberal democracy. If you take a look at his collected essays you'll see that they are subtitled something like 'A Progressive Theory of Liberal Democratic Thought'. Lippmann was involved in these propaganda commissions and recognized their achievements. He argued that what he called 'A revolution in the art of democracy', could be used to 'manufacture consent', that is, to bring about agreement on the part of the public for things they didn't want by the new techniques of propaganda. He also thought his was a good idea, in fact, necessary. It was necessary because, as he put it, ' the common interests elude public opinion entirely' and can only be understood and managed by a 'specialized class' of 'responsible men' who are smart enough to figure things out.

Pages 20–21

In the 1920s and early 1930s, Harold Lasswell, the founder of the modern field of communication and one of the leading American political scientists, explained that we should not succumb to 'democratic dogmatisms about men being the best judges of their own interest', because they're not. We're the best judges of the public interests. Therefore, just out of ordinary morality, we have to make sure that they don't have the opportunity to act on the basis of their own misjudgments. In what is nowadays called a totalitarian state, or a military state, it's easy. You just hold a bludgeon over their heads, and if they get out of line you smash them over the head. But as society has become more free and democratic, you lose that capacity. Therefore you have to turn to the techniques of propaganda. The logic is clear. Propaganda is to a democracy what the bludgeon is to a totalitarian state. That's wise and good because, again, the common interests elude the bewildered herd. They can't figure them out.

Public relations, pp. 22–29

[This piece also contains a small extract from *Necessary Illusions: Thought Control in Democratic Societies* by Noam Chomsky published by Pluto Press, London, 1993.]

The United States pioneered the public relations industry. Its commitment was 'to control the public mind' as its leaders put it. They learned a lot from the successes of the Creel commission[3] and the successes in creating the Red Scare and its aftermath.

The public relations industry underwent a huge expansion at that time. It succeeded for some time in creating almost total subordination of the public to business rule through the 1920s. This was so extreme that congressional committees began to investigate it as we moved into the 1930s. That's where a lot of our information about it comes from.

From *Necessary Illusions*, p. 16. 'In accordance with the prevailing conceptions in the US, there is no infringement on democracy if a few corporations control the information system: in fact, that is the very essence of democracy. In the *Annals of the American Academy of Political and Social Science*, the leading figure of the public relations industry, Edward Bernays, explains that "the very essence of the democratic process" is "the freedom to persuade and suggest", what he calls "the engineering of consent". "A leader", he continues, "cannot wait for the people to arrive at even general understanding . . . Democratic leaders must play their part in . . . engineering . . . consent to socially constructive goals and values", applying "scientific principles and tried practices to the task of getting people to support ideas and programs"; and although it remains unsaid it is evident enough that those who control resources will be in a position to judge what is "socially constructive", to engineer consent through the media, and to implement policy through the mechanisms of the state. If the freedom to persuade happens to be concentrated in a few hands, we must recognize that such is the nature of a free society. The public relations industry expends vast resources "educating the American people about the economic facts of life" to ensure a favorable climate for business. Its task is to control "the public mind", which is "the only serious danger confronting the company", an AT&T executive observed eighty years ago.[4]

Public relations is a huge industry. They're spending by now something in the order of a billion dollars a year.

The first trial was in 1937. There was a major strike, the Steel strike in western Pennsylvania at Johnstown. Business tried out a new technique of labor destruction, which worked very well. Not through goon squads and breaking knees. That wasn't working very well any more but through the more subtle and effective means of propaganda. The idea was to figure out ways to turn the public against the strikers, to present the strikers as disruptive, harmful to the public and against the common interests. The common interests are those of 'us', the businessman, the worker, the housewife. That's all 'us'. We want to be together to have things like harmony and Americanism and working together, Then there's those bad strikers out there who are disruptive and causing trouble and breaking harmony and violating Americanism. We've got to stop them so we can all live together. The corporate executive and the guy who cleans the floors all have the same interests. We can all work together and work for Americanism in harmony, liking each other. That was essentially the message. A huge amount of effort is put into presenting it. This is, after all, the business community so they control the media and have massive

[3]The Committee on Public Information, also known as the CPI and the Creel Committee, was intended to influence US public opinion regarding American intervention in World War I. It was established under President Woodrow Wilson as an independent agency by Executive order 2594, April 13, 1917. The committee consisted of George Creel (Chairman) and Secretaries of State (Robert Lansing), War (Lindley M. Garrison), and the Navy (Josephus Daniels) as ex officio members.

The purpose of the CPI was to influence American public opinion toward supporting US intervention in World War I via a prolonged propaganda campaign. Among those who participated in it were Wilson advisers Walter Lippmann and Edward Bernays, the latter of whom had remarked that 'the essence of democratic society' was the 'engineering of consent,' by which propaganda was the necessary method for democracies to promote and garner support for policy. Many have commented that the CPI laid the groundwork for the public relations (PR) industry. The CPI at first used material that was based on fact, but spun it to present an upbeat picture of the American war effort. Very quickly, however, the CPI began churning out raw propaganda picturing Germans as evil monsters. Hollywood movie-makers joined in on the propaganda by making movies such as *The Claws of the Hun, The Prussian Cur, To Hell with the Kaiser* and *The Kaiser, the Beast of Berlin*. These titles illustrated the message the CPI tried to convey.

[4]Alex Carey, 'Reshaping the truth', *Meanjin Quarterly* (Australia), 35: 4, 1976; Gabriel Kolko, *Main Currents in American History* (Pantheon 1984: 284) For extensive discussion, see Alex Carey, 'Managing public opinion: the corporate offensive', ms., U. of New South Wales, 1986

resources. And it worked, very effectively. It was called the 'Mohawk Valley formula'[5] and applied over and over again to break strikes. They were called 'scientific methods of strike breaking', and worked very effectively by mobilizing community opinion in favor of vapid empty concepts like Americanism. Who can be against that? Or harmony. Who can be against that? Or, as in the Persian Gulf War, 'Support our troops'. Who can be against that? Anything that's totally vacuous. But you don't want people to think about the issue. That's the whole point of good propaganda. You want to create a slogan that nobody's going to be against and everybody's going to be for. Nobody knows what it means, because it doesn't mean anything. Its crucial value is that it diverts your attention from a question that *does* mean something. Do you support our policy? That's the one you're not allowed to talk about. So you have people arguing about support for the troops? 'Of course I don't *not* support them.' Then they've won.

That's all very effective. It runs right up to today. And of course it is carefully thought out. The people in the public relations industry aren't there for the fun of it. They're doing work. They're trying to instill the right values. In fact they have a concept of what democracy ought to be: It ought to be a system in which the specialized class is trained to work in the service of the masters, the people who own the society. The rest of the population ought to be deprived of any form of organization, because organization just causes trouble. They ought to be sitting in front of the TV and having drilled into their heads the message, which says, the only value in life is to have more commodities or live like that rich middle class family you're watching and to have nice values like harmony and Americanism. That's all there is in life. You may think in your own head that there's got to be something more in life than this but since you're watching the tube alone you assume, I must be crazy, because that's all going on over there. And since there is no organization permitted – that's absolutely crucial – you never have a way of finding out whether you are crazy and you just assume it, because it's the natural thing to assume.

So that's the ideal. Great efforts are made in trying to achieve that ideal. Obviously, there is a certain conception behind it. The conception of democracy is the one that I mentioned. The bewildered herd is a problem. We've got to prevent their roar and trampling. We've got to distract them. They should be watching the Superbowl or sitcoms or violent movies.

[5]The Mohawk Valley formula was a corporate plan for strike-breaking to discredit union leaders, frighten the public with the threat of violence, use local police and vigilantes to intimidate strikers, form puppet associations of 'loyal employees' to influence public debate, fortify workplaces, employ large numbers of replacement workers, and threaten to close the plant if work is not resumed. The Mohawk Valley formula was described in an article by company president James Rand, Jr., and published in the *National Association of Manufacturers Labor Relations Bulletin* in the fourth month of the strike. The article was widely disseminated in pamphlet form by the National Association of Manufacturers (NAM) later that year.

The June 1936 issue of the NAM's *Labor Relations Bulletin* immortalised the 'Mohawk Valley formula' as a classic blueprint for union busting. The nine-point formula, as devised by James Rand, Jr., is as follows:

1. When a strike is threatened, label the union leaders as 'agitators' to discredit them with the public and their own followers. Conduct balloting under the foremen to ascertain the strength of the union and to make possible misrepresentation of the strikers as a small minority. Exert economic pressure through threats to move the plant, align bankers, real estate owners and businessmen into a 'Citizens' Committee'.

2. Raise high the banner of 'law and order', thereby causing the community to mass legal and police weapons against imagined violence and to forget that employees have equal rights with others in the community.

3. Call a 'mass meeting' to coordinate public sentiment against the strike and strengthen the Citizens' Committee.

4. Form a large police force to intimidate the strikers and exert a psychological effect. Utilize local police, state police, vigilantes and special deputies chosen, if possible, from other neighborhoods.

5. Convince the strikers their cause is hopeless with a 'back-to-work' movement by a puppet association of so-called 'loyal employees' secretly organized by the employer.

6. When enough applications are on hand, set a date for opening the plant by having such opening requested by the puppet 'back-to-work' association.

7. Stage the 'opening' theatrically by throwing open the gates and having the employees march in a mass protected by squads of armed police so as to dramatize and exaggerate the opening and heighten the demoralizing effect.

8. Demoralize the strikers with a continuing show of force. If necessary turn the locality into a warlike camp and barricade it from the outside world.

9. Close the publicity barrage on the theme that the plant is in full operation and the strikers are merely a minority attempting to interfere with the 'right to work'. With this, the campaign is over—the employer has broken the strike.*

*As quoted in R.G. Rodden, *The Fighting Machinists: a Century of Struggle*, Kelly Press, 1984.

In fact what does it mean if somebody asks you, Do you support the people in Iowa? Can you say, Yes, I support them or No I don't support them? It's not even a question. It doesn't mean anything. That's the point. The point of public relations slogans like 'Support our troops' is that they don't mean anything. They mean as much as whether you support the people in Iowa.

Of course there was an issue. The issue was, Do you support our policy? Every once in a while you call on them to chant meaningless slogans like 'Support our troops'. You've got to keep them pretty scared but unless they're properly scared and frightened of all kinds of devils that are going to destroy them from outside or inside or somewhere, they may start to think, which is very dangerous, because they're not competent to think. Therefore it's important to distract them and marginalize them.

That's one conception of democracy.

After the war came the unions declined, as did a very rich working class culture that was associated with the unions. That was destroyed. We moved to a business-run society at a remarkable level. This is the only state-capitalist industrial society that doesn't have even the normal social contract that you find in comparable societies. Outside of South Africa, I guess, this is the only industrial society that doesn't have national health care. There's no general commitment to even minimal standards of survival for the parts of the population who can't follow these rules and gain things for themselves individually. Unions are virtually nonexistent. There are no political parties or organizations. It's a long way toward the ideal, at least structurally. The media are a corporate monopoly. They have the same point of view. The two parties are factions of the business party. Most of the population doesn't even bother voting because it looks meaningless. They're marginalized and properly distracted. At least that's the goal. The leading figure in the public relations industry, Edward Bernays, actually came out of the Creel Commission. He was part of it, learned his lessons there and went on to develop what he called 'engineering of consent', which he described as 'the essence of democracy'. The people who are able to engineer consent are the ones who have the resources and the power to do it – the business community – and that's who you work for.

Reprinted with the kind permission of Professor Noam Chomsky.

Questions

1. How was public relations used in the examples given above by Professor Chomsky?
2. How are those examples reflected in the definitions given in this chapter?
3. From those quoted and discussed in this chapter, which academics and writers on public relations would criticise the examples given by Professor Chomsky?

CONCLUSION

This chapter has provided a number of definitions for public relations and indicated how to differentiate between the ordinary practitioner and the professional. It has also given a number of examples for debate and consideration, of when PR is used as a tool by practitioners with very different agendas. Various channels for messages have been discussed, including social media, to provide different models of communication for the different styles of public relations. Professor Chomsky's words stand as a warning to the would-be professional. Chapter 4 will make it clear why PR, as he describes it practised here, is not ethical and therefore not appropriate for a professional practitioner.

Answers to quiz

1. Advertising
2. Propaganda
3. Marketing
4. Publicity
5. Sponsorship
6. Lobbying
7. Social marketing
8. Public relations – which can, and often does, include any or all of 1–7 too.

REFERENCES

Andraeson, A. R. (1995) *Marketing and Social Change: Changing Behavior to Promote Health, Social Development and the Environment*, Jossey-Bass

Bates, D. (2006) www.instituteforpr.org/

Black, S. (1989) *An Introduction to Public Relations*, Modino Press

Cutlip, S. (1994) The Unseen Power: Public Relations, a History, Lawrence Erlbown Associates

Edwards, L. (2006) 'Public relations theories – an applied overview: alternative approaches' in R. Tench and L. Yeomans (eds), *Exploring Public Relations*, Financial Times Prentice Hall

Gerbner, G. (1967) 'Mass media and human communication theory', in F. E. X. Dance (ed.), *Human Communication Theory*, Holt, Rinehart & Winston

Grunig, J. and T. Hunt (1984) *Managing Public Relations*, Holt, Rinehart & Winston

Grunig, L., J. Grunig and D. M. Dozier (2002) *Excellent Public Relations and Effective Organizations*, Lawrence Erlbaum Associates

Heath, R. (2001) 'A rhetorical enactment rationale for public relations: the good organization communicating well', pp. 31–51 in *The Handbook of Public Relations*, Sage

Isaacs, W. (1999) *Dialogue and the Art of Thinking Together*, Currency Doubleday

Jensen, I. (1997) 'Understanding the organisation's raison d'être', Conference paper, Bledcom

Jensen, I. (2001) 'Emergent functions in the public sphere', Conference paper, Bledcom

Kirk, G. (2010) 'Nudging etc.', Unpublished paper

L'Etang, J. (2004) *Public Relations in Britain*, Lawrence Erlbaum Associates

MacFadyen, L., M. Stead and G. Hastings (1999) 'A synopsis of social marketing', www .management@stirling.ac.uk

McQuail, D. (1987) *McQuail's Mass Communication Theory*, Sage

McQuail, D. and S. Windahl (1993) *Communication Models for the Study of Mass Communications*, Longman

Mickey, T. J. (2002) *Deconstructing Public Relations: Public Relations Criticism*, Lawrence Erlbaum Associates

Molleda, J.-C. (2006) 'Global public relations', www.instituteforpr.org/topics/global-public-relations/

Morris, T. and S. Goldsworthy (2008) 'Girls, gurus, gays and diversity' in *PR – a Persuasive Industry?* Palgrave Macmillan

Peters, J. D. (1999) *Speaking into the Air*, University of Chicago Press

Pieczka, M. (1995) 'Symmetry in communication and public relations', Conference paper, Bledcom

Rodden, R. G. (1984) *The Fighting Machinists*, Kelly Press

Sharpe, M. L and B. J. Pritchard (2003) 'The historical empowerment of public opinion and its relationship to the emergence of public relations as a profession', in D. J. Tilson and E. C. Alozie (eds) pp. 14–36, *Towards the Common Good: Perspectives in International Public Relations*, Allyn & Bacon

Sieff, M. (1990) *Marcus Sieff on Management the Marks & Spencer Way* Weidenfeld & Nicolson

Sriramesh, K. and D. Verčič (eds) (2009) *The Global Public Relations Handbook: Theory, Research and Practice*, expanded and revised edition, Routledge

Tench, R. and L. Yeomans (2006) *Exploring Public Relations*, Financial Times Prentice Hall

Thaler, R. and Sunstein, C. (2008) *Nudge: Improving decisions about health, wealth and happiness*, Yale University Press

Verčič, D. (2000) 'Trust in organisations: a study of the relations between media coverage, public perceptions and profitability', Unpublished doctoral dissertation

Windahl, S. and B. Signitzer with J. Olsen (1992) *Using Communication Theory*, Sage

Chapter 2
What do PR practitioners do?
Kristina Laco

Learning outcomes

By the end of this chapter, you should be able to:

- Understand the role of a PR practitioner in the organisations where they work, and the classifications within which their roles have so far been defined
- Describe the scope of various activities and tasks performed by PR practitioners
- Compare the theoretical description of what practitioners do with the real-life experiences recorded in their diaries, both in-house and in consultancies
- Study what is needed to enter the world of PR practice and what is required in practice from practitioners today
- Apply all of the above in your personal reflection and perspective on PR practice

Introduction

Structure of the chapter:

- Clothes to fit the practitioners: roles in PR recognised by classic PR literature; the advantages and weaknesses of classifications.
- All the different things they do: reality of activities and tasks performed by practitioners in their day-to-day work contrasted with the theoretical descriptions we find in textbook classifications and job announcements.
- What it takes to become one: the knowledge and skills needed to succeed in the PR profession and the differences between in-house and consultancy work.
- First-hand experience: four detailed diaries written by PR practitioners employed both in-house and in consultancies, in Croatia, the Middle East and Nigeria.

Most PR professionals whose work does not include some of the stereotypes that are often used to superficially describe the profession, where they are either seen as spin doctors who manipulate the media or as publicists who work for celebrities and who constantly attend parties, have serious problems in trying to explain what they actually do even to their families, let alone to the less interested public. If they say that they work in communication, this is translated as 'marketing'; if they say that they write something, they are asked whether they are authors or journalists; if they are brave enough to try and explain that they work on improving how their organisation is understood by those with whom it interacts, they get puzzled faces and raised eyebrows that seem to ask, 'but what exactly do you do?' Feeding the stereotypes that connect public relations either with propaganda and manipulation or which reduce in the most banal terms its personnel to publicists in the worlds of politics, show business and celebrities cannot in the least help people understand what all the professionals in this job do throughout the world, except for a small minority who might perhaps belong to one of the two categories popularised through the BBC's *Absolute Power* or, indeed, *Sex and the City*.

The primary aim of this chapter is to enable you to research professional PR practice yourself by equipping you with the right tools and knowledge. The chapter does this by identifying the roles of PR practitioners as described by academics engaged in research of the practice of this field and then by giving an overview of the tasks and activities described in the literature and which we find in practice. The chapter ends with an overview of the knowledge and skills necessary to be successful in this profession. (Please also see Chapter 9 for further developments on the roles, knowledge and competences needed to take the profession up to the leadership level.)

The chapter contains four detailed diaries kept by PR practitioners, employed in-house in a bank and an NGO, and in consultancy in Croatia, UAE and Nigeria. The diaries are personal, sincere and detailed and present a unique view of the everyday practice of various practitioners, supplemented with brief CVs which show how these practitioners became involved in PR and explain why they do what they do.

The last Critical Reflection Box in this chapter calls for reflection on the role of PR practitioners in the organisations where they work and in society as a whole.

Mini case study

As an introduction to the chapter, read Diary 1 (below), the first of four detailed diaries describing a day, two days, three days or a week in the professional life of people who earn their living in PR.

Name	Marina Dijaković
Company	Zagrebačka Banka d.d.
Position	Director of Corporate Identity and Communications
Four days in my professional life	**Tuesday 20 April**

I begin each day in the same way: by reading all the relevant newspapers on the market. I have a tried and trusted system – I usually dive into the financial press first and then newspapers that deal with more general issues. I immediately go to the financial/business pages, and then to those where I can probably find an article about our bank or about the financial sector. When I've checked the topics related to our branch of activity, I go to other topics, primarily those that concern local politics which also often have a big impact on the economy and where consequences are quickly seen in the world of finance. Naturally, global events are also very important . . . actually, everything is important but the really key thing is to prioritise. The early-morning mailbox is also full of various media reports: for instance, the UniCredit clippings arrive regularly from our parent bank giving me information about happenings in the Italian and European financial market.

Today is going to be an 'interesting' day, because we have some critical articles related to our clients and business relationships. The situation does not require any further consultation with the president or with anyone else on the management board but this kind of news usually rings a warning bell – I immediately make a mental note and follow what today's online sites say about this, check whether this story goes deeper . . .

It soon becomes clear that the 'event of the day' is the government's new economic programme. All the media are buzzing, so I rush through the government's PowerPoint presentation to find parts of the programme dealing with fiscal changes, tax levies, and personal bankruptcies. I call the bank's chief macroeconomic expert and arrange a quick briefing on the new measures. We agree what he should highlight in his media statement, of course if and when the press call to get one. I conclude that it's best to consult the president of the management board and align our positions at bank level – so I request a quick meeting with him in the afternoon.

In the meantime, other meetings line up: one on the subject of a new prize, the Best Buy Award, that the bank has won; the second meeting is with the editor-in-chief of a business magazine, with whom I discuss some future projects. In any case, I'm really snowed under . . . I'm becoming aware that I won't have the chance to have lunch. In my free minutes, I search online sites, and now it is perfectly clear to what extent the news about the new economic programme has escalated – everyone has something to say on this issue . . .

The meeting with the president of the management board and the macroeconomic expert is relatively brief; we quickly agree on the key statements to give when answering questions from the press. The conclusion is that the measures are good, but that the greatest challenge will be knowing precisely when to apply them.

The end of the day is near and I only have to do a job interview with a new potential employee in the PR Department, or, more precisely, in Media Relations. The interview went really well; the girl comes from a renowned PR agency, has fresh ideas and seems ambitious. We'll probably come to an agreement that she moves to the bank.

Wednesday 21 April

Today at 10.00 we have a press conference on something that is particularly close to my heart – 'Green loans'! Tomorrow is Earth Day and the bank has decided to launch a new credit line with reduced rates for the construction of energy efficient real estate, or for solar panel systems that create renewable electricity.

Of course, we intentionally scheduled the press conference one day before Earth Day. The media will certainly be all over the place writing about energy and related topics on the environment and sustainability and there is also going to be some room to mention our innovative product. The press response is excellent; obviously there is interest in these subjects – and probably this also fits in well with their editorial concept for tomorrow's 'green' issues. We distributed some symbolic but useful gifts – devices to measure the power consumption of household appliances. What better way is there to begin this comprehensive environmental story than to raise public awareness of the value of even the smallest personal contribution to total energy savings?

Afterwards, I hurry to a previously agreed lunch with the director of a gallery that we have been sponsoring for years. She has a very interesting proposition for us – with the general lack of money for culture these days, the director has a really imaginative way of obtaining sponsorship for exhibitions. She suggests that we sponsor an entire season at a very reasonable price . . . I'll think about it, and will consider it in terms of the available budget and the foreseen benefits for the bank. I thank her for the offer and hurry away from an excellent lunch in a really cosy restaurant in Upper Town and I return to the office.

My last task of the day is a meeting with my staff: on the agenda are talks about their performance assessment for 2011. Fortunately, the discussion is pleasant – most of my staff have met their planned objectives, and we have been very successful overall as a team.

Thursday 22 April

I have a regular meeting at 10 o'clock with the president of the management board, where we usually go through all the current topics in my field. This time the topics include the coming EBRD conference in May, with the bank as one of the main sponsors. Then there are my planned objectives for 2012, first of all concerning PR but also the field of corporate culture, with regard to the coming rebranding project, which means repositioning the brand. In fact, there has been some significant change in the perceptions of banking institutions on the business market: banks have lost quite a lot of brand equity in terms of credibility, but also empathy for the client. Our group has therefore decided to change the brand promise, i.e. the idea that stands behind the key message for all our partners-stakeholders. This one will be much more realistic and 100% client focused – our ambition is to become a client-friendly bank that is easy to deal with. The meeting ends only two hours later, following a very constructive discussion. The guidelines are set, and I start work and try, as far as possible, to use Croatian terms. This isn't easy, because I work in a branch which is simply drowning in all kinds of Anglicisms . . . linguists, please forgive me.

In the afternoon, some visitors arrive who are organising an interesting festival that we are pleased to sponsor. The conversation develops around the incredible number of participants and the excellent effects for the bank in terms of the target group of students and the young urban population. They are already announcing the programme for 2013 – what's the hurry?

Friday 23 April

Today is the day for the staff meeting: we usually start at around 10 and end two hours later. Each of the teams *Media Relations*, *Corporate Sustainability*, *Brand Management*, *Corporate Culture*, *Web Identity* and *Event Management* gets the chance to present current projects, together with problems and solutions. I think it's extremely important that the entire department comes together at these staff meetings every fortnight, where they are informed first hand what their colleagues are doing, because it is not necessarily true that they can get to know about this in their everyday work. This is how we ensure a flow of information, good internal communication and what is perhaps most important, these meetings boost our creativity, our imagination runs free, we become innovative and ideas simply run wild.

After a quick lunch, I decide to devote my attention to all the received and neglected emails and correspondence, I make lots of phone calls and delegate tasks . . . Next, I also meet with the team in charge of sponsorships and donations and we draw up a plan for the whole year for sponsorship in culture. It's interesting to note that, in spite of the recession, the activity of cultural institutions is not slowing down. On the contrary, they have proposals for very high quality projects – but, naturally, they lack money. We are certainly going to support some of them – but we conclude, before we do so, we will have another round of talks with them.

Early tomorrow morning, I have a meeting with colleagues from Private Banking: they are coming from Milan, and we are going to draw up a platform upon which they wish to build their PR and marketing strategy. I find some old notes on this subject and do a bit of preparation . . . and what do you know, it's already 6 p.m. and another exciting day at the bank is over! I really love my job!

Brief CV	I began my career in the position of assistant in the American advertising company Saatchi & Saatchi where I spent my first 5 years of training in advertising and marketing. Subsequently, I moved to the then largest commercial chain for toys, fashion and sports in Croatia – Magma – where I worked as Marketing and PR director. The next step in my career was in Siemens, where I stayed for 5 years as director of Corporate Communications. Currently I work as director of Corporate Identity and Communications in Zagrebačka Banka, which is part of the UniCredit Group. I am a member of the Croatia PR Association and of the European Association of Communication Directors.
A few words about the company where you work	Zagrebačka Banka has for years been the leading banking institution in the Croatian market. It operates in Croatia with 80,000 corporate customers and over 1.1 million private customers. Since March 2002, it has been part of the UniCredit Group, one of the strongest financial groups in Europe, which operates in a total of 22 key markets with approximately 10,000 outlets and over 40 million clients. Zagrebačka Banka is a leader in the local market and one of the most successful members of the UniCredit Group.

Question

Think how, after reading this diary, you would describe what PR practitioners do to a member of your family.
To what extent does this person's activities relate to the perception of PR practitioners as persons who manipulate the media or as publicists in the world of show business?

CLOTHES TO FIT THE PRACTITIONERS

PR roles are often classified into those done by communications 'managers' and 'technicians'. This division has its roots in research conducted by Broom and Smith (1979) and Broom and Dozier (1986), identifying two dominant roles of PR, which, although criticised by many (White et al. 2009: 392), are also used and described in a number of PR textbooks on both sides of the Atlantic. The dual typology defines two roles to describe the work of practitioners:

- Communications manager, who plans and manages PR programmes, gives advice to management, makes decisions on communications policy and supervises its implementation; they act more like thinkers.

- Communications technician, who is not involved in decision-making in the organisation, but implements PR programmes, or conducts activities to implement them, such as writing press releases, organising events, producing contents for various publications, the internet, intranet, etc. According to this classification, technicians are not usually engaged in the preliminary research for the programme or in any evaluation following its implementation; they act more like doers.

The division of roles into managers and technicians does not in any way mean that there is a clear dividing line, because most practitioners perform a combination of these tasks, which you can see in the actual cases of the practitioners' diaries which form part of this chapter. Nevertheless, it can be stated that at the very beginning of their career, most practitioners are assigned mainly technical tasks and when they advance in the profession and gain experience and knowledge, they gradually move towards management tasks, which, at the top of the pyramid, include participation in key decisions for their organisation.

More clothes to fit the practitioners

Roles (Dozier and Broom 1995; Cutlip et al. 2006) may be further divided into:

- Expert prescriber who defines the problem, develops a programme for solving it and assumes full responsibility for its execution. When the role of the professional in charge of PR in the organisation is established in this way, what frequently happens is that the top management of the organisation assumes a relatively passive role and leaves public relations in the hands of the experts. Although this might flatter the practitioner, such a division of roles within the organisation might lead to a situation where the expert prescriber becomes responsible for the results of the PR programme he or she is implementing even when he or she has very little or no influence on all the factors which have led to something becoming a PR problem. In organisations that are not prepared to deal with the causes of a problem but expect the PR professionals to offer solutions with PR tools, one PR expert is easily replaced by another, but this does not solve the core problems.

- The communication facilitator works in practice as a type of information broker and sensitised listener who maintains two-way communication between the organisation and its publics, who connects them and interprets and mediates between them. The aim of communication facilitators is to provide the management of the organisation for which they work and its publics with the information they need to make decisions in their mutual interest. They work under the assumption that high-quality two-way communication improves the quality of the decisions that an organisation and publics make about mutually important procedures, activities and policies.

● The problem-solving facilitator on one hand helps others resolve communication problems, and on the other hand functions as a programme planning and implementing consultant. PR professionals who have this role collaborate with other managers in the organisation in defining and resolving problems and become part of the organisation's top management. Problem-solving facilitators become part of the management team because they have shown and proven their skills and have contributed to the organisation in helping other managers either avoid or resolve problems. The result of their work is often to include public relations thinking in management decision-making at all levels within the organisation.

Of course, within each of the above roles there is further great variety, which, in addition to the knowledge and skills of an individual practitioner, is largely defined by the type and size of the organisation where they work, the positioning of PR as a function within that organisation, the top management's awareness and conviction of the importance of the role of PR, etc. Thus, for example, a technician who was given a job in PR because he or she writes well may work on an entire range of tasks that include writing, from press releases and blogs to speeches to internal and external publications, but his or her job may also be limited, for instance, to writing content for the corporate website. On the other hand, a highly positioned PR manager may be in charge of external and internal communication, investor relations, sponsorships and donations, social responsibility and corporate identity, or, if he or she works in an equally high position for a very large organisation, may cover, for instance, only one of these areas.

Most roles in an organisation may be performed by an in-house expert or an external consultant, i.e. a consultancy company (agency), or a combination of both. Generally, all the jobs in PR are either:

● In-house, within an organisation, whether in the private or public sector, or in companies or public bodies, state administration, local self-government, non-governmental and humanitarian organisations, and the NGO sector; or

● In consultancies where PR professionals work as consultants for the clients of these agencies, or as freelance practitioners whose work is not much different from that of agency consultants, apart from the fact that they are one-man bands and, as such, are taken on for projects by in-house departments or agencies.

Critical Reflection

Read the following quotation from the article 'The United Kingdom: advances in practice in a restless kingdom' by White et al. (2009):

Much of the discussion about the role of the practitioners, within academic circles, has focused on debates about the extent to which practitioners fulfil a predominantly 'manager' or 'technician' role. The use of this dual typology of manager–technician roles to explain the work of practitioners has been criticised on a number of grounds, not least that these role typologies only represent abstractions for studying the wide range of activities that practitioners perform in their daily lives.

When reading the practitioners' diaries included in this chapter, can you draw a line in individual cases between the 'manager' and 'technician' roles? Can you clearly recognise an expert prescriber, a communication facilitator and a problem-solving facilitator among these practitioners? Or are these *abstractions*, as the above criticism calls them, difficult to transfer into reality?

ALL THE DIFFERENT THINGS THEY DO

When we think of the work of practitioners through the activities and tasks they perform, this contributes to a better understanding of the practice. Thus, Cutlip et al. (2006: 34–5) categorised work in public relations according to its tasks, and came up with ten elements that summarise what PR practitioners do in their job. According to them, the following ten categories summarise what public relations specialists do at work.

1. **Writing and editing**: Composing print and broadcast news releases, feature stories, newsletters to employees and external stakeholders, correspondence, website and other online media messages, shareholder and annual reports, speeches, brochures, film and slide-show scripts, trade publication articles, institutional advertisements, and product and technical collateral materials.

2. **Media relations and placement**: Contacting news media, magazines, Sunday supplements, freelance writers and trade publications with the intent of getting them to publish or broadcast news and features about or originating from an organisation. Responding to media requests for information, verification of stories and access to authoritative sources.

3. **Research**: Gathering information about public opinion, trends, emerging issues, the political climate and legislation, media coverage, special-interest groups and other concerns related to an organisation's stakeholders. Searching the internet, online services and electronic government databases. Designing programme research, conducting surveys and hiring research firms.

4. **Management and administration**: Programming and planning in collaboration with other managers; determining needs, establishing priorities, defining publics, setting goals and objectives, and developing strategy and tactics. Administering personnel, budgets, and programme schedules.

5. **Counselling**: Advising top management on the social, political and regulatory environments; consulting with the management team on how to avoid or respond to crises; and working with key decision makers to devise strategies for managing or responding to critical and sensitive issues.

6. **Special events**: Arranging and managing news conferences, 10 km runs, conventions, open houses, ribbon cuttings and grand openings, anniversary celebrations, fund-raising events, visiting dignitaries, contents, award programmes and other special observances.

7. **Speaking**: Appearing before groups, coaching others for speaking assignments and managing a speaker's bureau to provide platforms for the organisation before important audiences.

8. **Production**: Creating communications using multimedia knowledge and skills, including art, typography, photography, layout and computer desktop publishing; audio and video recording and editing; and preparing audio-visual presentations.

9. **Training**: Preparing executives and other designated spokespersons to deal with the media and to make other public appearances. Instructing others in the organisation to improve writing and communication skills. Helping introduce change in the organisational culture, policy, structure and processes.

10. **Contact**: Serving as liaison with media, community and other internal and external groups. Listening, negotiating, managing conflict and reaching agreement as mediator between an organisation and its important stakeholders. Meeting and acting as host to guests and visitors.

Going a step further in connecting activities and tasks with practice, Johanna Fawkes describes the common PR areas with examples of what practitioners do in each field:

Public relations activity	Explanation	Examples
Internal communications	Communicating with employees	In-house newsletter, suggestion boxes
Corporate PR	Communicating on behalf of whole organisation, not goods or services	Annual reports, conferences, ethical statements, visual identity, images
Media relations	Communicating with journalists, specialists, editors from local, national, international and trade media, including newspapers, magazines, radio, TV and web-based communication	Press releases, photocalls, video news releases, off-the-record briefings, press events
Business to business	Communicating with other organisations, e.g. suppliers, retailers	Exhibitions, trade events, newsletters
Public affairs	Communicating with opinion formers, e.g. local/national politicians, monitoring political environment	Presentations, briefings, private meetings, public speeches
Community relations/ corporate social responsibility	Communicating with local community, elected representatives, headteachers, etc.	Exhibitions, presentations, letters, meetings, sports activities and other sponsorship
Strategic communication	Identification and analysis of situation, problem and solutions to further organisational goals	Researching, planning and executing campaigns to improve ethical reputation of organisation
Issues management	Monitoring political, social, economic and technological environment	Considering effect of US economy and presidential campaign on UK organisation
Crisis management	Communicating clear messages in fast changing situation or emergency	Dealing with media after major rail crash on behalf of police, hospital or local authority
Copywriting	Writing for different audiences to high standards of literacy	Press releases, newsletters, web pages, annual reports
Publications management	Overseeing print/media processes, often using new technology	Leaflets, internal magazines, websites
Events management, exhibitions	Organisation of complex events, exhibitions	Annual conference, press launch, trade shows

Source: Johanna Fawkes (in Theaker 2004, p. 7)

These activities and tasks intermingle in everyday practice under the very varied job titles given to PR professionals, although quite similar jobs – made up of a similar mix of activities and tasks – usually lie behind pretty different titles. To them we must now also add monitoring, writing and responding to issues on various social media platforms.

A 'thicket' of titles and requirements in PR job ads

The PR jobs on offer give us a brief overview of the variety of titles, and a hint about what activities and tasks may be involved in the work of these practitioners.

Exercise 1

1. Find and search websites with job announcements in your country or the websites of professional PR associations, which generally have a 'jobs section' and see what jobs are offered. What do they require from candidates? What qualities, knowledge and skills are apparently requested and why?

2. You will probably notice that even very similar PR job descriptions bear very different job titles. Why do you think this is?

3. In some cases, job announcements stress the 'capability to develop strategy' but the description of tasks seems to be fully focused on something tactical, such as developing content and materials. What do you think is happening here?

There are many ways to enter public relations. Although this chapter does not deal with PR education, it should certainly be mentioned that one of the paths is to enrol in regular studies, which last three or four years, following which it is possible to do postgraduate courses up to PhD level. On the other hand, experts who come to public relations from other areas will be wise to enrol and complete a differential PR programme and then, just like the students who gain more comprehensive education, engage in continuous professional development and life-long learning in their field of interest.

Necessary knowledge	Necessary skills
Communication and persuasion concepts and strategies	Research methods and analysis
Communication and public relations theories	Management of information
Relationships and relationship building	Mastery of language in written and oral communication
Societal trends	Problem-solving and negotiation
Ethical issues	Management of communication
Legal requirements and issues	Strategic planning
Marketing and finance	Issues management
Public relations history	Audience segmentation
Uses of research and forecasting	Informative and persuasive writing
Multicultural and global issues	Community relations, consumer relations, employee relations, other practice areas
Organisational change and development	Technological and visual literacy
Management concepts and theories	Managing people, programmes and resources
	Sensitive interpersonal communication
	Fluency in a foreign language
	Ethical decision-making
	Participation in the professional PR community
	Message production
	Working with a current issue
	Public speaking and presentation
	Applying cross-cultural and cross-gender sensitivity

Exercise 2

For more insight into the CIPR's (Chartered Institute of Public Relations) CPD (continuous professional development), go to www.cipr.co.uk/cpd/index.html

CPD is a record of individual annual learning and development, completed by accruing points across different activities. Taking part in the CIPR's CPD leads to Accredited Practitioner status – professional recognition of skills and ability, primarily in the UK. With the spread of CIPR-accredited educational centres abroad, more and more CIPR members, not only British but also international members, can now also benefit from this well-structured CPD.

Roadmap to success

All who have agency experience will agree that agencies are ideal working environments for adrenalin junkies, who, by the way, can certainly count on long hours and hard work. Hinrichsen (2001: 451–3) says about the job descriptions in agencies,

> the typical agency job might not exist but there are some common factors among agencies: they tend to be fast-paced, exciting, demanding and challenging. . . . If public relations is seen as a glamorous field, then public relations firms may be viewed as 'Glamour Central'. There can be prestige and excitement, and there is always a fast pace. Some other advantages are . . . variety . . . big budgets . . . a team of professionals; perhaps the biggest advantage is being able to work with peers who understand public relations . . . many of the most skilled practitioners work in agencies" . . . On the flip side, agency life can also be rigorous, stressful and demanding. Some of the issues are . . . the long hours . . . the agency environment is like a pressure cooker, with what can seem like constant hammering to stay billable, produce excellent work under a time crunch, stay on budget, satisfy the client, and manage the ever changing workload . . .'

Cropp and Pincus (2001: 200), referring to the future requirements of public relations practitioners in terms of skills, say that they will also have to be 'strategic thinkers and doers, with a premium attached to those with the business training, knowledge, and acumen to position their organizations favourably among the people comprising the stakeholder groups whose loyalty the organizations cannot do without'.

Concerning the question of what is needed to succeed in PR, Grunig and Hunt (1984: 92) wrote over a quarter of a century ago something that is confirmed by today's practice:

> You may occupy only one public relations role at a time, but whether you are the senior public relations professional in an organization or the most junior communication technician, you will perform that role more effectively if you understand how it contributes to meeting both public relations department objectives and overall organizational goals.

Typical of the systems theory school that they represent in their works, these authors viewed the role of PR practitioners and the 'something' that is needed for success in this job primarily from the perspective of the organisation and its goals.

L'Etang (2008: 6–7), in her critical reflections on PR from 'alternative perspectives', contextualises the profession very broadly when she says:

> Inter-disciplinary thinking draws upon a wide range of subjects to try to understand a problem. It is central to public relations education and to its practitioners who need to engage with multiple interested parties, perspectives and relationships. At present public relations is an emergent discipline with porous boundaries to a range of other disciplines: marketing, management, organization studies, communications, journalism, media studies. . . . It is because public relations cuts across these disciplines that it is

important to read beyond public relations books and journals and think more broadly about problems. . . . For example, can we really think properly about 'strategy' without reading some sources in strategic studies . . . ? Can we talk about 'persuasion' without reading psychology and political science? . . . Thinking divergently can help our creativity (a facility much prized in public relations) by forcing the pathways in our brains to work in unusual ways. Working in different areas is challenging, hard but rewarding. Public relations students need to be curious and intellectually brave, not just clever!

Critical Reflection

Compare the above quotations from Grunig and Hunt (1984) and L'Etang (2008). What does it take in your opinion to succeed in the public relations profession?

Job announcements reflect one picture, the practitioners' diaries another, and some of the theory elaborated here a third. Describe in your own words, using one example, what public relations practitioners do, how they contribute to the organisation where they work, and what their broader social roles are.

Name	Ben Verinder
Company	Association of Colleges (AoC)
Position	Communications Director
Four days in my professional life	**19 February** On Saturday a 19-year-old sitting in a parked car was shot dead by two masked men in East London. The attack is probably a case of mistaken identity. Newspaper reports describe him as a university student. He was studying a two year foundation degree at a college and this evening the college's head of marketing and communications rings asking for advice – a second opinion – on handling media enquiries. The BBC and *Evening Standard* have called in the past half an hour. We discuss what should and should not appear in a reactive statement, the protocols of checking with the victim's family, steps to ensure that other journalists get the information they need. The college has established a counselling service for staff and students. Social media channels flood with tributes. In a decade of advising education institutions, this has probably been the most common crisis management call – young people as victims of crime, often by virtue of being in the wrong place at the wrong time. What is happening to the young man's family, friends and tutors trivialises what frames it. I struggle to describe my working day without sounding shallow. The rest of today is dedicated to my consultancy business. I write: a summary of findings and recommendations at the end of a three-month-long reputation research project; notes for a client workshop on developing communications and brand; slides for a talk about how a national research project into business trends can be used for curriculum planning. **20 February** An early train to Birmingham, where I am an observer at a digital communications training session, helping an Association of Colleges colleague

assess the workshop and advising on the likely market among education communicators. It is a healthy mix of the tactical and strategic, well structured, and we are regularly invited to participate. 'We want to use this exercise to check that you have understood everything so far', repeats the trainer. I pick up technical and training titbits.

The remains of the day are dominated by the search for a communications conference speaker. The last piece of the programme's jigsaw is an expert on influencing senior management teams and boards. I speak to an occupational psychologist, two life coaches and a university director whom I have previously heard speak, purposefully and inspirationally, on the topic. People are either unsuitable or unavailable. The search continues.

As with every working day I monitor emails and respond where necessary, which is rare. The 'CC' button is usually an instrument of courtesy among the teams with whom I work.

21 February

Somewhere within the labyrinth of Government meeting rooms I am among a group discussing a new loans system with the team responsible for its implementation. Loans will replace many fully-subsidised courses, and they are controversial. The response is frank – in the current economic climate and a Treasury seeking more savings from each department, this is the least worst choice. My task is to understand the state of play and pass on college concerns to the team managing loans communications; AoC runs nine regional PR, communications and marketing networks and these channels have buzzed with the issue for months. We have also been monitoring LinkedIn group discussions and Twitter comments. Marketing directors call to express their concerns. Many communication problems have already been addressed by the Government team, it appears, but the task for colleges remains very difficult: they are expected to be the main communication channel 'to market'; there is, hitherto, no plan or funding for a national awareness campaign; colleges must walk a tightrope between introducing the scheme and avoiding giving financial advice. Poor communication will blight second chances.

I am reassured by the speaker that more of the market research is soon to be placed in the public domain – communicators need to see the wiring, to understand better the attitudes to debt among different groups and see more of the results of earlier message-testing focus groups.

In the afternoon I organise college visits for a national newspaper education editor. He is interested in new higher education and pre-16 provision in colleges. Later, I spend an hour working through the mechanics of recruiting a new press officer with the colleague who manages the post. She has already done most of the hard work, updating the job description, refreshing the advertising copy, booking interview dates. The current incumbent has spent 18 months with us and excelled. He moves on to a much bigger organisation and the opportunity to rotate between different press offices, an offer he says he cannot refuse and we sadly cannot match.

22 February

A college marketing and communications director calls me for advice on his new patch. He has moved south to take up this senior post at a much bigger institution. Minutes later his former manager – Vice Principal of a college in the North East – emails asking for data to help support a presentation on the impact of education communications, for a senior management team. I think of the time when they were both working in a small team in a small college and the day they both decided to sit the Chartered Institute of Public Relations Diploma. There, in my estimation, began their ascent.

As with every Friday morning, the senior team spends several hours on the business of managing the organisation – member issues, our people, finances, buildings, projects, commercial activity, policy headlines. The forward planning section is invaluable. Later I use it as the skeleton for a planning conversation with the editor of a trade journal. A reporter on the same title also calls, asking if I know of any Principals willing to comment about local councils 'cutting' funding for some students with special needs. All the colleges I speak to are still negotiating with councils and hopeful that they can correct the problem. Appearing in a national newspaper, they say, will not help their local cause.

It's late and I make time for a meeting with the project manager for our new website. Accepted practice says that we should aim to reduce our bounce-rate. Research, contrarily, tells us that a significant set of our audience wants to find the document they are looking for and leave the site straight away. Thus ends the week as many begin, wrestling with the paradoxes of membership communications – how to meaningfully measure success and represent collective concerns without affecting individual relationships and reputations.

Brief biography

Ben Verinder works part-time as communications director for the Association of Colleges (AoC) and runs a consultancy specialising in reputation and relationship management, strategic communications and market intelligence. Ben's career started as a senior print journalist in the north west of England, a BBC radio producer and, later, education editor with online portal Freeserve. He moved into marketing and public relations with a software development company, then travelled to South America with development charity Raleigh International, before joining AoC. Ben is an accredited Chartered Institute of Public Relations practitioner, a judge on a number of PR and journalism awards, and a regular speaker on public relations. His biography of Cumbrian writer Mary Burkett – *I Felt Like An Adventure* – was published in 2008.

Case study
Ahmad Odeh's diary from the Middle East

A crisis in a crisis management training course

Riyadh, Saudi Arabia, 2009

That was a memorable day! I was invited by the institute of Prince Ahmed Bin Salman for Applied Media in Riyadh, to run a training course on media crisis management. Trainees were the chief editors of different Yemeni newspapers and the course was sponsored by the Saudi Ministry of Information.

Things went normally at the beginning, just until it was time for each of the trainees to introduce themselves to the others. Then I was in the middle of a real crisis where I would need to apply the theories I had already planned to teach in this course. The trainees represented a wide range of political standpoints in Yemen. They belonged to almost every political party, for and against the regime, and there were very few beliefs in common.

Different religious, governmental, liberal and national ideologies were all represented in that training room, for four days, on a course where each one was supposed to share and discuss their work with his enemies. Most of the trainees believed that their party's problems were actually caused by other trainees in the group who were defending their opponent's positions, and yet here they were sitting right next to them.

Although I believe that there is an opportunity in every crisis, this training course gave me a number of opportunities. I had to learn how to negotiate with opponents and communicate with people with different thoughts and cultural backgrounds.

That training course took my actual experience to a new level and enhanced my belief that a public relations expert should learn the skill of communication in a multicultural environment. While I was the trainer for that course, I believe that I was also a trainee in a course I will never forget!

Libya – 42 years of ignorance

Tripoli, January 2012

My first visit to Libya was a fruitful one in every sense of the word. At a human level I had the chance to see the suffering the Libyan people were forced to endure for 42 years of ignorance and repression. I had the chance to listen to Libyan people for the first time and to hear stories about their lives, which were much worse than I had understood before.

Yet, this visit was also fruitful at a professional level. I recognised how mistaken a regime is when it closes all means of communication for the public for a long period of time and how such behaviour increases misunderstandings and distorts the image of the state and the statesmen. It gave me a good feeling of the importance of my role as a public relations expert in the reformation and rebuilding of the Libyan state. Public relations is as vital as water and air for the new Libya.

Terms such as opinion, point of view, communication channels, public opinion, level of awareness, credibility, trust, mutual understanding, the publics' aspirations, publics' reactions, influencing opinion and so on were simply forbidden terms. The use of any of those terms was punishable by a prison sentence. The regime was also against any kind of celebrity or fame for any individual apart from Colonel Gaddafi. Even sports commentators were forced to refer to famous football players by their numbers only and were forbidden to use their names. The people also had no idea who anyone else in government was.

During my visit I conducted a number of meetings with government officials and members of the Transitional National Council, working for an agreement on the initiatives and projects based on using public relations to help the new Libyan state. Talks were about internal communication and also connecting members of the government within a wireless communication system to enable them to keep in contact with all geographic areas. Other meetings focused on elections and the necessary means of communication to encourage people to participate after 42 years without elections or political parties. We also discussed the training of spokespeople and helping the people to make use of social media and learn journalism and public relations skills. Talking about such topics would have been impossible before the revolution but Libya is at last entering into an era of media and communication.

Brief CV

Ahmad Odeh of Turjuman, MCIPR, CIPR Course Leader, UAE

- Course leader of Chartered Institute of Public Relations CIPR in the UAE.
- President of the Arab Forum for best practices in public relations and corporate communications.
- A certified instructor in public relations (Beginner, Intermediate, Advanced) from the CIPR.
- Approved Trainer in Diploma in Diplomatic Studies/Emirates Center for Strategic Studies and Research in Abu Dhabi.
- General Manager and founder of Turjuman Consultancy UAE, Tripoli, Saudi Arabia and Jordan.
- The former Director of Corporate Communications, Nobles Holding Company, United Arab Emirates.
- The former projects manager at Al Jazeera Media Training and Development Centre/ Al Jazeera Channel.
- Provided advisory services in public relations and corporate communications for a number of major institutions in the region.
- Designed many working papers at international conferences specialising in public relations and corporate communications.

Working for Turjuman Consultancy

Turjuman is a limited liability company based in the UAE, Tripoli, Saudi Arabia and Jordan, which specialises in providing professional training and consultancy in corporate communication and public relations, according to the latest professional practices in the world.

The company slogan is 'Translating knowledge into practice'.

Turjuman is an exclusive agent in the UAE for the Chartered Institute of Public Relations CIPR.

Case study
The German had my lunch! Frank Tamuno-Koko, FNIPR

Frank Tamuno-Koko is a leading PR consultant and campaigner for the public relations profession in Nigeria. He chairs the committee of Fellows of the Nigerian Institute of Public Relations, rigorously working to uphold their standards.

Prologue

Blessed is the man (woman?) who first mixed and drank the concoction now known as coffee. Nothing helps to start a day better than sipping a hot cup of this wonderful juice while watching television to get news of what had transpired in the few hours you spent out of this world sleeping. So another day started for me on this fateful day in May of 2010. The 'to do' list was typical of most of my days: meeting at 9.30 am with Orlean Invest (West Africa) Ltd, press interview at 12 noon and lunch at 2.00 pm, Community Development Committee Council meeting at 5.00 pm and meeting with Chief Inimgba at 8.00 pm.

Background

For over thirty years I had practised and taught Public Relations, especially managing Community Relations from behind the corporate desk. However, in 2008 this changed when I became the Chairman of my Community's Development Committee – a statutorily recognised development platform. This meant for me, practising Public Relations in the field.

The main responsibility of the CDC is the daily administration of the community, including managing relationships with companies for the development and good of the community in a peaceful, transparent and sustainable way. Situated at the Trans-Amadi industrial area of Port Harcourt in the Niger Delta of Nigeria, my Community Amadi Ama, with a population of about 10,000, has as guest companies the NLNG (Nigerian Liquefied Natural Gas Company), Chevron, Total, Orlean Invest West Africa (with its subsidiaries) Van Oord, Trevi Foundation, Hyundai, Julius Berger, Idekke Shipping and several others including many banks. All of these companies are either in the oil and gas or construction sectors of the economy.

It is pertinent to understand the environment that dictates or rather heavily influences such a daily schedule. The UNDP (United Nations Development Programme) *Niger Delta Human Development Report 2006* rightly asserts that a major concern in the Niger Delta is the long standing exclusion of the communities from the mainstream of Nigeria's socio-economic and political activities. Economically, the region is heavily invested in by the oil and gas industry, but despite the fact that this is a non-renewable resource, economic diversification has been limited. Local people cannot tap directly into oil industry benefits because they lack skills or capital resources or both. The once rich agricultural fields and fishing creeks have been polluted or abandoned, and so the majority of the people live on the margins. The Niger Delta today is a place of frustrated and deep-rooted mistrust. Long years of neglect and deprivation have fostered a siege mentality among the youth – some very well educated – who feel they are condemned to a future without hope and see conflict as means of redressing the deprivation and an escape from it.

While turmoil in the Niger Delta has many sources and motivations, the pre-eminent underlying cause is the historical failure of governance at all levels. The result is that communities such as mine have now resorted to holding the nearest 'government' hostage to provide basic amenities of life. 'It matters not that you pay your taxes and so forth, you must provide to uplift our lives or you operate over our dead bodies.' This might sound extreme, but it is the environment in which community relations is practised in the Niger Delta of Nigeria. Businesses are now the main providers of basic necessities, sometimes under duress and with many in the communities thinking and feeling it is their right and the responsibility of the companies so to provide. This is the terrain that shapes your daily to-do list in these parts.

The day starts

9.30 am

I arrive at Orlean Invest as pre-arranged to continue discussion on increasing the amount of the company's commitment to projects in the community. We (the community's representatives) 'insist' on an increase of 100 per cent and the company (represented by its Community Relations/Public Affairs Manager and his team) say the economic climate is such that no increase would be possible 'for now'. After some seasoned reasoning by both sides the company offers a 50 per cent increase. Inwardly we are happy, as this was our target. But we suspend discussion, agreeing to come back with final answer to their offer after reporting the outcome of the meeting to the Chiefs and Elders Council.

12.00 noon

In the previous week an article had appeared in a local newspaper alleging that Amadi Ama was a den for cultists and militants, quoting the proprietor of a local business to give credence to its story. This report sent panic waves in the community because in the recent past it has been a victim of military high-handedness. On the pretext of flushing miscreants, cultists and militants from the community based on 'intelligence' received, the military and the police had invaded the community, looted properties and destroyed social cohesion. At a meeting between the CDC and the Chiefs and Elders Council to discuss the implications and necessary counter-actions, the majority proposed that we should publish an 'advertorial' in a rival local newspaper in order to debunk the allegation. It was felt that the advertorial would expose the lie and forestall any possible reprisal actions from security agencies. To me, this was inadequate and not the appropriate channel to communicate with the right quarters, nor was it the right strategy. My submission was to send letters to the Commissioner of Police in the state, the Commander of the Joint Military Force (JTF) in the state, the State Governor and the Chief of Defence Staff in Abuja, debunking the allegation and pledging our commitment as responsible citizens to continue to uphold the peace and act within the law. In addition, all the letters were to be delivered by hand immediately, except the one to the Chief of Defence Staff at Abuja which would be sent by courier. Furthermore, the editor of the local newspaper which published the story should be invited to observe first-hand the peace in the community, the unavailability of bush where militants could make their home and that the address of the business proprietor quoted in the original story did not exist. This was accepted and actions started immediately.

The editor came, went round the community, talked to a few people and sat down with me for an interview. He was thereafter given a copy of our side of the story to the various authorities. (He subsequently built his story on my interview and this became our 'rebuttal'.)

2.00 pm – the lunch the German ate

So far the day had gone well. There would certainly be a good atmosphere at the CDC Council meeting later in the day and I was certain Chief Inimgba, the community's most senior Chief, would give the CDC a pat on the back. With this good feeling, I sat down to eat lunch with my friend Victor, a bottle of wine to go with the meal. Victor was in the process of saying grace for the meal – then the phone rings and rings again. We say amen and I pick up the phone . . . *There is fire on the mountain!* The caller, the Community Relations Officer from the NLNG, quickly narrates the source of the fire and there goes my lunch – abandoned!

The NLNG maintains an operations base at the Amadi Creek opposite my community. Boats of different draughts commute in a military-led convoy twice daily to Bonny, the NLNG's operational headquarters some 40 nautical miles away. The impact of the waves on the community are many and varied: boats sunk, fishermen inconvenienced, our shoreline eroded by the pounding waves; these have been the source of disaffection between the community and the NLNG. The complaint box is always abuzz with one or other of these sources of disaffection. It got worse.

At low tide, two brothers aged 8 and 10 went swimming down the creek and, oblivious of the current the waves generated by the NLNG boats could cause, continued to play in the water. Unfortunately the undertow of the waves swept them off and they drowned before any help could reach them. Some young men of the community who rushed to the scene following the alarm recovered one boy and gave up on the other and waited for the body to naturally float to the surface. Here was an opportunity to get even with the NLNG for defoliating and polluting our environment and 'doing nothing' to remedy these actions. This was an opportunity to make some money out of the miserly NLNG that 'does nothing for the community'. So, six boat-loads of about 40 young men rowed across the creek and berthed at the NLNG jetty with the recovered corpse as a present to the company. You could hear the chants of the war songs above the din and bustle of a busy jetty. 'NLNG come and carry your corpse', they demanded, or 'fire would burn'. Please come and help prevent the fire starting, the NLNG Community Relations man on the phone pleaded.

First, I got in touch with the youths and assured them I was coming right away. I requested that they should withdraw all the boats from the NLNG jetty except the one with the corpse. Two boats must stay, they demanded, and I accepted. The CDC Vice Chairman was immediately summoned and within minutes he was with me for the short walk to Chief Inimgba as I briefed him on the situation. We soon had the blessings and guidance of the Chief.

The Vice Chairman of the CDC, Sir Peter Roberts, went to see the bereaved parents who happened to come from another state, making them strangers at Amadi Ama. I headed for the NLNG – a four-minute drive. Sir Peter was to assure the parents of the community's support in the 'fight' with the NLNG and convey the condolence of the Chiefs and Elders Council on behalf of the community to them.

The NLNG was asked to waive the admittance procedure for me. On my arrival, a senior staff member met me and wanted me to come in right away for talks. You could not pretend the two boats and the agitated youths did not exist. I went across to the youths, greeted them and asked what they wanted. Having noted their demands, I asked that they should appoint three amongst them to accompany me to the meeting. These exchanges took place in the hearing of the NLNG officials who had wanted to deal with me alone. I didn't want to be accused of having been bought off by the NLNG or pocketing what was due to the community. Besides, they were mature enough to understand and follow the proceedings. Furthermore, it created a community versus NLNG atmosphere – I wasn't going to be alone.

The meeting kicked off with my rejection of the offer of tea or coffee or any form of refreshment. This rejection was predicated on the fact that in my previous meetings my polite requests had always been turned down for administrative reasons. For me and the boys, this was not time for tea, and I did not want to support the impression that most in the community had that whenever CDC members had meetings with companies on matters affecting the community, we spent the time eating and drinking, accepting whatever was offered even when it was to the community's disadvantage. We flatly rejected the attempt by the NLNG to pass the buck to the company contracted by them for ferry services; and also their attempt to push us to the military escorts who they alleged constantly ignore the NLNG speed limit across our creek.

At this point Sir Peter arrived to join us and inform us that about 100 youths spoiling for war were on their way to NLNG. He had stopped and appealed to them to abandon the path of violence and terminate their march at the entrance to the NLNG. He reasoned with them to wait till the end of the meeting before taking any further action. He also privately informed me that the bereaved parents wanted no compensation but assistance in the burial of the boys. Quickly we agreed – quickly because reports kept coming in that the boys at the gate were wondering what on earth was keeping us – perhaps the NLNG was entertaining us with a sumptuous meal and drinks, and their numbers were increasing by the minute. The terms of the agreement covered 'appreciation' of the divers who recovered the corpse and would recover the second when it floated, drinks for the boys at the gate, burial expenses and water to 'cleanse the corpse carriers and their boats'. The representatives of the youths demanded on-the-spot payment. Because of payment procedures the 'immediate demand' was shelved. However, some amount acceptable by the boys was raised 'on the spot' for the 'cleansing'. A terminal date was agreed for the payments. In return, we promised that no further issues, legal or otherwise, would be raised and there would be no blockade of the creek. The representative of the boys announced the outcome to their peers.

We departed with a timetable to discuss further issues raised by this calamity and review our relationship with the NLNG and their contractors.

Sir Peter and I went to thank the young men for their peaceful conduct, and to brief the Chiefs and Elders on the outcome and finally the bereaved parents. I got home and asked for my lunch to be heated and served. We gave it to the German, came the reply. The dog ate my lunch? No answers! Thankfully the German abhors wine. It was 8.00 pm as I sat down for what was brought before me. As I ate, I wondered if the German did indeed eat all that fish in the soup, considering that he loves his meat so much more. For the abandoned meetings in the to-do list? We could reschedule. Thankfully the fire didn't roll down the mountain.

SUMMARY

In this chapter, we have surveyed the battleground of public relations practice, from the description and classification of roles, through the activities and tasks of PR practitioners, to the knowledge and skills required to enter the profession and to succeed in it. The roles developed by academics, the diaries of authentic PR practitioners and the overview of selected job announcements from three continents have often not been easy to connect into a single picture under the broad title 'What do PR practitioners do?'

In general, the role-model PR practitioner considered in this chapter would be a person who skilfully manages the complex relations within the organisation he or she works in and the relations of the organisation with its environment; who facilitates communication internally and externally; and who, on one hand, has a seat at the table of the top management and advises the leaders of the organisation but also has excellent skills ranging from, for example, writing to problem-solving and negotiating, while also possessing outstanding technological and visual literacy. This PR professional will also certainly have a professional certificate or diploma, if he or she came into PR from another profession, and will actively participate in the PR community and continue reading and learning as widely as possible, never ceasing to be 'curious and intellectually brave'. If you read job announcements, you will see that it is often stressed that the person is required to remain calm even under great pressure.

Questions

1. How much does such a practitioner differ from the stereotypes mentioned in the introduction to this chapter?
2. How would you write your CV if you were applying tomorrow for a PR job?
3. What choices would you make to gain the knowledge and skills to succeed in this profession?

REFERENCES

Broom, G. M. and D. M. Dozier (1986) 'Advancement for public relations role models', *Public Relations Review* 12(1): 37–56

Broom, G. M. and G. D. Smith (1979) 'Testing the practitoner's impact on clients', *Public Relations Review* 5(3): 47–59.

Chartered Institute of Public Relations (2010) www.cipr.co.uk

Cropp, F. and J. D. Pincus (2001) 'The mystery of public relations' in *Handbook of Public Relations*, R. L. Heath (ed.), Sage

Cutlip, S. M., A. H. Center and G. M. Broom (2006) *Effective Public Relations*, 9th edition, Prentice-Hall

Dozier, D. M. and G. M. Broom (1995) 'Evolution of the managerial role in public relations practice', *Journal of Public Relations Research* 7(1): 17–18

Grunig, J. E. and T. Hunt (1984) *Managing Public Relations*, Holt, Rinehart & Winston

Hinrichsen, C. L. (2001) 'Best practices in the public relations agency business' in *Handbook of Public Relations*, R. L. Heath (ed.), Sage

L'Etang, J. (2008) *Public Relations: Concepts, Practice and Critique*, Sage

Public Relations Consultants Association (2010) www.prca.org.uk

'Public Relations Education for the 21st Century: A Port of Entry' report (1999). Accessed at www.commpred.org/aportofentry/

Public Relations Institute of Australia (2010) www.pria.com.au

Public Relations Society of America (2010) www.prsa.org

Tench, R. and L. Yeomans (2006) *Exploring Public Relations*, Financial Times Prentice Hall

Theaker, A. (2004) *The Handbook of Public Relations*, Routhedge, p. 7

White, J., J. L'Etang and D. Moss (2009) 'The United Kingdom: advances in practice in a restless kingdom' in *The Global Public Relations Handbook*, K. Sriramesh and D. Verčič (eds), Routledge

Chapter 3
What is a public?

How does it lead to issues management and why is the term necessary to public relations practice?

Sue Wolstenholme

Learning outcomes

At the end of this chapter you should be able to:

- Understand how public relations work is informed by the working relationships needed by the client or organisation involved

- Realise why the needs of those relationships might more usefully dictate the measures of success, for the client or organisation, rather than the financial ambitions of shareholders

- Understand how to define those with whom relationships are needed (publics) from their points of view, using positive and negative standpoints

- Be familiar with identifying the best language and channels of communication, from posters to posting on the internet, to make contact with publics

- Know how to use issues management as a tool to open the conversations from which to build working and meaningful relationships

- Be familiar with the planning needs for social responsibility and sponsorship strategies

Introduction

This book has been written at a normal time in the development of ideas and public relations practice – that is, at a time of change. During change people can feel bewildered and confused about where their lives are going, whether at work or socially, and so it is vital that they are communicated with, as much as possible, to inform and possibly reassure them. This chapter deals with relationships and language, channels and style. It will ask whether we should adapt to make relationships work, but above all, how we choose with whom to make them.

It might seem too obvious or to sound like a truism but for communication to be effective, for trust to be established and relationships to be formed, everyone involved must understand each other.

Understanding is affected by many things: the language that is used, whether it is written, illustrated or spoken, the channel through which it is delivered and the circumstances of the people involved at the time. This chapter will explore some theories behind effective techniques that can increase understanding and thereby improve trust and relationships.

The chapter will cover the following issues:

- The misuse of jargon
- What is a public and why its definition from a broad perspective of attitudes, for each campaign or set of messages, is important to building relationships
- Why defining stakeholders might not work as well
- How closely defined publics help to expand the usefulness of issues management
- The importance of identification with messages
- How corporate social responsibility and sponsorship fit better when they grow out of issues management

There are two main points to this discussion in this chapter that challenge much of the accepted academic wisdom. Publics can represent opportunities as well as threats, especially before they are aware of an issue, and defining stakeholders instead or as well is an unnecessary and possibly confusing exercise.

Mini case study
Jargon

Many people working in specialist fields are inclined to lace their language with their specialism's particular jargon. This can make their work only accessible to others within their field and make it difficult for those outside to understand what they are saying.

In public relations we should know all about the importance of understandability and yet the following are extracts from the industry's main publication, *PRWeek*, in the UK:

Matt Cartmell, *PRWeek* 6 July 2011
Quoting Leigh Daynes of Plan UK, 'The apparent deficit in describing the difference charities make is disappointing. Often charities bamboozle the public with jargon and faux management speak when they're sitting on a gold mine of human interest stories.'

George Eustice, *NHS story needs clear treatment, PRWeek*, 7 April 2011
. . . and jargon, fit only for consumption by managers in the middle of the system, is high.

PR Week UK, 18 March 2011
. . . seen how a great idea or a central narrative is lost in jargon and corporate messaging.

Dominic O'Reilly, *Why don't you say what you mean? PR Week*, 22 June 2006
Public sector press releases full of jargon and buzzwords make me think, 'Heaven facilitate us'.

Not only because of the jargon used, but in many instances because information does not translate automatically into knowledge and that is why the public relations practitioner has to be more sophisticated rather than just act as a sender of messages. Information must be accessed, processed, absorbed, understood, interpreted and integrated by those needing to know it before they can accept or act upon it. Table 3.1 indicates some questions to ask, as a communicator, to improve the success of communication:

TABLE 3.1 Questions before communicating

First question	Following questions
Is it accessible?	What format is it in? Can all the publics see, read or hear? Where is it being made available?
Is it understandable?	What are the publics' first languages? What are their reading ages or capability? How much jargon is known well to them?
Is it absorbable?	Has enough time been allowed at the various stages for the information to sink in or to make sense?
Is it identifiable with?	Does the subject matter reflect the publics' interests? Can the publics identify with and thereby personalise the information?
Is it relevant or timely?	Is the information necessary or interesting to the publics at the moment?
How is it going to be interpreted?	How will you evaluate how the information has been interpreted?
Will it be integrated?	What will the publics do with the information within their daily lives?

WHAT IS A PUBLIC?

Stakeholders or audiences must be subdivided into publics for public relations to be effective

The term 'public' is attributed to John Dewey's 1927 book *The Public and its Problems*, which is possibly why publics are most often defined by the problems or issues they share and those that they might create for an organisation.

A public is a group of people, who need not know each other or even live in the same town, but they are a public because they:

face a similar problem – for example they can be single parents on low incomes with disabled teenagers or occupants of a street that has been designated for demolition

enjoy/support/follow the same things – such as fans of a particular football team, type of music or style of art

share the same concerns – for example those who worry about the environment, human rights issues or the welfare of young children or animals.

Publics can be at different stages in their development – in fact they might not yet know that they are about to become a public.

James Grunig discussed his situational theory of publics in 1984 and it is helpful in defining them in these terms because they will need different types of communication to involve them in conversations.

When a public faces a problem but does not realise it yet (they might live in a street that has been designated for demolition so that a new motorway can be built) they can be described as being *latent*.

When they recognise the problem's existence (perhaps a notice in the local library, a blog or an item on the news has alerted them) they have become *aware* and when they organise to do something about it (maybe they will arrange a meeting of some kind, create a petition against the motorway or even set up some kind of protest demonstration) they have become *active* (Grunig and Hunt 1984).

As indicated above, because publics can share problems, interests or concerns, the same individual can be a member of a large number of publics at the same time, but according to what is going on around them (for example, the imminence of the proposed flattening of their street, the football world cup final or an announcement about a new epidemic that might harm young children) they will be differently sensitised to pay attention to stimuli which might become their main concerns at that time.

It is important to note that the purpose of defining publics in this way is to enable you to generate a conversation with them in their terms rather than in yours. Therefore there is no value in defining them according to their age, gender, race, ethnicity, religion, sexuality, employer or location. It is impossible to have a meaningful conversation with all middle-aged, British, white, Christian, heterosexual males who work in sales, but if you refined the definition to add in some problems, interests or concerns, you would be able to open a discussion with them easily. For example, if you know that many of your organisation's employees are parents of teenage school children, who are capable of winning a place at university, you can immediately strike up a conversation with them that they will most likely be interested in joining.

However, if you just think of them as employees your conversation will not necessarily attract their attention.

Task

The author of this chapter raised three wonderful people as a single parent, living in an old and crumbling rural house. She likes the Rolling Stones, supports Plymouth Argyle Football Club, hates injustice, is very concerned about the plight of Palestinian people, is worried about the overfishing of the seas and wishes people would waste less of the world's resources, etc. Write down ten publics to which you belong.

It is also important to note that publics can behave differently according to their relationship with an issue.

James Grunig (Grunig and Hunt 1984) categorised them into being:

- All issue – those for whom anything goes so long as they can raise an audience or gain attention
- Apathetic – no matter how much they might be going to be affected they will remain unconcerned
- Single issue – they put their all energy into one cause, such as animal rights
- Hot issue – they will go for the latest ideas and jump on to the bandwagon.

No matter what the concerns, passions or positions of your publics, you need to know them because, for example, if you were to spend a month showing genuine interest in someone else's interests or concerns you will be likely to form a friendship, but if you spend ten years only discussing matters of concern to you, you are likely to remain lonely.

This is what business and most organisations fail to understand, in that they design most of their communication or public relations efforts around talking about themselves. However, as

Ledingham said in 2003, 'An organization's livelihood is affected by its ability to develop mutually satisfying relationships'.

There will be more on this later in the chapter, but first we have a short digression.

What about stakeholders?

The Bled Manifesto is a report on a Delphi study (as discussed in Chapter 1) and one of the areas considered was to ascertain whether or not there are any differences between the approach to the subject of public relations in the US and in Europe. The results were presented in July 2002 at the 9th International Public Relations Research Symposium in Bled, Slovenia (Van Ruler and Verčič 2002).

The whole study is well worth reading for a number of insights into the subject and it informs far more fully than the short extracts given here for the purposes of this chapter. Essentially it found that, generally, the US approach is commercially focused and the European one more interested in public service. Also and possibly in line with that finding, the Europeans tend to be more reflective and the Americans more pragmatic.

Concepts were discussed during the research and, while it can be tedious to be continually defining and redefining the terms used in public relations, it is vital for mutual understanding to know what all parties in a conversation mean by the terms that they use.

Key concepts for building a European definition of public relations were taken from the European Delphi study to determine the parameters for the European body of knowledge (EBOK). This was created for academics wanting to carry out research that could be useful to the development of the profession and of interest to students of the subject. The 20 concepts in order of choice were:

=1 Communication	=11 Stakeholders
=1 Relationships	=11 Environment (in terms of the organisation)
=3 Publics	=13 Ethics/integrity
=3 Mutual understanding	=13 Activity
5 Management	15 Society
6 Public trust	=16 Information
7 Organisation	=16 Philosophy
=8 Profession	18 Promotion
=8 Mutually beneficial	19 Informing people
10 Strategy	20 Engineering support

The concept of legitimacy has since been added to the list. Put simply, legitimacy means having undisputed credibility or legal endorsement. In communications terms a legitimate spokesperson has the right to speak or write on a matter by virtue of their genuine position of knowledge on the subject.

To investigate further into the use of legitimacy, as a concept in PR, readers might choose to study the work of Jürgen Habermas and his communicative action theory (as mentioned in Chapter 1). This is not an easy task, even for the most highly tuned or adventurous academic mind, and so he might more easily be accessed through clever people who understand him and his relevance to public relations. His work on the concept has been well investigated by a number of academics and especially Inger Jensen. As a result of her pioneering work, legitimacy has become regarded as a necessary prerequisite for trust.

In the Bled Manifesto the authors were discussing the split between those who felt that the subject was mainly about communication and those who put relationships to the fore, and they showed here how those two concepts came out of the survey for the EBOK. (The relationship–communication discussion has been aired in Chapter 1.)

The reason for showing the list of concepts here is to illustrate the concept of publics in relation to stakeholders. In 2002 it was considered that publics was as important a concept to public relations as mutual understanding.

As discussed above, without knowing your publics' interests it would be difficult to arrive at any level of mutual understanding. Sam Black said: 'Under modern conditions no government, industry, company or organisation of any kind can operate successfully without the cooperation of its publics, these publics may be both at home and overseas but mutual understanding will be a potent factor for success in every case' (Black 1989: 8).

Since 2002 the term 'stakeholders' has become more widely used, as practitioners have worked alongside those coming from political or management schools and academics have created theories to try and accommodate the term (Julia Jahansoozi in L'Etang and Pieczka 2006: 86; Grunig et al. 2002: 144; Anne Gregory in Theaker 2008: 55).

David McKie in 2006 expressed concerns about the increasing use of the term stakeholders in public relations. He found, in an analysis of journals, there were the following uses of the term: 22 in *Public Relations Review*; 27 in the *Journal of Communication Management*; 90 in the *Journal of Public Relations Research*; 94 in *Public Relations Quarterly*; 114 in *Public Relations Tactics*.

Dominic O'Reilly, quoted above complaining about the use of jargon, said: 'Whenever I hear "stakeholder", I just think of *Buffy the Vampire Slayer*' (*PRWeek*, 22 June 2006).

Their concerns are justified. In most public relations textbooks, written in English since 1984, the term 'stakeholders' is often used interchangeably with 'publics' or it is defined as being a number of things, including 'a group whose collective behavior can directly affect the organization's future but which is not under the organization's control' (Emshoff and Freeman in Grunig and Hunt 1984: 297).

Stakeholders can only ever be defined in the terms of the organisation doing the defining rather than in their own terms, and therefore their existence is in the realm of the organisation and any relationship with them is fashioned according to the organisation's intentions for them.

In fact, most organisations, whether private, public, charitable or just existing to put pressure on others to change, set up their communication plans and strategies in their own interest and go on to define those upon whom they want to have an effect. So it has been logical for them to focus on stakeholders. It helps them to identify those who matter most by the interest or impact they might have upon the organisation's success. However, by working in this way they are establishing a situation that is based upon one-way communication, as it is driven entirely from and for only one side's interests and not upon any hope to establish or develop relationships.

There are a number of different types of relationships that need to work for organisations to succeed. They can be grouped as follows (and the categories are not exhaustive):

- commercial – customers, suppliers, agents;
- socio-economic – employees and their families, potential employees, the communities local to any factories, offices or operating areas;
- political – decision-makers at local, regional, national and international levels;
- legal – organisations who have legal power, such as tax collectors, health and safety enforcers or environmental officers;
- professional – other members of the PR profession or allied groups, such as journalists, lawyers or marketers;
- moral – society at large in small or large part who might be affected by the actions or behaviour of the organisation.

All relationships will be built more successfully if they are based upon a good understanding of the others' point of view and can be open to the possibility for effective dialogue. Therefore these generic groups need to be further broken down into the publics they contain.

We are told that stakeholders become publics when they become active and thereby a more real threat to the organisation. Grunig et al. (2002) refer to them then as strategic publics, and when describing stakeholders, Gregory writes: 'When an individual or a group does become active and interested, then they may be regarded as a public' (Anne Gregory in Theaker 2008: 55).

This approach denies James Grunig's earlier situational theory of publics described above, in which publics move from latent (unknowing) to aware and then active.

This concept is still important because the way in which a public becomes aware often dictates the way in which it might become active.

Publics are defined as being groups of people sharing an interest or concern, which makes them ideally suited for engaging in conversations that could lead to relationships, so long as we are prepared to discuss their concerns and interests first rather than just our own at any point in the conversation. Please see the Brent Spar case study below.

ISSUES MANAGEMENT

Case study
Brent Spar

Use the timeline below to track how awareness was raised and what activity took place as a result. Consider how it might have been different if others had made publics aware and provided them with full information.

- **1976**: Brent Spar (or Brent E) was built, largely out of concrete and steel, and commissioned for service as a North Sea oil and tanker loading buoy, operated by Shell UK.

- **September 1991**: Brent Spar was considered to be of no further use and so it was decommissioned.

- **1991–3**: Shell considered what to do with it and carried out full risk and environmental impact assessments. Based upon the results of those assessments, Shell decided to sink Brent Spar at the North Feni Ridge, in the deep Atlantic (approximately 250 km from the west coast of Scotland, at a depth of around 2.5 km).

- **February 1994**: An independent environmental consultancy, Aberdeen University Research and Industrial Services, endorsed Shell's decision for deep sea disposal. Shell began formal consultations with conservation bodies and fishing interests and submitted an application for permission to sink.

- **December 1994**: The UK government approved the plans for sinking.

- **April–May 1995**: Greenpeace activists (as well as journalists) occupied the Brent Spar platform for three weeks, to prevent its being sunk. Greenpeace International organised an international media campaign (the first information about the issue to enter the public domain), leading to a boycott of Shell products and services across northern Europe.

- **30 April 1995**: While on the platform, Greenpeace carried out its own tests and wrongly reported that the Brent Spar still contained 5,500 tonnes of crude oil (Shell's estimate was of 50 tonnes) and a variety of toxic chemicals and heavy metals. The BBC showed film footage, taken by Greenpeace of the occupation, on their main news bulletin.

- **5 May 1995**: The British government granted a disposal licence to Shell UK for the sinking of Brent Spar.

- **9 May 1995**: The German Ministry of the Environment protested to the UK government against the disposal plan.

- **23 May 1995**: Having been trying for some time, Shell finally won an eviction order for the protesters on board the platform. They were taken away by helicopter to Aberdeen, where they held a press conference.

- **11 June 1995**: Shell UK began to tow Brent Spar to the disposal site in the deep Atlantic Ocean.

- **15 June 1995**: The German Chancellor Helmut Kohl joined the protest and complained personally to the British Prime Minister, John Major, at the G7 summit.

- **14–20 June 1995**: Protesters in Germany damaged Shell petrol stations, including one that was fire-bombed. Greenpeace condemned these actions.

- **20 June 1995**: Shell took the decision, due to falling sales and a drop in share price, to withdraw their plan to sink Brent Spar. Shell UK released the following statement:

  Shell's position as a major European enterprise has become untenable. The Spar had gained a symbolic significance out of all proportion to its environmental impact. In consequence, Shell companies were faced with increasingly intense public criticism, mostly in Continental northern Europe. Many politicians and ministers were openly hostile and several called for consumer boycotts. There was violence against Shell service stations, accompanied by threats to Shell staff.

Despite the fact that Shell had carried out risk and environmental impact assessments in full accordance with the law at that time, which informed their view that their actions were in the best interests of the environment, they had severely underestimated the Greenpeace-led development of public opinion and emotion. The final cost of the Brent Spar operation to Shell was estimated to be between £60 million and £100 million, taking the loss of sales into account.

- **7 July 1995**: As the plan for deep-sea disposal had been abandoned, Norway granted permission to moor Brent Spar in Erfjord.

- **12 July 1995**: Shell UK commissioned the independent Norwegian consultancy Det Norske Veritas (DNV) to conduct an audit of Brent Spar's contents and investigate the validity of the Greenpeace allegations.

- **5 September 1995**: Greenpeace admitted their inaccurate claims that Brent Spar contained 5,550 tonnes of oil and apologised to Shell ahead of the publication of the DNV report. However, they made it clear that their actions were taken against waste disposal at sea, as a general principle, rather than because of the contents of the platform.

- **18 October 1995**: DNV presented the results of their audit, which endorsed Shell's original inventory of the contents of Brent Spar. DNV stated that the amount of oil claimed by Greenpeace to be in Brent Spar was 'grossly overestimated'.

- **29 January 1998**: Shell announced that Brent Spar would be disposed of onshore and recycled, to be used as foundations for harbour developments at Stavanger in Norway to provide a ferry terminal. While much of the structure went to form part of the harbour development, there was also a large amount of material sent to landfill in Norway.

- **23 July 1998**: Although no connection has been proved between these events, OSPAR's (originally the Oslo and Paris Conventions for the protection of the marine environment of the North-East Atlantic) fifteen member states announced agreement on onshore disposal of oil facilities in the future.

- **February 1999**: The BBC's main TV News screened an interview with the Conservative, former environment minister, John Selwyn-Gummer, in which he accused Greenpeace campaigners of telling lies and, as a result, causing damage to the whole environmental movement.

- **10 July 1999**: The breaking up of Brent Spar was completed and the first stages of constructing the ferry terminal were started.

A damp occupation by
Greenpeace – but the Spar
was not dumped
Source: Photofusion Picture Library/
Alamy

QUESTION

How was awareness generated, by whom and to whom? And what were the resulting activities? How might it have been different if Shell had brought Greenpeace and other interested publics in for discussions before deciding what to do or if Shell instead of Greenpeace had made their publics aware?

The manner in which a public becomes aware will affect how it might go on to be active and issues management helps us to plan to ensure that our views take others' into consideration and are put forward at the right time in the debate.

In order to build strong relationships there has to be mutual understanding.

Issues management is a system that is most often used to monitor ideas and thinking to inform public affairs activity. In other words, as ideas develop in society, issues managers create strategies to affect the way in which their government will react to them. The term is considered to have been coined by Howard Chase (1984), who defined an issue as being an unsettled matter which is ready for decision.

An unsettled matter can be of great interest as those concerned debate the issues and try to win favour for their point of view. In an election far more effort is made to persuade the undecided rather than spending time with those who are definitely won over or lost. Like

There is a powerful African proverb, which translates as, 'if lions had written histories the tales of hunters would be differently told'.
Source: John Foxx Images

an unsettled matter an undecided person can go either way and therefore is given greatest attention.

In his *Introduction to Public Relations*, Sam Black discusses the need for organisations to be aware of public trends and possible threats to their success, which he summed up as follows: 'issues management is a better term as it suggests that one does not merely monitor change but plans to take it into continuing consideration in planning corporate strategy' (1989: 10).

Monitoring the issues of our publics, as well as our own, helps us to consider and incorporate others' views in our planning and thinking. It can also inform the development of appropriate corporate social responsibility strategies, to ensure that we are being inclusive and responsive to those with whom we need to have good relationships.

Issues management has been written about by many academics and writers, including Robert Heath and Richard Nelson (1986), James Grunig and Todd Hunt (1984) and others, who have considered it to be about working with the concerns of the client or the organisation involved. They too described how working with publics at an early stage can reduce the impact of their concerns but not in terms of acting to develop their interests favourably for them. They also discussed addressing issues as part of public affairs, to influence politicians in their decision making, as mentioned above.

This chapter encourages readers to extend the practice to include gathering knowledge and understanding of our publics' concerns and interests as well as those of the organisation involved, so that a more balanced conversation can take place.

The importance of issues management is discussed in the Introduction to the *Public Relations Digest*:

if there is going to be any level of excellence in public relations practice, there has to be issues management, which Heath asserts grew out of the fertile ground of the 60s and 70s when deference withdrew and criticism or activism against business grew. He sums issues management up as monitoring, identifying, evaluating, prioritising, creating response and implementing. Well applied issues management is most likely to lead to a company becoming more socially responsible as it endeavours to build relationships with its publics and Heath here discusses how CSR might take an organisation above reproach by engaging interlocking cultures and building coalitions, keeping the firm ethically attuned to the community. 'People identify because they share symbolic substance that reflects their shared identity and mutual interests' (2009: 75).

The first task for the issues manager is to define the publics with which the organisation needs to have good relationships, to function well. As explained above, 'publics' is a term that academics have debated and many practitioners have abandoned in favour of the now much more commonly used 'stakeholders'. We can be forgiven for losing some patience with academe for its confusion over the terms, as the *Digest* Introduction continues:

> Gerard Choo, in Tench and Yeomans, gives a thoughtful and much needed discussion on audiences, stakeholders and publics in chapter seven. Despite thought provoking discussions on reception analysis, audience activity, the linear communication model and a useful consideration of the differing views of media effects, the chapter is still slightly confusing with the assertion that publics need not be stakeholders but that stakeholders become publics. The chapter suggests that publics are always active and therefore stakeholders are latent publics, which will hopefully set some bright minds thinking as to why we need to refer to stakeholders at all.

How does this different style of issues management work?

An organisation's issues management group should be made up of a cross section of the staff, to try to represent, as far as possible, the publics employed there.

They will be monitoring all of their information sources between meetings. The information sources will include a variety of news and social media channels, conversations with friends and family, local gossip and rumours, and contacts that they may have with clubs, societies or pressure groups to which they might belong. This process can be referred to as media tracking and environmental scanning.

In this huge amount of data, much of what each individual sees and hears is ignored, possibly because it is not understood, but most likely because it is of no interest to the individual. Unless there is some identification with a story it has little relevance to the viewer or listener.

Case study
The news for parrots

In the 1970s *Monty Python's Flying Circus* brought us the News for Parrots and for various other creatures such as wombats and gibbons. Michael Palin was the newsreader, with a parrot on his shoulder. The news was similar to broadcasts seen every day except that, when air crashes, natural disasters or events were related they were concluded with the phrase 'but no parrots [or other creatures as applicable] were involved'.

Taken from the script: 'Good evening. Here is the news for parrots. No parrots were involved in an accident on the M1 today when a lorry carrying high-octane fuel was in collision with a bollard. That's a *bollard* and not a *parrot*. A spokesman for parrots said he was glad no parrots were involved. '

Each item is read in matter-of-fact terms until, at the end of the bulletin, there might have been a news flash concerning a parrot that has sneezed at number 11, Acacia Avenue and, with great urgency, the action would go live to an outside broadcast to find out the latest on what is happening. This is the first time in the news that the parrots would have identified with a story and therefore the viewers (parrots) would become interested.

Source: jhamlon/Fotolia.com

This is a parody on the way that our news is brought to us, identifying with us as much as possible to keep us interested. Most businesses and organisations, in communicating about matters of key interest to themselves, rather than to their publics, are repeating this metaphor but without realising that very few people will be interested or concerned enough to take notice.

Individuals become aware of issues of concern or interest to them as they go about their lives interacting with others and reading and listening to ideas, news and features. As mentioned above, only a few will be inclined to take the issue into the next phase of its life – the public debate phase.

People talk about the issue in restaurants, at the school gate, on Twitter, at work, in the news media and so on. During this phase, as people are talking they are also listening for more information and if these people matter to an organisation it can be a vital moment to build or enhance a relationship with a stance, a position or a very public act that connects the organisation with the issue.

Once the debate takes hold and a public of interest forms around it the situation can quickly move from awareness and debate into action, as the declaration is so often made, 'something must be done!'

As the Brent Spar example above shows, because it was Greenpeace that made us aware of Shell's intention to dump the oil platform in the sea, the publics formed around their view point and looked to them for guidance of how to act. Shell was heavily boycotted around Northern Europe and a petrol station in Germany was attacked. Had Shell taken the trouble to communicate their intentions first and explain their reasons it would more likely have been to them that the interested publics would have looked for indications on how to act. It is likely that Greenpeace would have joined the debate but only after Shell's reasons had been calmly communicated. Once the debate has been led and heated by a particular point of view, it is much more difficult for the other side to put its points across.

The news and social media thrive on sensation and a Shell scientist explaining their data on environmental impact will always have less effect than protestors with flags aboard an oil platform in the North Sea being sprayed with water cannons.

There was probably some arrogance on the part of Shell, in deciding not to bother to explain their intended action, but they would certainly have regretted it as so much emotion was stirred that national leaders became involved in standing against them.

It should not be surprising that governments became involved as they are always watching issues carefully. Because of that, if an issue has attracted national public attention it can

Case study
The Post Office

In 1997, the Post Office (now the Royal Mail Group) in the UK set out to devise a corporate social responsibility strategy.

A number of pieces of research were carried out (using issues management techniques, employee questionnaires and discussions at staff meetings) to create a tool to help them to assess the most appropriate investments to make in the community, in sponsorships and in charities.

The Royal Mail Group was then a vast organisation with over 190,000 staff. It was the biggest retail chain in Europe, with 14,300 outlets. When delivering the post, many of its staff visit people's homes every day, which is given as an explanation (Verčič 2000) for its high standing as a very personal, trustworthy and strong brand.

At the beginning of the review, they were sponsoring the Olympics, a very crowded arena in which it is extremely difficult for such a small sponsor, giving just £4 million, to command attention. They were in competition with giants like IBM and Coca-Cola, whose sponsorship of the games is so large that it affects their bottom line. Whatever a company does, unless it is acting philanthropically, it needs to try to be distinctive. The Olympics also had little relevance to the Post Office's business objectives.

A matrix was devised for them, which took account of their core values, their business objectives, key publics' issues and employee support or opportunities for employee involvement. This matrix was used to score applicants and ideas for corporate support in terms of their relevance under these headings.

The Post Office was already working hard at community involvement with 1 in 6 of their staff doing voluntary work, often in the company's time and with financial support. The research for the matrix put the theme of literacy at the top of all categories. Clearly of great business importance to an organisation dealing so much with the distribution of the written word but also of particular interest to a large number of their employees. It was discovered that staff were already involved in over 200 ad hoc schemes concerning literacy. They were unconnected and had no system by which they could learn from or build upon each other. The board also wanted projects that would help to reduce social exclusion and begin to tackle crime.

In the UK, at that time, 12% of the population had literacy problems, whereas 60% of the prison population was functionally illiterate. The scheme brought together a wide range of staff projects, giving better opportunities for sharing good practice and building on success. It was reinforced by a fund, established by the Post Office, for a wide range of groups, from a small number of asylum seekers to a cooperative of leisure facilities and a national theatre, to successfully apply for funding to help with literacy projects.

As there were very few other companies working in the literacy arena, with by far the majority being involved in sport or education more generally, the Post Office could be distinctive as well as relevant to their business and a source of pride for their employees.

CSR policies have to be well researched and managed, as shown above and they have to go deep and be built for the long term, as there are many journalists and pressure groups watching very closely and commenting publicly, to test and contest any shallow claims.

Each public, according to its social, cultural, political or economic situation has a different interpretation of risk and indeed of reputation. Issues management is needed to identify what matters to every one of an organisation's key publics and to analyse how to use the information learned to build communication plans involving CSR appropriately.

THE CHANNELS

Just as each public is responding differently to different stimuli so it is checking and engaging with different channels from which to gather and through which to share information.

The news and social media can almost be described as being tribal, in this respect, with publics choosing different channels according to taste, politics, language and interest. It is difficult for someone to read a newspaper for monitoring purposes that is markedly different from their own, as the style of language will be unusual to them and the choice of stories and articles will seem strange. For example, in the UK the reading age of the language in the printed news media ranges from 7 to 16 and they use an equally diverse range of editorial and pictorial styles and subjects.

Most press officers understand the need to target news releases carefully (as discussed in Chapter 6) according to likely interest groups, but several are still making mistakes where social media are concerned.

The print news media have a range of reading ages, which suggest that they are read by young people, but that is decreasingly the case. The reading ages are those of their adult readers. Large numbers of young people and adults now access their news and comments entirely online through websites and opinion forums such as Twitter and Facebook, where they can see the attitudes of their peer groups instantly reflected.

The editor of the *Guardian* newspaper in the UK, Alan Rusbridger, entitled a recent essay aimed at journalists on the subject: 'If you want to find out where most things happen first – go to Twitter' (Alan Rusbridger, quoted in Mair and Keeble 2011: 4–8).

In the essay he gives 15 reasons for the importance of Twitter – here summed up as:

1. An amazing form of distribution

2. Things happen there first

3. An excellent search engine

4. A formidable aggregation tool (if you are following the most interesting people they will bring you the most interesting information, having searched and gathered it for you (2011: 5)

5. A great reporting tool

6. A fantastic marketing tool

7. A parallel universe of common conversations

8. It's more diverse – letting anybody in

9. It changes the tone of writing, involving listening as well as talking

10. It's a level playing field for the 'knowns' and the 'unknowns'

11. It has different news values – influencing the mainstream news media

12. It has a long attention span with subjects being chewed over for far longer

13. It creates communities – or publics

14. It changes notions of authority

15. It is an agent for change (and sometimes influences changes in authority – see case study above on the Arab Spring)

There is nowhere where people are exchanging ideas or gathering information that can be ignored by the PR practitioner hoping to build relationships with those people. This means that issues management groups might have to grow bigger to accommodate access to all of those out there writing, filming, blogging, posting and scanning what everyone is doing at the same time.

RELATIONSHIPS

Reputation and relationships exist whether or not someone is paid to build, shape or manage them. Positive differences can be made by executive boards, which include public relations directors chosen according to their depth of knowledge and breadth of experience.

Those who choose ex-journalists to advise them (www.guardian.co.uk/commentisfree/2011/jul/29/phone-hacking-inquiry-unanswered-questions and www.guardian.co.uk/media/2011/jul/15/metropolitan-police-chief-forced-to-explain-why-he-hired-neil-wallis), in the hope that they will be better able to influence news editors, are only going to achieve a small part of the influence that they seek and very few, if any, of the relationships that they need.

CONCLUSION

This chapter has outlined the aspects of PR practice that have come to define and differentiate the subject and which also benefit from continuous study and development.

Most especially, the use of the term 'publics' and the model of issues management that have been described, are needed to help the practitioner to understand how to establish relationships with key publics and thereby build lasting reputations. It has to be learned and it has to evolve, along with the best research methods needed to find information; the best analytical tools to employ to interrogate that information and make plans from it; and the most appropriate evaluation methods needed to ensure that what has been said and done has been appreciated.

Therefore professional public relations practitioners need to keep studying their subject and to keep a critical eye on what the PR academics are telling us.

REFERENCES

Black, S. (1989) *An Introduction to Public Relations*, Modino Press

Chase, H. (1984) *Issue Management – Origins of the Future*, Issue Actions Publications

Crowther, D. (2000) *Social and Environmental Accounting*, Financial Times Prentice Hall

Dewey, J. (1927) *The Public and its Problems*, Holt

Emshoff, J. R. and R. E. Freeman (1979) 'Stakeholder management', Applied Research Center, Philadelphia, May, in J. Grunig and T. Hunt (eds) (1984) *Managing Public Relations*, Holt, Rinehart & Winston

Friedman, M. (1962) *Capitalism and Freedom*, University of Chicago Press

Friedman, M. (1970) 'The social responsibility of business is to increase its profits', *New York Times Magazine*, p. 32, 30 September

Gregory, A. (2008) 'Public relations and management', in A. Theaker (ed.), *The Public Relations Handbook*, Routledge

Grunig, J. and T. Hunt (1984) *Managing Public Relations*, Holt, Rinehart & Winston

Grunig, L., J. Grunig and D. M. Dozier (2002) *Excellent Public Relations and Effective Organizations*, Lawrence Erlbaum Associates

Heath, R. and R. Nelson (1986) *Issues Management*, Sage

Holmstrom, S. (2002) 'The reflective paradigm', Master's thesis, Roskilde University, Denmark

Ledingham, J. A. (2003) 'Explicating relationship management as a general theory of public relations', *Journal of Public Relations Research* 15(2): 182

L'Etang, J. and M. Pieczka (2006) *Public Relations. Critical Debates and Contemporary Practice*, Lawrence Erlbaum Associates

McKie, D. (2006) 'Dis-integrating public relations', Conference paper at Euprera Annual Congress hosted by University of Central Lancashire in Carlisle, September

Müller, F. M. (tr. and ed.) (2000) *Wisdom of the Buddha, the Unabridged Dhammapada*, Dover Publications

Peters, R. (1967) *Hobbes*, Penguin Books

Public Relations Digest (2009) Pearson

Rusbridger, A. (2011) in J. Mair and R. Keeble, *The Internet and Journalism Today Face the Future: Tools for the Modern Media Age*, Abramis

Smith, A. (1778) *The Wealth of Nations*

Verčič, D. (2000) 'Trust in organisations: a study of the relations between media coverage, public perceptions and profitability', Doctoral dissertation, London School of Economics

Van Ruler, B. and D. Verčič (2002) *Bled Manifesto on Public Relations*, Pristop d.o.o., Ljubljana

Wolstenholme, S. (2009) 'Introduction', in CIPR, *Public Relations Digest* (2009) Pearson

Chapter 4
Ethics and public relations

Sue Wolstenholme

Learning outcomes

By the end of this chapter you should be able to:

- Discuss ethical theory
- Understand how morals have informed laws, which have been developed through education and the spread of knowledge
- Understand the CIPR Code of Conduct
- Identify how morals create social responsibility
- Know some international perspectives on ethics and understand the Global Compact

Introduction

This chapter will consider ethics and public relations, which may seem contradictory after reading the words of Professor Noam Chomsky in Chapter 1. However, for public relations, like so many tools, the morality is in how it is used and to what purpose it is put, rather than just in its existence or its potential. An ethical practitioner will understand how that potential is managed or even controlled.

As previous chapters have shown, public relations is practiced in a wide range of ways (see Heath in Chapter 1). For the sake of this discussion the chapter will be considering professional public relations schools of ethical theory (three Western and two Eastern) and it will all be taken together to consider public relations practice.

There will be a further discussion about social responsibility, not only as a possible expression of an ethical position for public relations but also as a potential smokescreen for an unethical position.

At the end of each section, as each moral code or ethical theory is discussed, selected principles from the CIPR code will be repeated and a question posed for you to answer. There will be a number of questions in this chapter to encourage you to reflect upon your own moral standpoints and those of others in the news and in business.

WHAT ARE ETHICS AND MORALS?

Ethics and morals are often confused with each other but, in fact, although they are linked, they mean slightly different things.

At a CERP (European Confederation of Public Relations) education conference in 1995 Professor Anne van der Meiden, of Utrecht University, described his research into ethical behaviour among public relations practitioners. Having established their views on what is, put simply, good or bad behaviour he asked them if they would resign their jobs rather than go against what they felt to be right. The majority said that they would stay in their jobs and do as they were asked because by going they could change nothing as they would be replaced by somebody who would behave unethically and they would be unemployed.

At what point does a person feel ready to act ethically?

Chartered Institute of Public Relations Code of Conduct

Principles

1. Members of the Chartered Institute of Public Relations agree to:

i. Maintain the highest standards of professional endeavour, integrity, confidentiality, financial propriety and personal conduct;

ii. Deal honestly and fairly in business with employers, employees, clients, fellow professionals, other professions and the public;

iii. Respect the customs, practices and codes of clients, employers, colleagues, fellow professionals and other professions in all countries where they practise;

iv. Take all reasonable care to ensure employment best practice, including giving no cause for complaint of unfair discrimination on any grounds;

v. Work within the legal and regulatory frameworks affecting the practice of public relations in all countries where they practise;

vi. Encourage professional training and development among Members of the profession;

vii. Respect and abide by this Code and related Notes of Guidance issued by the Chartered Institute of Public Relations and encourage others to do the same.

Principles of good practice

2. Fundamental to good public relations practice are:

Integrity

- Honest and responsible regard for the public interest;
- Checking the reliability and accuracy of information before dissemination;
- Never knowingly misleading clients, employers, employees, colleagues and fellow professionals about the nature of representation or what can be competently delivered and achieved;
- Supporting the CIPR Principles by bringing to the attention of the CIPR examples of malpractice and unprofessional conduct.

Competence

- Being aware of the limitations of professional competence: without limiting realistic scope for development, being willing to accept or delegate only that work for which practitioners are suitably skilled and experienced;
- Where appropriate, collaborating on projects to ensure the necessary skill base.

Transparency and avoiding conflicts of interest

- Disclosing to employers, clients or potential clients any financial interest in a supplier being recommended or engaged;
- Declaring conflicts of interest (or circumstances which may give rise to them) in writing to clients, potential clients and employers as soon as they arise;
- Ensuring that services provided are costed and accounted for in a manner that conforms to accepted business practice and ethics.

Confidentiality

- Safeguarding the confidences of present and former clients and employers;
- Being careful to avoid using confidential and 'insider' information to the disadvantage or prejudice of clients and employers, or to self-advantage of any kind;
- Not disclosing confidential information unless specific permission has been granted or the public interest is at stake or if required by law.

Maintaining professional standards

3. CIPR Members are encouraged to spread awareness and pride in the public relations profession where practicable by, for example:

- Identifying and closing professional skills gaps through the Institute's Continuous Professional Development programme;
- Offering work experience to students interested in pursuing a career in public relations;
- Participating in the work of the Institute through the committee structure, special interest and vocational groups, training and networking events;
- Encouraging employees and colleagues to join and support the CIPR;
- Displaying the CIPR designatory letters on business stationery;
- Specifying a preference for CIPR applicants for staff positions advertised;
- Evaluating the practice of public relations through use of the CIPR Research & Evaluation Toolkit and other quality management and quality assurance systems (e.g. ISO standards); and constantly striving to improve the quality of business performance;
- Sharing information on good practice with Members and, equally, referring perceived examples of poor practice to the Institute.

Interpreting the Code

4. In the interpretation of this code, the Laws of the Land shall apply.

Source: Chartered Institute of Public Relations Code of Conduct,
http://www.cipr.co.uk/sites/default/files/CIP%20Code20%of Conduct%2029-06-2011.pdf

Anita Roddick, the founder of Body Shop, once said that if you think you're too small to make a difference you've never been to bed with a mosquito.

An individual's morals come together to form their moral code, which is based upon what they believe to be right or wrong. With the few exceptions of totalitarian dictatorships, where laws are established from the standpoint of maintaining power, cultures and societies build their laws to reflect the moral codes of the citizens. That way they can be more easily enforced and any resulting criminal or extreme behaviour can be more easily dealt with through the justice system. Thereby harmony is maintained and the legal systems provide the citizens with a sense of well-being and safety.

Also, because moral codes are built upon ideas of right and wrong, which are handed down through generations and influenced by experience, they are different in different cultures with differing histories. Education, religion and experience also influence the moral codes of individuals and the societies that they share, so morality changes over time. There is, however, just one principle common to all of the world's religions across time and geography, and that is to do unto others as you would be done by – to treat others as you would like to be treated, only give out what you are prepared to take back – it doesn't matter how it is said, it amounts to the same thing and yet, with this great principle at the heart of all religions, it is so often religion that is used to encourage people to fight and to kill one another.

As Simon Blackburn wrote, an ethical environment determines our conception of what is due to us and what is due from us, as we relate to others (Blackburn 2003: 1).

Therefore, as we are discussing public relations, it is of paramount importance to understand how ethical environments affect relationships.

Case study
Laws and sexuality

An example of the changing and differing nature of morality is homosexuality. There is much evidence in Greek and Latin literature (Sappho, Plutrarch, Alaeus, Solon, Hadrian) to suggest that homosexuality was accepted in those societies; however, for the Romans it was only lawful so long as a slave was the recipient of the sexual act.

The year 1290 saw the first recorded common law punishment for being homosexual in England. By 1300 they were burned alive. In 1533 sex between men, or buggary, was punishable by hanging, which remained the penalty until 1861. In 1967 homosexuality became legal between consenting males over the age of 21, and in private, though this had been recommended by the Wolfenden Report ten years earlier, when society was not considered, by the government, to be ready for the law to be enacted. In 1973 the first gay rights conference was held. In 1984 the age of consent was lowered from 21 to 18. In 2000 the government removed the ban against homosexuals in the armed forces and the age of consent was lowered to 16. In 2005 the Civil Partnership Act was implemented, giving same-sex partnerships the same legal status as for married heterosexuals, with the first gay 'weddings' taking place in December that year. Over 700 years of change and development were dependent on the evolving education and attitudes of the populous.

In 1295 the age of consent for heterosexuals was 12 and it was raised to 16 in 1885, where it has remained ever since. The map in Figure 4.1 indicates how the variation in the age of consent for heterosexual sex, across the world, goes from no minimum to 20.

Homosexuality is still illegal in many countries and punishable by death in a few. The laws are made according to the people's teaching and their experience, which builds their moral codes.

Question

CIPR Code

Respect the customs, practices and codes of clients, employers, colleagues, fellow professionals and other professions in all countries where they practise . . .
How might adherence to this professional code create a possible conflict of interest and thereby introduce a moral code into the frame?

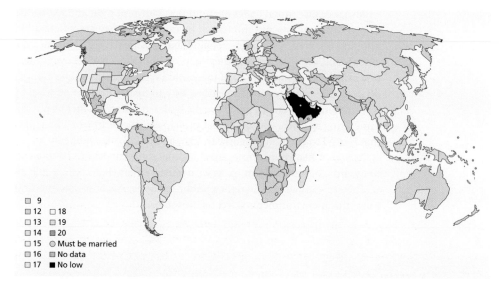

□ 9
□ 12 □ 18
□ 13 □ 19
□ 14 ■ 20
□ 15 ○ Must be married
□ 16 ■ No data
□ 17 ■ No low

FIGURE 4.1 Age of consent

Ethics

Ethics is the subject of morality, as studied and much discussed by moral philosophers. As cited in the *Oxford English Reference Dictionary* (1996):

> There has long been debate as to whether moral action can be justified or demonstrated to be rational; discussion is also centred on whether such a thing as moral truth exists. Schools of ethics in Western philosophy can be divided, very roughly, into three sorts. The first, drawing on the work of Aristotle, holds that the virtues (justice, charity and generosity) are dispositions to act in ways that benefit both the person possessing them and that person's society. The second, defended particularly by Kant, makes the concept of duty central to morality: humans are bound, from a knowledge of their duty as rational human beings, to obey the categorical imperative, to respect other rational human beings. Thirdly, Utilitarianism asserts that the guiding principle of conduct should be the greatest happiness or benefit of the greatest number.

Other ethicists and scholars discuss the three approaches under the headings of ontology, deontology and teleology, where Aristotle, the Kantian and the Utilitarians would be grouped; also as non-consequentialists and consequentialists, as in Table 4.1.

TABLE 4.1 Ethical schools

Ontology	Deontology	Teleology
Being/existence	Non-consequentialist	Consequentialist
Virtue	Duty	Utilitarian
Aristotle	Kant	Mill, Bentham

Aristotle 384–322 BC

As with many great thinkers, Aristotle's ideas have been widely interpreted by different cultures and during different periods in history. Referred to as Aristu or the 'wise one' in Islamic philosophy his teaching was commented upon by Ibn Rushd and later translated from the Arabic by Gerard of Cremna in the twelfth century (Routledge 2000).

Aristotle considered ethics to be a practical rather than a theoretical subject for study; in other words, one which was focused on doing good rather than just knowing about good for its own sake. He is cited (Routledge 2000) as having written several treatises on ethics: the Nicomachean Ethics, Eudemian Ethics and Magna Moralia, but the last two are considered to have been written by his pupils and only the first, the Nicomachean, is thought to be, in the main part, his own original work (Russell 1961: 185). He put forward the idea that by being made to do good or virtuous things we will learn to have pleasure from only doing good things.

Aristotle developed the idea of the golden mean, which was that every virtue is at the mean point between two extremes, both of which are vices, for example, courage is at the mean point between cowardice and rashness; liberality between prodigality and meanness and truthfulness between boastfulness and mock modesty. Russell points out that, in his opinion (ibid.), this can only apply to truthfulness about oneself but there could be an application for the truthfulness to the pronouncements made, sometimes through the public relations departments, by organisations and individuals in public and political life every day. Aristotle believed that happiness or well-being come from virtues, which are actions tending to produce good or success.

Russell points to the fact that 'a considerable part of Aristotle's Ethics is occupied with the discussion of friendship' (Russell 1961: 191). He points out that perfect friendship can only occur between the good. 'Friends are a comfort in misfortune but one should not make them unhappy by seeking their sympathy' (ibid.). That could have interesting implications during crisis management, but that is not for this book.

In an essay by the Slovenian writer Aleš Debeljak, entitled 'Lonesome heart and the failed community', there is an interesting way of looking at Aristotle's definition of friendship. In the Nicomachean Ethics Aristotle devotes two of the ten books to a discussion on *philia*, the feeling which friends have for one another. He explains that it is one of the things which life can least afford to be without and that 'the rich men in positions of power and authority, are believed to stand, more than other people, in need of friends'. So what is friendship and why is it a most appropriate subject for students and practitioners of public relations ethics?

According to Aristotle it depends upon three pillars:

the sharing of pleasures;

being useful to one another;

being committed to a common good.

According to Debeljak, too often in the West, friendships have become restricted to the sharing of common pleasures, as he says: 'in a world in which gifts, duties and obligations are paid for and not symbolically returned' we will become lost and lonely. This is not just at a personal level. Like the rich, powerful and those in some authority, which globally many businesses now are, the corporate world needs friends too. Debeljak is not putting forward the view that socialism is the only way for community but he does reject the interpretation of 'the claim that man does not live by bread alone represents an argument for starvation' (2000).

How might this be applied to public relations?

It is fairly straightforward to stage mutually enjoyable events or to sponsor the arts or sports, which identified publics will enjoy and through that enjoyment will feel closer to the sponsor, as many companies do.

Being useful to publics and genuinely sharing a commitment to their value systems is much more difficult and requires an understanding of what they think and believe, which requires careful research.

When he was the chairman of Royal Dutch Shell, Mark Moody-Stuart stated in a 1997 speech 'in the future, the successful companies will be those who work hardest to make sure that they are in tune with the needs and aspirations of society'.

Questions

If you search for Shell online, do you think that the company is living up to its former Chairman's predictions? Can you find a company that does reflect the needs and aspirations of the society in which it functions?

If public relations is going to be ethical, it needs to consider how it is going to develop and sustain all of the three pillars of friendship with its publics. It is the moral dimension of commitment that turns a superficial relationship into something meaningful – 'so does our only hope remain in the preservation of the consciousness of the broader community to which we belong?' (Debeljak 2000). Or, as Hegel put it, 'our consciousness of ourselves is largely or even essentially a consciousness of how we stand for other people' (in Blackburn 2003: 1).

Questions

Consider these views in terms of your personal friendships.

1. If you meet somebody with whom you have nothing in common (for example, she only likes watching football on television and you are passionate about going to the theatre to see modern ballet) do you think that the friendship is likely to develop happily?

2. If a good friend needs help, don't you want them to call on you as an expression of the trust that you hope they place in you?

3. When you find that someone you regarded as a friend has extreme and opposite views from you about an important issue, such as religion, immigration or capital punishment, might you reconsider the depth of that friendship?

In A. C. Grayling's *The Good Book*, he reflects the thoughts of 'hundreds of authors and over a thousand texts' and when discussing friendship he promotes Aristotle's view when he states: 'all I can do is to urge you to regard friendship as indeed the greatest thing in the world, for there is nothing which so fits human nature, or is so exactly what we both desire and need, whether in prosperity or adversity. But I must at the very beginning lay down this principle: that true friendship can only exist between good people.' And he goes on to clarify: 'Let us mean by "good people", those whose actions and lives leave no question as to their honour, sense of justice and generosity both of hand and heart; who have the courage to stand by their principles and are free from greed, intemperance and violence' (Grayling 2011: 57).

CIPR Codes

Maintain the highest standards of professional endeavour, integrity, confidentiality, financial propriety and personal conduct

Deal honestly and fairly in business with employers, employees, clients, fellow professionals, other professions and the public

Fundamental to good public relations practice [. . .] Honest and responsible regard for the public interest

Task

Try to create a golden mean for the key virtues in these three parts of the codes.

Question

If friendship is ethical and relationships are intrinsically important for the building of reputation, how could a public relations exercise be a bad thing?

Bentham and Mill

Jeremy Bentham (1748–1832) and John Stuart Mill (1806–73) were leading proponents of Utilitarianism in the UK.

Jeremy Bentham believed that human and political behaviour is based around pleasure and pain, being the pursuit of pleasure and the avoidance of pain. He set forward the ideal goal as being producing the greatest happiness for the greatest number, which came to be the focus of Utilitarianism.

It was quite a sophisticated approach to law in that it was clear to him that rather than an individual setting out just to enjoy their own pleasure, they would reap more happiness by trying to create happiness for others at the same time. His views on punishment were similarly drawn. To punish a person for their wrongdoing, to have an effect on just that person, would not be of any advantage to the many. It would only make sense to administer punishments that would deter others. Bentham also believed that people needed to be protected from government and he designed what was, at the time, a forward-thinking system of constitutional law in which the only fair form of government was democracy. Central to that system were theories of public opinion, suggesting that public opinion had the power to ensure that rulers would rule for the greatest happiness of the greatest number.

Utilitarians saw happiness as being the sole human goal. Mill stated that if happiness was not 'in theory and in practice, acknowledged to be an end, nothing could ever convince any person that it was so'. In his 1859 essay 'On liberty' (Warnock 1970) he put forward the principle that people should be able to define their own version of happiness, within the law, that, in pursuing it, they must not interfere in any way with the legal choice for happiness of another.

CIPR Code

Take all reasonable care to ensure employment best practice, including giving no cause for complaint of unfair discrimination on any grounds

Question

Employment is an area where advantage can be taken of employees by employers, who might be pursuing their own happiness goals at the expense of their employees'. Can you think of a situation where an organisation's reputation has been damaged in this way?

Also, consider how the opinion-formers, described by Chomsky in Chapter 1, might persuade themselves that they were taking care of the greatest number's happiness. How might properly researching public opinion overcome that potential problem?

The Utilitarians might have been early believers in democracy but perhaps they hadn't accounted for spin.

> when a subject appears to be all around him, a person tends to accept it and take it for granted. It becomes part of the atmosphere in which he lives. He finds himself surrounded by it and absorbs the climate of the idea . . . it must be deftly developed and reach into the subconscious of the person and tune to his urges, interests and desires. Mere expression of the communicator's point of view will not succeed; so it must be attuned to the mental and emotional bent of the audience (Philip Lesly 1974, quoted in Ewen 1996: xv).

How can public opinion be left to find its own way forward to choose that which will create the most happiness? Politicians and their supporters, in the news and social media, want to secure their own happiness and win elections and so they lure, or mould, public opinion to support them. According to Abraham Lincoln 'public opinion needs to be molded'. And he went on:

> When the conduct of men is designed to be influenced, persuasion, kind, unassuming persuasion, should ever be adopted. It is an old and true maxim 'that a drop of honey catches more flies than a gallon of gall'. So with men. If you would win a man to your cause, first convince him that you are his sincere friend. Therein is a drop of honey that catches his heart, which, say what you will, is the great high road to his reason, and which, when once gained, you will find but little trouble in convincing his judgment of the justice of your cause, if indeed that cause really be a just one. On the contrary, assume to dictate to his judgment, or to command his action, or to mark him as one to be shunned and despised, and he will retreat within himself, close all the avenues to his head and his heart; and tho' your cause be naked truth itself, transformed to the heaviest lance, harder than steel, and sharper than steel can be made, and tho' you throw it with more than Herculean force and precision, you shall no more be able to pierce him, than to penetrate the hard shell of a tortoise with a rye straw' (1860, quoted in Zarefsky 1994: 40)

Case study
The Tehran Declaration

In 2005 an international conference was held in Tehran, the capital of the Islamic Republic of Iran. The theme for the conference was public opinion and speakers from Europe, Asia and Iran gave papers on various ways to research or reflect and respect public opinion. There were over 800 Iranians in the audience, men and women, PR practitioners, professors, students and journalists. At the end of the conference a meeting took place, which included the author of this chapter, to distil the ideas that had been expressed into the Tehran Declaration of Public Opinion, which is reproduced here, translated from Farsi by the administrator of the conference, Amir Rastegar. It is a set of codes for public relations and it is appealing to governments to support them for democracy and the proper practice of public relations.

Draft of Tehran Declaration on the Significance of the Position and Application of Research and Public Opinion Studies in Public Relations

مؤسسه تحقیقات روابط عمومی

Public Relations Research Institute

موسسه فرهنگی روابط عمومی آرمان

(19–20 December, TEHRAN, I.R. IRAN)

Assembled in The First International Symposium on Research and Public Opinion Studies in Public Relations, we – the participants – highlight the significance of both scientific research and public opinion studies as fundamental and indispensable principles in the public relations profession and have agreed on the following propositions:

A. Research

1. The participants hold that research is the principal instrument in the public relations profession, and believe that it should be the basis for taking every action and carrying out every communication program. After carrying out each program, we should conduct evaluation in order to measure the effectiveness and success of the program.

2. The participants consider all aspects of research (including the selection of topic, research method, research plan and research implementation and evaluation) as a scientific process. Conducting research in the following fields as a means to developing the scientific basis of public relations is considered essential:

   A. Image analysis
   B. Message or content analysis
   C. Media analysis
   D. Interlocutor analysis
   E. Satisfaction analysis
   F. Effectiveness analysis
   G. Opinions analysis

3. The participants consider the selection of the ideal model for public relations activities as a necessary and complementary factor for research in public relations. Such a model must recognize the importance of the receiver of communication, pay attention to his/her satisfaction, and avoid one-sidedness. Public relations must communicate with people in a way which enables them to give feedback to – and influence – the organization. Undoubtedly, this ideal model is the two-way symmetric form of communication which emphasizes the importance of mutual understanding between an organization and its publics. The two-way symmetrical model gives especial attention to research and uses it as a means for allowing people's voices (public opinion) to be heard – and to influence – senior managers.

4. The participants believe that in addition to paying attention to applied research in the area of public relations, practitioners and academics in this field of knowledge should constantly endeavor to create new and pure views which are based on global studies in public relations.

B. Public opinion

5. The participants consider that respect for public opinion is a humanitarian and democratic principle. Such respect is considered a prerequisite for scientific, non-discriminatory and targeted studies. Any distortion or alteration of public opinion studies is viewed as being contrary to the ethical principles of the public relations profession. Protecting the reliability and validity of public opinion studies is also considered a sacred professional responsibility.

6. The participants request governments to expand and promote these types of studies through civil and private bodies in order to allow the people to influence society and government. We expect that the managers of public relations programs will increasingly participate in the activities of such bodies, and thus invest in their profession.

7. The participants consider the development of civil bodies for public opinion studies and the protection of correct and scientific procedures for conducting such studies to be among the features of a democratic society. We consider the application of these results in policy planning to be a human right. We request government to create a fund for the protection of public opinion studies through specialized civil bodies in this profession.

Questions

Can you find any similarities between the Tehran Declaration and the CIPR Code of Conduct? Can you see any of the themes in the Tehran Declaration, which would find sympathy with the Utilitarians?

Kant

Immanual Kant (1724–1804) took the position that an individual, alone, is responsible for his or her actions and that human reason could and should live by the basic principles of behaviour without needing the help of a higher being. He had a liberal view of justice, which he put in a cosmopolitan context. He said: 'There can be nothing more dreadful than that the actions of a man should be subject to the will of another' (in Russell 1961: 678). Kant was against democracy, describing it as despotism: 'the "whole people", so called, who carry their measures are really not all, but only a majority; so that here the universal will is in contradiction with itself and with the principle of freedom' (ibid.).

Although often cited as being preoccupied with rule and duty and as creating the categorical imperative (Gregory 2009: 278; Oxford English Reference Dictionary) it is also thought that those ideas were attributed to Kant much later and that they were not a part of his own ethical approach (Routledge 2000: 433).

When you carry out your own research on Kant, you will find that most writers have him firmly leading the duty-based approach in which the means cannot be justified by the end (as the Utilitarians would assert they could) but that it is an individual's duty to do the right thing all of the time, regardless of the end result. As an example, murder is wrong categorically and yet if murdering one person meant that many thousands would be saved, would that be wrong? According to the categorical imperative, it most certainly would be.

Blackburn thought that Kant went too far, insisting that the 'centre of ethics must be occupied with things we can reasonably demand of each other'.

CIPR Code

Deal honestly and fairly in business with employers, employees, clients, fellow professionals, other professions and the public

Questions

If a person is found to have lied and it is made public it can be damaging to their reputation. In public relations the telling of the truth is held up as important in every code of conduct. Can you think of an example when the telling of the whole truth might not lead to the greatest happiness for the greatest number? Which of the ethical schools discussed above do you think best suits the practice of public relations?

And what of flexibility? In an emergency rules change, as considered by Hume (Blackburn 2003: 78) and described by Inger Jensen who spoke about the queue in the pharmacy that will step aside for the urgent case and resume their positions when it has been dealt with (Jensen 2009). Hume said: 'emergencies permit exceptions because the old stabilities and certainties return as soon as the emergency is over' (Blackburn 2003: 78).

Question

Can you think of other demands that could be made to require a more flexible approach?

Chinese philosophical schools

As the study of an ethical frame is useful to public relations, those living and working in the East need a different range of references to make sense of their decisions within relationship building and reputation management. Like in all things, there is also much that can be transferred to other cultures. As each culture and religion sets differing moral codes for their people to live by, so do they also give rise to differing philosophical schools. When working in a different culture it is important to have an understanding of how those schools of thought have defined ethics and by how much they are regarded as being influential.

Some leading examples from China are briefly described here.

Tao te Ching (or *Daodeching*), written between 350 and 250 BC by Professor Lao Tze, was the foundation for the Daoist religion (Dao means 'the way'), which in turn became the basis for Buddhism. It became very popular in the West in the 1960s, with many a student consulting the *I Ching*, or *Book of Changes*, before making decisions on all kinds of light and serious dilemmas (e. g. whether or not to go out for the evening, get married, leave the country). This might seem fanciful, but making the right decision about the future can be daunting and many people check

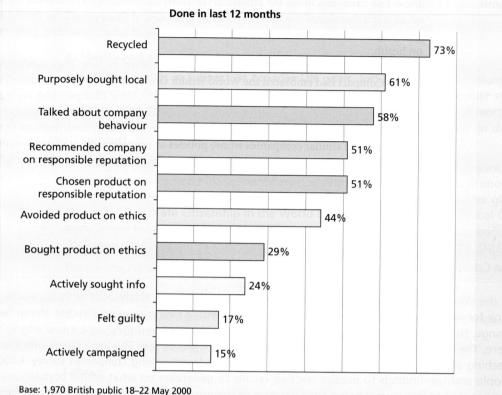

Done in last 12 months

Recycled	73%
Purposely bought local	61%
Talked about company behaviour	58%
Recommended company on responsible reputation	51%
Chosen product on responsible reputation	51%
Avoided product on ethics	44%
Bought product on ethics	29%
Actively sought info	24%
Felt guilty	17%
Actively campaigned	15%

Base: 1,970 British public 18–22 May 2000

FIGURE 4.4 Ethical behaviour
Source: Ethical Consumerism Research, Ipsos MORI http://www.ipsos-mori.com/researchpublications/researcharchive/1496/Ethical-Consumerism-Research.aspx

The bank reports annually on how well it is doing against often challenging targets set for them by their customers, which can also be seen on their website.

The policy has been a success in business terms as well as in creating strong customer loyalty. In 2010 the bank also won the Which? award for the best financial services provider.

During a time of economic downturn for most, the bank's profitability almost tripled, from £45.5 million in 1996 to £122.5 million in 2002, just ten years after the introduction of the policy.

As the bank grows the research will continue to add to our knowledge of the ethical values of its customers. Those expressing values-led decisions are moving up to come closer to those whose choices are value-led – in other words more people are beginning to ask the true cost of products and services (in social and environmental terms) rather than just what is written on the price ticket.

In a MORI poll for the Co-operative Bank in 2000 it was found that 29% of respondents have actively chosen to buy from responsible companies and, where they knew, 51% of customers had chosen the responsible and 44% had boycotted the irresponsible (see Figure 4.4).

The MORI report goes on to analyse the findings for the Co-operative Bank

In fact through detailed factor and cluster analysis, there seems to be five distinct segments of the British public in relation to ethical consumerism. These are:

- Global Watchdogs
- Conscientious Consumers

- Brand Generation
- Do What I Can
- Look After My Own

The 'global watchdogs' account for approximately 5% of the population. These are more likely than average to be ABs, aged between 35 and 54 and live in the South of England. They tend to be broadsheet newspaper readers and socio-political activists. While they obviously place high importance on ethical factors when purchasing, it is the influence of these in persuading them to buy one product over another, and the lack of concern about getting value for money which really distinguishes this cluster. They are also particularly likely to seek information on companies' ethical behaviour, and be influenced by consumer watchdog organisations, charities or NGOs.

Those who place importance on ethical issues when purchasing – from perceived impact on the environment to community involvement, and are fairly active from recycling to recommending companies to others and either choosing or avoiding products on ethical grounds have been classified as 'conscientious consumers' (18% of population). While this group are traditionally classified as CSR activists, the cluster analysis shows that this group fall short of the hardcore activists as they are less likely to actively seek information or campaign on ethical issues. Although resembling the hardcore activists, they are more likely to own a car or read a 'mid market' tabloid.

The 'brand generation' make up approximately 6% of the British public. They are likely to be aged under 35 and single, C1C2s and read 'redtop' tabloids. They are less likely to own their own home or have shares. Although they tend to feel empowered as consumers, they do not like the tag of 'ethical consumers'. A company's treatment of its employees, the customer service provided and brand names are the key persuading factors when choosing between products of similar price and quality. Although they are unlikely to shop locally, recycle or seek GM free or organic labels, ethical issues are engrained and they regularly discuss ethical issues and companies' ethical reputations with friends and family and recommend or avoid companies because of their responsible reputation. However, corporate involvement in the community or corporate policies are seen as less important than reputation and proven ethical track record.

'Do what I can' account for half (49%) of the British adult population, accounting for the largest segment. As they make up half the British public, their geo-demographics reflect the population as a whole. Although four in five regularly recycle and seven in ten have purposely bought to support local shops and suppliers, they tend not to do any more ethically-challenging activities. This lack of substantial ethical behaviour, and the fact they place less importance on ethical factors when purchasing is reflected in their own perceptions of not being particularly ethical consumers.

Twenty-two per cent are 'look after my own', who rarely, if ever, recycle, support local shops or take ethics into account when purchasing – value for money is the key over riding factor. Inactives are more unlikely than average to not vote, and only one in four have talked to friends and family about a company's behaviour (compared to three in five of the public as a whole). They tend to be often aged under 35, rent from local authorities, unlikely to own shares, and are unlikely to be trade union members. This group are honest about the perceived importance of ethical standards and its impact on their purchasing behaviour. It has little relevance to their daily lives.

Source: Ethical Consumerism Research, Ipsos MORI http://www.ipsos-mori.com/researchpublications/researcharchive/1496/Ethical-Consumerism-Research.aspx

CSR policies have to be well researched and carefully initiated and managed as there are a number of journalists and pressure groups watching very carefully, who are intent upon exposing any false claims.

Public relations practitioners with small research budgets would be well advised, if their publics match in any way, to check online with the Co-operative Bank and see the values that they too should be reflecting in their policies.

Case study
The Cornish Crisp Company Ltd

Source: The Cornish Crisp Company Ltd

It is not only large corporates that should be trying to create a value system to meet that of their publics.

Introduction

The Cornish Crisp Company was established in May 2009: a product, name and marketing idea devised by a public relations consultant who lives in Cornwall. Seeing that much of the county's potato crop was exported or used in processing, she saw an exciting opportunity for adding value to and celebrating a locally grown crop whilst building upon the successful Cornish food brand. The Cornish Crisp would also help to achieve a personal goal to prove that a commercial product can be a success when promotion and publicity are led by public relations and a good reputation.

Background

The food and drink sector is the leading industry in Cornwall and (in 2011) worth £1.5 billion per year.

Values

A strong commitment to social responsibility was placed at the heart of the Cornish Crisp business model. This was expressed by:

- Reducing the environmental impact of the business whilst being a positive addition to the town in which the business operates
- Celebrating the charities and organisations, which make the company proud to be a part of the Cornish community

- Providing or commissioning full staff training in anything identified by them and advisers as being required
- Involving (and often following) staff in all decision making

Always paying full attention to quality and customer feedback

Minimising waste

The flavours

Each different flavour was allocated a different charity to support and given a 'tater' nickname to add character and a local dimension to the crisps. (In Cornwall, potatoes are locally named 'taters' and the strapline 'it's the taters that make the flavour' was done to indicate the reliance on their good quality.) A penny from every bag that the company sold would be donated to their charity and space is also given on the packet for the logo and a paragraph about their work. This was considered, by the organisations, to be the biggest benefit.

- Salt and vinegar, the 'agitater', supports Surfers Against Sewage (SAS), a non-profit-making organisation campaigning for clean, safe recreational waters, free from sewage effluents, toxic chemicals, marine litter and nuclear waste. SAS also campaigns to protect surfing areas from environmental damage and negative impacts on wave quality and to safeguard recreational water users right of access (www.sas.org.uk).
- Cheese and onion, the 'gratertater', supports Cornwall Community Foundation, a charity committed to supporting local projects in Cornwall and the Isles of Scilly that engage local people in making their communities better places to live (www.cornwallfoundation.com).
- Salt and black pepper, the 'spectater', supports the Hall for Cornwall, the county's award-winning performing arts venue, which relies upon donations from businesses and individuals to continue to bring world-class productions to Cornwall and to continue with community and education work with thousands of people locally every year (www.hallforcornwall.co.uk).
- Chilli, the 'devastater', supports Shelter Box, a charity set up by the Rotary Club of Helston in Cornwall to send emergency supplies such as tents, sleeping bags, water purification tablets and cooking equipment, to areas devastated by natural disasters.
- Unflavoured, the 'resuscitater', supports the Cornwall Air Ambulance, which was the first of its kind in the country to supply a helicopter service to take seriously ill or wounded people to hospital.
- Ready salted, the 'commontater', promotes ashesandsparks.com, an online tool for capturing people's opinions on topical issues with the aim of promoting change in governments, organisations and companies.

The link between flavours and charities was an opportunity to build new working relationships and highlight the ethical stance of the company. Raising awareness for the charities was given as much importance as raising funds for them.

Cornwall Community Foundation actually contacted the Cornish Crisp Company and asked for a flavour as they were keen for the opportunity to reach new audiences through the crisps.

As crisp packaging is one of the most littered items, an anti-littering message on behalf of Clean Cornwall (www.cleancornwall.org) was included on all of the packaging. Waste is minimised by recycling where possible, most notably the waste sunflower oil, which is converted into bio-diesel. All office paper is used on both sides and, when finished with, is recycled. Cardboard is also recycled and the company has a green electricity tariff. All materials and ingredients needed for the running of machinery and making of the crisps are, where possible, sourced locally.

Case study
Can you work for everybody?

Below are three personal positions from public relations practitioners to offer some ideas and ways of thinking about a controversial subject. One writer explains why they could not work as a PR practitioner for a tobacco company, a second (who had been a student of the first writer) tells us briefly why she has felt able to do the work, and a third presents some work that she has done to try and persuade smokers to take up the safer option of 'electronic cigarettes'.

Opportunity declined – why I will not accept tobacco industry clients by Myroslaw Kohut

As Managing Director, shareholder and board member of a professional PR firm founded 1992, I am acutely aware of the need for clients. Those seeking big-budget campaigns are especially desirable. The tobacco industry is large and profitable, and spends a lot of money on advertising and promotion. Market capitalisation in the third quarter of 2010 of cigarette companies publicly traded in the US was in the range of $240 billion, with a further $1 billion for those producing tobacco and associated products (http://biz.yahoo.com/ic/350.html and http://biz.yahoo.com/ic/351.html [04.08.2010]). These sums exclude a tobacco firm owned by the Chinese government which is nearly double the size of the second largest publicly traded multinational tobacco company.

Our PR firm in Ukraine had previously conducted work for a tobacco company. The prospects for promoting tobacco products in Ukraine are very good – the adult daily smoking prevalence rate is 39%, well above the rates of 15-18% in Canada, Sweden, the US and the UK, and the rates of 26–7% in Denmark, France and Germany (WHO report on the global tobacco epidemic, 2009: implementing smoke-free environments, World Health Organization, 2009).

When I joined our firm in 2001, I took the personal position not to provide professional services to any tobacco firm and not to permit my name to be associated in any way with such engagements.

This case study explains my reasons for the action I have taken.

The problem

Tobacco use is not a new practice. Initially socially restricted to men in Western countries, it has seen rapid growth in the twentieth century that continues on a global scale, even with declines in developed countries. Seeking new clients to fulfil obligations to shareholders of increasing profits, leading tobacco industry firms realised that women were an untapped market on their door-step. The famous public relations campaign by Edward Bernays, 'Torches of freedom', in 1928, for a major US tobacco firm expanded the market for cigarettes to women. Smoking became fashionable, evoking mystery and sensuous sexuality. Film scenes with glamorous stars smoking in sophisticated company or as tough guys, and reposing languidly in a smoky aura after intimacy were common in the World War II era.

Torches for freedom – women smoking in public were a surprising sight

Source: Mary Evans Picture Library

The number of smokers rose sharply, although smoking among men continued to be significantly more prevalent than among women.

Tobacco use kills – 100 million deaths in the twentieth century. At the close of the first decade of the twenty-first century, tobacco use is acknowledged as a risk factor in six of the eight leading causes of death in the world. Illness and death from tobacco continues to be at epidemic levels (Figure 4.5).

WHO Fact sheet N°339
May 2010

Tobacco

Key facts

- Tobacco kills up to half of its users.
- The annual death toll of more than five million could rise to more than eight million by 2030 unless urgent action is taken to control the tobacco epidemic.
- More than 80% of the world's one billion smokers live in low- and middle-income countries.
- Total consumption of tobacco products is increasing globally, though it is decreasing in some high-income and upper middle-income countries.

Leading cause of death, illness and impoverishment

Tobacco use is one of the biggest public health threats the world has ever faced. It kills more than five million people a year – an average of one person every six seconds – and accounts for one in 10 adult deaths. Up to half of current users will eventually die of a tobacco-related disease.

More than 80% of the one billion smokers worldwide live in low- and middle-income countries, where the burden of tobacco-related illness and death is heaviest.

Tobacco users who die prematurely deprive their families of income, raise the cost of health care and hinder economic development.

In some countries, children from poor households are frequently employed in tobacco farming to provide family income. These children are especially vulnerable to 'green tobacco sickness', which is caused by the nicotine that is absorbed through the skin from the handling of wet tobacco leaves.

Gradual killer

Because there is a lag of several years between when people start using tobacco and when their health suffers, the epidemic of tobacco-related disease and death has just begun.

- Tobacco caused 100 million deaths in the 20th century. If current trends continue, it will cause up to one billion deaths in the 21st century.
- Unchecked, tobacco-related deaths will increase to more than eight million per year by 2030. More than 80% of those deaths will be in low- and middle-income countries.

Surveillance is key

Good monitoring tracks the size and character of the epidemic and indicates how best to tailor policies. Two-thirds of countries – more than four in five of them low- and middle-income – do not have even minimal information about tobacco use.

Second-hand smoke kills

Second-hand smoke is the smoke that fills restaurants, offices or other enclosed spaces when people burn tobacco products such as cigarettes, bidis and water pipes. There is no safe level of second-hand tobacco smoke.

Every person should be able to breathe smoke-free air. Smoke-free laws protect the health of non-smokers, are popular, do not harm business and encourage smokers to quit.

- Only 5.4% of people are protected by comprehensive national smoke-free laws.
- In 2008, the number of people protected from second-hand smoke increased by 74% to 362 million from 208 million in 2007.
- Of the 100 most populous cities, 22 are smoke free.
- Almost half of children regularly breathe air polluted by tobacco smoke.
- Over 40% of children have at least one smoking parent.
- Second-hand smoke causes 600,000 premature deaths per year.
- In 2004, children accounted for 28% of the deaths attributable to second-hand smoke.
- There are more than 4000 chemicals in tobacco smoke, of which at least 250 are known to be harmful and more than 50 are known to cause cancer.
- In adults, second-hand smoke causes serious cardiovascular and respiratory diseases, including coronary heart disease and lung cancer. In infants, it causes sudden death. In pregnant women, it causes low birth weight.

FIGURE 4.5 Extent of the tobacco epidemic

Source: WHO (2012). *Tobacco*. Geneva, World Health Organization (Fact Sheet no. 339; www.who.int/mediacentre/factsheets/fs339/en, accessed 2 September 2012)

International action

Since up to half of all tobacco users will die, tobacco companies must seek replacements. Young people are a target group for marketing by the tobacco industry. With the campaign posters below, Smokefree Southwest set out to remind young people that hard-rolling tobacco is just as dangerous as ready made cigareetes

Source: Creative from Smokefree South West's 'Wise-Up to Roll-Ups' campaign

Building a conceptual model of interference

The list of interfering tactics and their goals in Table 4.3 is revealing; however, a conceptual model that covers these tactics would enable researchers to better analyse the nature of industry interference. Such a model was developed by a research group of 34 Americans, with previous experience in the field, who participated in a study published in 2003. Fifteen were academics, seven represented advocacy organisations, seven contract research organisations, four government agencies, and five were from tobacco control funding organisations.

Concept mapping was used to develop the model. This methodology is a participatory mixed-method approach that integrates group activities (brainstorming, unstructured pile sorting and rating of the

TABLE 4.3 Tobacco industry tactics for resisting effective tobacco control

Tactic	Goal
Intelligence gathering	To monitor opponents and social trends in order to anticipate future challenges
Public relations	To mould public opinion, using the media to promote positions favourable to the industry
Political funding	To use campaign contributions to win votes and legislative favours from politicians
Lobbying	To make deals and influence political processes
Consultancy	To recruit supposedly independent experts who are critical of tobacco control measures
Funding research, including universities	To create doubt about evidence of the health effects of tobacco use
Smokers' rights groups	To create an impression of spontaneous, grassroots public support
Creating alliances and front groups	To mobilise farmers, retailers, advertising agencies, the hospitality industry, grassroots and anti-tax groups with a view to influencing legislation
Intimidation	To use legal and economic power as a means of harassing and frightening opponents who support tobacco control
Philanthropy	To buy friends and social respectability from arts, sports, humanitarian and cultural groups
Corporate social responsibility	To promote voluntary measures as an effective way to address tobocco control and create an illusion of being a 'changed' company and to establish partnerships with health interests
Youth smoking prevention and retailer education programmes	To appear to be on the side of efforts to prevent children from smoking and to depict smoking as an adult choice
Litigation	To challenge laws and intimidate tobacco industry opponents
Smuggling	To undermine tobacco excise tax policies and marketing and trade restrictions and thereby increase profits
International treaties and other international instruments	To use trade agreements to force entry into closed markets and to challenge the legality of proposed tobacco control legislation
Joint manufacturing and licensing agreements and voluntary policy agreements with governments	To form joint ventures with state monopolies and subsequently pressure governments to privatise monopolies
Pre-emption	To overrule local or state government by removing its power to act

Source: WHO, 2008. *Tobacco Industry Interference with Tobacco Control*, Geneva, World Health Organization (Table 2: Tobacco industry tactics for resisting effective tobacco control, pp. 12–13, ISBN 978 924 1597340, http://www.who.int/tobacco/resources/publications/; accessed 5 November 2012)

brainstormed items) with several multivariate statistical analyses (multidimensional scaling and hierarchical cluster analysis) to yield both statistical and graphic representations of a conceptual domain.

Participants brainstormed a list of 226 specific tactics or activities the industry uses to oppose tobacco control. These were edited and consolidated into a set of 88 mutually exclusive statements with the objective of no loss of information content from the original set. Each tactic on the final list was rated according to its importance in undermining tobacco control on a scale of 1 (least) to 5 (most). The results were statistically analysed to obtain average ratings and clustering, and mapped using suitable software.

Eight clusters were identified and given a label that summarised their contents. In order of descending average importance and their mean scores out of 5, the clusters were:

- lobbying and legislative strategy (3.71)
- legal and economic intimidation (3.46)
- usurping the agenda (3.39)
- creating illusion of support (3.27)
- harassment (3.26)
- undermining science (3.26)
- media manipulation (2.91)
- public relations (2.85).

The public relations cluster is listed separately but the other clusters could fall under the PR umbrella. The top five specific PR tactics and their mean scores were:

- using philanthropy to link their public image with positive causes (4.00)
- using philanthropy to build a constituency of support among credible groups (3.62)
- diverting attention from the health issues by focusing attention on the economic issues (3.48)
- distracting attention from the real issues with alternative stances such as accommodation and ventilation (3.38)
- asserting that restrictions on tobacco could lead to restrictions on other industries and products (3.38).

Reasons for the decision not to accept tobacco industry clients

The Global Protocol on Ethics in Public Relations published in 2008 by the Global Alliance includes Appendix A, Guiding principles for the ethical practice of public relations. Appendix A presents a six-point decision-making guide. The six-point guide follows:

1. Define the specific ethical issue/conflict
2. Identify internal/external factors (e.g. legal, political, social, economic) that may influence the decision
3. Identify key values that are in question
4. Identify the parties who will be affected by the decision and define the public relations professional's obligation to each
5. Select the ethical principles to guide the decision-making process
6. Make a decision and justify it to all parties affected by the decision and to the public if necessary.

Task

Looking at this list and the factual evidence provided above, is it easier to make a case for or against working in PR for a tobacco company?

Relating the decision to the CIPR Code of Conduct requires a more subjective approach. Awareness and judgement of the tobacco industry's business objectives and practices need to be weighed against the following clauses:

Principles, 1.i: To maintain the highest standard of professional endeavour, integrity, confidentiality, financial propriety and personal conduct, and

Principles of Good Practice 2, first bullet: Integrity – honest and responsible regard for the public interest.

Last words

Ethics does not necessarily provide unique answers. What it does is oblige one to think about one's actions, motives and any consequences arising from them, how they affect the rights of others and ultimately whether they are good and right, or bad and wrong.

Question

What would your ethical conclusions be?

A few thoughts of a PR practitioner working in an international tobacco company (Ukraine) – personal views of Kateryna Zasoukha

In spite of the fact that all of us now have more freedoms to express our own thoughts and ideologies, made more possible by Web 2.0, we still depend on many powerful global trends. One of them is the big war against tobacco in society. I'm not a smoker, but many of my colleagues and relatives enjoy smoking. So I can observe the behaviour of my company's consumers every day and make my own judgements about the issue of smoking.

Tobacco products were invented ages ago. And long, long ago those products were enjoyed, very often as an anti-headache remedy or antidepressants. During my visit to Saint-Petersburg (Russia) the museum guide told me that Tsar Peter I was a very heavy smoker who used to say that smoke made his head clearer. A few decades ago almost every movie star was a smoker. I have even found a picture of Ronald Reagan, the actor who later became President of the USA, on a cigarettes advertising poster on the internet. And that was a time when tobacco products were not as technologically developed as they are today. There were no charcoal filters, for example.

Tobacco is a legal product around the world. There is only one small state (Bhutan) where smoking is absolutely prohibited. So what about the rights of the smokers? Smoking is their adult choice and if they are tolerant of non-smokers, why make them feel underprivileged? Why make them stand in the cold streets outside bars instead of providing good ventilation facilities and separate rooms for smokers and non-smokers? I am very proud to say that my company invests millions into smoking stations at airports. Smokers can feel absolutely comfortable there and not disturb anybody else.

The world's biggest tobacco producers are socially responsible companies. None of them direct their marketing initiatives at underage people; all of them pay huge taxes and organise charity initiatives. In Ukraine, for example, tobacco companies are big investors and among the most admired employers. During the economic downturn a lot of companies had job cuts and haven't even paid any compensation to those affected. My company consolidated the manufacturing processes a month before the credit crisis, and I was privileged to work upon a very serious and detailed factory closure plan. We considered each and every worker and we approached all the families. The company has carefully created outplacement packages and calculated a very high compensation budget. As a result, we have not had any strikes or complaints. I received an excellent training in change communication and I was very proud to be a part of such a professional and socially responsible team.

Cigarette prices grow tremendously and international organisations happily share the statistics about the tobacco market decrease. However, people haven't necessarily quit smoking but instead of legal, more expensive cigarettes they have started buying illegal products coming from Eastern Europe. The illicit trade affects my company's operations around the world, so the company invests hundreds of millions to fight against it. I am a part of this project in Ukraine and I really feel proud to be a part of it.

There is a global trend now to avoid cooperation with tobacco companies, as well as with weapon producers and other 'evil' industries. But it is interesting to consider the companies who were knocking at our door and fighting for our money just a decade ago, which is a very short time for such a dramatic change. These companies now cooperate with drug producers, GM food producers and other possibly dangerous industries.

My grandfather is 86. He started smoking during World War II. When I ask him what he will do if cigarette distribution becomes forbidden, he says that he will start growing tobacco plants himself because there was a time when his father did that. It's useless to tell my grandfather about how harmful smoking is. He says he has always known about that, but made his personal choice long ago. I also had a friend who died because of lung cancer. He had never smoked. He was a painter.

To summarise my thoughts, I'd like to say that as a PR person and CIPR graduate I'm really proud to work in a socially responsible and transparent company. I consider, with pride, that I have never acted unethically as a professional. And my employer has never violated the law. The company puts all the information required about the health risks on the packs. Smoking is always an adult choice of a legal product. So I think there is nothing about ethics in PR to worry about in my job.

Question

The above is a personal point of view, which is supported by anecdote and legal considerations. Does reading this affect your answer to the previous question and if so, why?

Case study
The promotion for e-cigarettes in Poland

Katarzyna Gontarczyk

Background information

The electronic cigarette or e-cigarette is a relatively new device invented in China, available in Europe for about five years and in Poland for about three years. It is a sophisticated inhalator usually produced in a shape of a cigarette, consisting of a battery, a heater called an atomiser and a cartridge that may or may not contain nicotine. Electronic cigarettes are quite often used by smokers to quit or reduce smoking.

In Poland we have currently about 9 million smokers in a 40 million nation. Three years ago our Parliament set forward an Act protecting inhabitants from being affected by 'passive smoking'. Unfortunately, in this Act, one sentence suddenly appeared regarding electronic cigarettes: they were to be made illegal in Poland.

Electronic 'smoking' – that is inhaling nicotine or artificial flavours without nicotine, has become more and more popular in Poland. At the end of 2009 we had about 30,000 e-smokers and over 1,500 electronic cigarettes were sold every month. According to the daily *Puls Biznesu*, these numbers were growing rapidly. In February 2010 electronic cigarette producers and distributors began their attempts to stop the tobacco lobbying, just a few weeks before voting was due to take place, on the Act, in Parliament.

Tools

The tobacco lobbyists had been working on the Act for two years, using top lawyers, several special-ised public relations consultants, media communications companies and public affairs companies. The news media and individual politicians were targeted with strong and constant information flows. For the e-cigarette lobby, it was not easy to build a communication strategy with their limited budget and under the enormous time pressure.

The market for electronic cigarettes was considerably underdeveloped. There were only a few companies in existence that were strong enough to cooperate. The first challenge was to convince the e-cigarette producers that despite the fact they are competing against each other on a daily basis in the market, there were common goals that had to be addressed to achieve a common purpose for the whole sector. After surmounting a number of obstacles, an association of e-cigarette producers and distributors was formed under the name of 'Alternatywa' (an alternative for smoking, www. alternatywadlapalaczy.pl). This Independent body undertook to communicate exclusively with members of parliament. The news media were not targeted, due to the lack of time; however, there were several news print, radio and television interviews that took place, as a side effect of the strong information campaign that had been aimed at decision makers only.

Some other NGOs (non-governmental and non-profit organisations) joined the action, like Instytut Innow-acji (Institute of Innovation, www.ii.org.pl), which is focused on innovative products and services, and BezDymu. com (without a smoke, www.bezdymu.com), a social action group led by a journalist who is campaigning for public space to be free from cigarette smoke. Those organisations, as well as individuals, including a few medical doctors who supported electronic cigarettes, spontaneously joined Alternatywa, sharing ideas on the blog created by BezDymu.com and attending several commission meetings just before the final vote.

At the same time Alternatywa was distributing e-cigarettes, sponsored by the producers to influential people, like actors, TV presenters and journalists, with the hope that this not very well-known product would be tested and evaluated by them. That resulted in several positive opinions being published before the vote. A letter was also sent to the Minister of Health, who apparently was a dedicated smoker, with an invitation to receive an electronic cigarette and have several lessons on how to use it.

Finally, Alternatywa undertook a very effective communication campaign aimed at the parliamentarians.

The parliamentary work on amendments to the Act put forward by the Health Commission was supported by 26 members from various parties.

Alternatywa, together with an e-cigars company, hired a professional lobbyist, who held the required certificates and registrations required by Polish law, and with his support a special folder of information was created.

The folder included a few pages of information about the e-cigarette market in Poland, its turnover and tax paid and an analysis on the impact of e-smoking on human health. There was also a question-and-answer sheet describing influences of e-smoking on human health, which was supported by a full medical analysis.

The above documents were handed to parliamentarians while the Health Commission was meeting. Additionally, representatives of Alternatywa talked to numerous parliamentarians on the issue.

As there were journalists waiting for the conclusion of the Health Commission meeting, the documents were also given to them.

This turn of events was crucial to the campaign as the journalists learned about the analysis and started their own campaign to discuss the case and all of the pros and cons.

The noise in the media was so loud that the parliamentarians refrained from discussing e-smoking in the commission and rejected the issue from the Bill.

Results

An amendment to the Act was introduced that cancelled the inserted sentence about electronic cigarettes being illegal in Poland. The battle with tobacco companies was won by a small group of e-cigarette producers but the war is still going on.

Questions

This case study takes another position within the ethical debate about tobacco. While still providing nicotine but eliminating passive smoking, might this case be easier to undertake for an ethical PR practitioner?

Considering the issues management discussion relating to the Brent Spar oil rig in Chapter 3, by how much do you think the government in Poland was responding to the facts presented to them or the noise in the media?

REFERENCES

Barton, H. (2010) 'ISO 26000 and the UN Global Compact: introduction to the linkages between the Ten Principles and ISO26000 Core Subjects', 27 May

Blackburn, S. (1999) *Think*, Oxford University Press

Blackburn, S. (2003) *Ethics, a Very Short Introduction*, Oxford University Press

Cai Xiqin (ed.) (2006) *Confucius: The Analects*, Sinolingua

Crofts, T. (ed.) (1995) *Confucius: The Analects*, Dover

Debeljak, A. (2000) 'Lonesome heart and the failed community', in M. Kos (ed.), *The Slovenian Essay of the Nineties*, Litterae Slovenicae, Ljubljana

Ewen, S. (1996) *PR! A Social History of Spin*, Basic Books

Fombrun, C. J., N. A. Gardberg and Barnett, M. L. (2000) 'Opportunity platforms and safety nets: corporate citizenship and reputational risk', *Business and Society Review* 105(1): 85-106

Freeman, S. (2000) 'John Rawls', in *Routledge Encyclopaedia of Philosophy*, Routledge

Fu Yunlong and Cai Xiqin (2007) *A Selected Collection of the Great Learning*, Sinolingua

Fung Yu-Lan (1976) *A Short History of Chinese Philosophy* (ed. D. Bodde), The Free Press

Grayling, A. C. (2011) *The Good Book: a Secular Bible*, Bloomsbury

Greenwood, J. (2003) 'Trade associations, change and the New activism', in John and Thompson, *New Activism and the Corporate Response*, Palgrave MacMillan

Gregory, A. (2009) 'Ethics and professionalism in public relations', in R. Tench and L. Yeomans, *Exploring Public Relations*, Financial Times Pearson

Hazlehurst, J. (2013) 'Spin masters: How PR is taking over the world', *Management Today*, http://www.managementtoday.co.uk/features/1164615/spin-masters-pr-taking-world/, 1 January

Jensen, I. (2009) 'Mutual dependency of communication and legitimate institutionalise mechanisms of social coordination', Conference paper, Milan

Lao Tzu (1963) *Tao Te Ching*, Penguin

L'Etang, J. (2006) 'Corporate responsibility and PR ethics', in J. L'Etang and M. Pieczka (eds) *Public Relations: Critical Debates and Contemporary Practice*, Lawrence Erlbaum Associates

L'Etang, J. and M. Pieczka (2006) *Public Relations: Critical Debates and Contemporary Practice*, Lawrence Erlbaum Associates

London Benchmarking Group (1997) 'Companies in community: getting the community investment measure', prepared by David Logan Corporate Citizen International

Oxford English Reference Dictionary (1996) Oxford University Press

Peters, J. D. (1999) *Speaking into the Air*, University of Chicago Press

Pieczka, M. (1995) 'Symmetry in communication and public relations', Conference paper, Bledcom

Rousseau, J.-J. (1998) *The Social Contract* (tr. H. J. Tozer), Wordsworth Classics

Routledge Encyclopaedia of Philosophy (2000) Routledge

Russell, B. (1961) *History of Western Philosophy*, Allen & Unwin

Sartre, J.-P. (1946) *Existentialism is a Humanism* (tr. P. Mairet), Public lecture

Warnock, M. (1970) *Utilitarianism*, Fontana

Zarefsky, D. (1994) '"Public sentiment is everything": Lincoln's view of political persuasion', *Journal of the Abraham Lincoln Association*, Summer

Part 2
Skills in public relations

Chapter 5
An introduction to international communication

Eva Maclaine

Learning outcomes

By the end of this chapter, you should be able to:

- Identify the key definitions of international communication and its role
- Recognise the debates around the nature of international communication and the role of ethics in it
- Understand the importance of cultural differences and how to accommodate them
- Have a grounding in the teachings of Hofstede
- Have considered the role of social media in international communication and how technology can help when running a virtual office

Note: For the purposes of this chapter the terms 'communication' and 'public relations' are interchangeable.

WHAT IS INTERNATIONAL COMMUNICATION?

In today's shrinking world, where we are fed a diet of 24-hour news, where radio and television programmes do not analyse what has happened but consider the outcomes of what will happen as the news unfolds, when telephoning someone in New Zealand on Skype is as easy as talking to your mother down the road, the world is suddenly immensely accessible.

With this accessibility, though, come challenges.

International communication seeks to ensure that the challenges do not turn into problems, that our perceptions are shared or at least explained, that we all understand each other and that we can work and live together harmoniously.

Broadly speaking, there are two types of work associated with international communication. The first is that done by employees who look after communication for large multinational companies with subsidiary companies throughout the world. They may travel abroad frequently but they are usually based in the country of the company's headquarters.

The other type of international communication is executed by practitioners who obtain assignments in a specific country to carry out a specific project. Often consultants rather than employees, they can live in the country of work for anything between one month and two years or may travel in and out for short periods.

Some definitions

According to Robert Wakefield in *International Public Relations* (1996) only a few scholars have tried to define international practice. Wilcox, Ault, and Agee (1998: 409–410) called it 'The planned and organized effort of a company, institution, or government to establish mutually beneficial relations with publics of other nations'.

James Grunig in Wakefield (1996: 18) defined it as a 'broad perspective that will allow [practitioners] to work in many countries or to work collaboratively with people in many nations'.

The study of international communication touches on many different subjects: psychology, linguistics, ethics, culture, behavioural change and even anthropology. And, of course, it is grounded in communication theories and practices.

It has many things in common with intercultural communication. For example, Karlfried Knapp, the German linguist, defines intercultural communication as 'The interpersonal interaction between members of different groups, which differ from each other in respect of the knowledge shared by their members and in respect of their linguistic forms of symbolic behaviour' (Knapp et al. 1987: 190).

Stella Ting-Toomey states: 'Intercultural communication takes place when individuals influenced by different cultural communities negotiate shared meanings in interaction' (1999: 310).

The World Bank global programme, the Communication for Governance and Accountability Program (CommGAP), explains intercultural communication by defining what it does. 'By applying innovative communication approaches that improve the quality of the public sphere – by amplifying citizen voice; promoting free, independent, and plural media systems; and helping government institutions communicate better with their citizens – the program aims to demonstrate the power of communication principles, processes and structures in promoting good and accountable governance, and hence better development results'.[1]

In many respects there is little difference between intercultural and international communication. One could argue, however, that intercultural communication can be between government departments in one country, between different ethnic backgrounds in one country or between different religions. International communication is by definition between different countries and on a global scale.

---

[1] CommGAP – Towards a new Agora; Intercultural Communication http://siteresources.worldbank.org/EXTGOVACC/Resources/InterculturalCommweb.pdf

Challenges

An attempt to define the ideal international public relations programme, however, reveals some barriers to its development.

First, political, economic and cultural climates of the nations all shape the way PR is practised. What is, therefore, understood by public relations and communication is very varied and uneven.

Politically repressive regimes suffer from underdeveloped communication. Russia, China, North Korea, for example, erect powerful communication barriers, which inhibit any public relations work.

The Committee to Protect Journalists[2] has documented the killings of 33 Russian journalists since 1992, most of them business and political reporters.

In North and South Korea the differences in behaviour and culture are striking. BBC journalist Sue Lloyd-Roberts reported in her film *Life inside the North Korean Bubble* in June 2010: 'South Koreans can use their mobile phones to pay in the supermarket, there are more and faster broadband connections per person than in any other country in the world and, if you are feeling frivolous, there are cameras and touch screen keyboards along the main shopping streets to allow you to send a photo to a friend. All new arrivals from North Korea spend months in special government schools to learn how to cope with the twenty-first century.'

Even mass grief in North Korea is communicated in a way completely foreign to the West. The death of the North Korean president, Kim Jong-il, resulted in highly emotional public expressions of grief on a huge scale: tears, wailing and fists beaten against the pavement by tens of thousands of people.

China's restrictive media make it extremely difficult to communicate honestly. The *New York Times* reported[3] in December 2011 about the prominent Chinese blogger and heart-throb Han Han. Previously controversial, he produced three new essays which revealed a more conciliatory stance towards the government. This had angered the dissidents, including the internationally respected artist Ai Weiwei. The authorities, on the other hand, appeared to be heartened.

Even when political systems have opened up, however, a legacy of reluctance to embrace communication persists. Polish PR companies are, for example, a relatively new phenomenon due to the political constraints faced by the country until 1989. A 2005 report[4] showed there were about 500 companies in Poland claiming to practise public relations but, in reality, only about 70–100 of them actually offered services that could be called public relations (Czarnowski, 2003; Laszyn, 2001). The majority of PR agencies only offered primitive advertising and event planning services.

Gaps in the teaching of international public relations also prevent an ideal PR programme. Elizabeth Toth and Linda Aldoory found a great variety of standards throughout the world, with some university courses in PR being no more than a major in advertising and practitioners calling PR an 'addition to marketing communication' (2010: 12).

Many cultural factors affected the teaching in particular countries, making uniformity impossible:

> In Figure 5.1, cultural factors are listed that participants shared that they felt affected public relations education in their country. For example, in Nigeria there is a strong emphasis on relationships and politics, which is tied with the country's focus on health and development. In New Zealand there was a similar focus on development and

---

[2] www.cpj.org/killed/europe/russia/murder.php
[3] http://thelede.blogs.nytimes.com/2011/12/27/with-essays-on-democracy-chinese-blogger-stirs-debate-among-reformers/
[4] www.instituteforpr.org/wp-content/uploads/Bribery_Poland.pdf Bribery for News Coverage: Research in Poland, by Katerina Tsetsura; Copyright © 2005, The Institute for Public Relations

Africa
Law and ethics in Nigeria
Democracy and freedom of speech is new in Nigeria
Strong emphasis on relationships
'There are various levels of development across Africa. One must deal with
health, development, politics, and relationships. Relationships are extremely important.'

Americas
Conscious of history, role of country in its region
Roots in colonisation
Licensing: Study public relations for 30 credits to obtain a licence to practise or have BA or MA in Brazil

Eurasia
More attention to harmony as a principle, and tradition of the Chinese culture
Emphasis on IMC (integrated marketing communication)
Target publics are journalists and consumers
Perceived lack of social acceptance of public relations; public relations = media relations
Building relationships is important
Size of the PR industry is still small
Different media system

Europe
Social responsibility and ethics are important
Finland emphasis on public sector and non-profits
Lack of internship opportunities
UK: 'Slightly more commercial, stronger emphasis on corporate enterprise'
Strong regulation from the ministries of education

Oceania
Intercultural, international focus
Development communication, poverty, solving social problems
Globalised outlook

FIGURE 5.1 Cultural factors influencing public relations education by continent
Source: Adapted from Toth and Aldoory (2010)

solving social problems, while also looking globally for public relations strategies. In China, participants talked about Confucian traditions and the ongoing framework of harmony working within public relations and other professions in the country. Participants also expressed a negative reputation in the country for public relations, which is viewed as merely media relations and publicity. Finally, the European countries seemed to highlight social responsibility and ethics.

While most participants suggested a moderate emphasis on Western ideals for public relations, some participants actively resisted known Western ideologies in their courses and programming. One participant claimed that public relations had a negative reputation due to its ties to assumed Western ideals and therefore, his program chose other labels for its public relations courses. (2010: 16)

Why bother communicating internationally?

There are many reasons why it has become necessary to communicate internationally. The rapid expansion of the internet, 24-hour news media, increased speed of travel and decreased distances, the growth of social media, global markets where the same products are sold worldwide have all increased the need for global understanding.

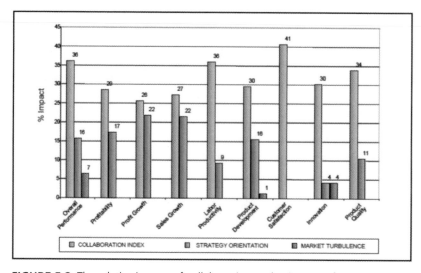

FIGURE 5.2 The relative impact of collaboration on business performance
Source: Frost & Sullivan, www.frost.com

Yet effective international communication is not simply needs-based. It is desirable in itself. Research shows that companies that collaborate globally perform better.

A report done by Frost and Sullivan[5] based on three regions (Europe, Asia and the US) reveals that companies which have a strong collaborative culture, which is decentralised and open, also benefit from greater innovation, provide higher quality, and more growth and profitability than others.

The way we conduct public relations has changed considerably from imparting information to our selected audiences, through adopting two-way communication with publics, to today's conversations with all our varied publics. It is no longer enough simply to provide information; we need to collaborate, to influence and above all to listen in order to reach them all effectively.

On a global scale that provides particular challenges there is no doubt that international communication is vital. On 10 August 2011 *PRWeek* published, in conjunction with the consultancy APCO Worldwide, the results of a survey of 96 in-house communication professionals (Figure 5.3). It found that international experience, although not currently considered important, is deemed to be important for the future for people in PR. '. . . it is obvious why international experience will become increasingly valuable. The web is also breaking down borders, often requiring campaigns to speak to global audiences. As well as experience of working with different clients and understanding different cultures . . . language skills will be important.'

Task

Why do you think it important that we practise effective global communication?

---

[5]Frost & Sullivan White paper: Meetings Around the World: The Impact of Collaboration on Business Performance, sponsored by Verizon Business and Microsoft http://newscenter.verizon.com/kit/collaboration/MAW_WP.pdf

During the period 6 June–6 July 2011, *PRWeek* and APCO asked 96 in-house comms professionals in the UK for their views on the issues they face in daily work life:

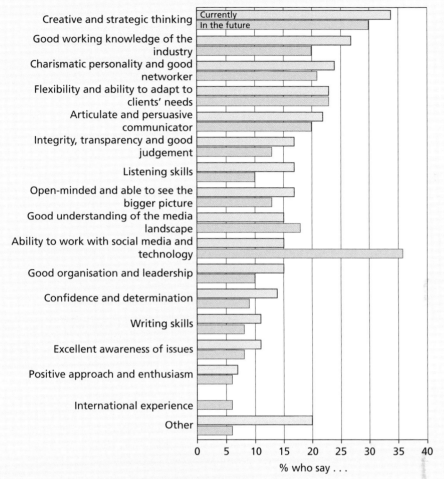

FIGURE 5.3 Most important attribute for a successful PR person

Source: *PRWeek*, 10 August 2011, reproduced from *PRWeek* magazine with the permission of the copyright owner. Haymarket Business Publications Limited

PRODUCTS ARE GLOBAL BUT PEOPLE ARE NOT

Key bodies are now working internationally to promote the understanding of international communication.

The Global Alliance, for example, announced that its theme for the Seventh World Public Relations Forum, in Melbourne, Australia from November 2012 will be 'Communication without borders'. Global Alliance Chair Daniel Tisch said: 'This reflects the global nature of the World Public Relations Forum and of communication today. Communication is transforming global society, and the Forum is an opportunity to break down barriers, enhance intercultural understanding, and consider how to enhance our profession's contributions to our organizations – and to our world' (22 November, 2011 Global Alliance release: 'Communication without borders: One year until Melbourne welcomes the World PR Forum').

Although we all understand the term 'global' and products may be sold globally, we ourselves are not global; neither are we motivated globally. We have not created a globally uniform consumer. We operate within a very precise local environment, with responses that are particular to our experience and our upbringing. We might eat Big Macs, drink Coca-Cola and use the internet, but our behaviours are, in fact, very different. To consumers, local is more meaningful than global. Whilst we may all like to use the same face cream, for example, or drink the same orange juice, the way we might be persuaded to do so could be quite different.

The human element involved in the process of persuasion should never be forgotten. Although products are often sold using technology accessible to millions, they are sold by people to people. That is why public relations is maturing to a conversation which seeks to engage the publics continuously, to listen to what they say and to respond as immediately as possible to their needs and wants. This is not from an inbuilt altruism towards the end user. It is, of course, sound business sense. However, customers themselves have found their voice and now expect and demand to be heard and listened to. Although the world has shrunk the number of publics has increased and they are more diverse than ever.

Professor Geert Hofstede says: 'In our globalized world most of us can belong to many groups at the same time. But to get things done, we still need to cooperate with members of other groups carrying other cultures. Skills in cooperation across cultures are vital for our common survival.'[6]

How then can you manage messages in a large global organisation which is autonomous on a global scale yet whose offices are scattered throughout the world and where both workforce and customers differ in every possible way: in education, sophistication, finances, economy and societal structures? On the one hand the product or service may be rolled out on a global scale, but reality demands that the public relations is tailored to each market and then to each market segment. Hence the mantra 'Act global, think local'.

There are huge differences between mature markets such as America, the UK and Japan, high-growth markets such as Brazil and China, and emerging markets like Vietnam and Thailand. In addition there is much diversity within each country as well. The inhabitants of Shanghai, for example, have little in common with those living in the far reaches of the north by the Mongolian mountains. Added to this there are often language, religious and cultural differences.

Some actions are taken for financial reasons. Advertisers, in particular, are guilty of trying to cut costs. They argue that by using one standardised campaign throughout the world they save on photo shoots, models, translations and the like. International ad guru Simon Anholt says, however: 'Translating ad copy is like painting the tip of an iceberg and hoping it all turns red' (2000: 5).

You may have a global product but unless you persuade the people by using arguments and rationale that appeal to them, your product will fail. In *International Marketing Blunders: Marketing mistakes made by companies that should have known better*, Michael D. White (2009) relates how Colgate-Palmolive tried to launch Pepsodent toothpaste in South East Asia with a campaign to make teeth whiter. The campaign failed dismally. Not only did locals chew betel nuts to make their teeth darker but the ad was considered by many to be a racial slur.

A question of ethics

In public relations the idea of free 'Tasters' and gifts comes with the territory. Many journalists receive sweeteners: music reviewers get free CDs, beauty writers receive skin care products and treatments, and fashion editors find parcels crammed with designer clothes landing on their desks. Travel editors can plan their holidays round travel offers. Although many media companies now stipulate maximum gift allowances and are much tougher on the practice of freebies, few are quite as honourable as LBC's presenter of *The Travel Show*, Simon Calder, whose tag line is 'The man who pays his way'.

However, if the lie of the land is cloudy in the UK, which considers itself to be an ethical country in the world, how much more difficult are decisions internationally.

In spite of our reputation, UK PR companies have come in for considerable criticism regarding their work for foreign regimes.[7] 'An investigation by the *Guardian* revealed that the capital's public relations firms are earning millions of pounds a year promoting foreign regimes with some of the world's worst human rights records, including Saudi Arabia, Rwanda, Kazakhstan and Sri Lanka', claims the *Guardian*.

---

[6]www.geerthofstede.nl/
[7]*PR firms make London world capital of reputation laundering*, Robert Booth, guardian.co.uk, Tuesday 3 August 2010

One sometimes hears the argument 'When in Rome do as the Romans do'. Does that mean then that we should work with corrupt regimes, that we should pay bribes to obtain business, or that ethics should be put aside when working internationally?

Whatever anyone thought until recently has been put under the spotlight of the Bribery Act, which came into force in the UK in July 2011. Under this, companies, individuals and even service providers for or on behalf of an organisation could face severe penalties if found guilty. Individuals can face up to 10 years' imprisonment and organisations can incur unlimited fines.

The Bribery Act also created a new crime – failure to prevent bribery, irrespective of where commercial organisations carry on a business. This means companies now need to delve far deeper into their customers' backgrounds and business practices. They need to know who their partners, clients or agents are before aligning themselves in a business relationship with them. Not always an easy thing to do at a distance.

Although the CIPR, the UK's Public Relations Consultants Association, the Public Relations Society of America and the Global Alliance all have guidance and/or codes of conduct that address this issue, it is still a centrally important topic, exercising all international practitioners.

Where corruption and bribery are endemic, public relations is particularly vulnerable.

Transparency International publishes an annual Corruption Perceptions Index.[8] The 2011 index revealed first places taken as follows:

1.	New Zealand	9.5
2.	Denmark	9.4
2.	Finland	9.4
4.	Sweden	9.3
5.	Singapore	9.2
6.	Norway	9.0
7.	Netherlands	8.9
8.	Australia	8.8
8.	Switzerland	8.8
10.	Canada	8.7
11.	Luxembourg	8.5
12.	Hong Kong	8.4
13.	Iceland	8.3
14.	Germany	8.0
14.	Japan	8.0
16.	Austria	7.8
16.	Barbados	7.8
16.	United Kingdom	7.8
19.	Belgium	7.5
19.	Ireland	7.5

Note: The Corruption Perceptions Index measures perceived levels of public sector corruption. In 2011, the index looked at 183 countries and territories around the world.

The 2011 index ranked Russia at 143 out of 183 countries for levels of corruption. Nigeria was also placed at 143 while Venezuela was worse at 172.[9] Worse, the Committee to Protect Journalists has documented the killings of 52 Russian journalists since 1992, most of them business and political reporters.

[8]Reprinted from *Annual Corruption Perceptions Index 2011*, http://cpi.transparency.org/cpi2011/results. Copyright © 2011 Transparency International: the global coalition against corruption. Used with permission. For more information, visit http://www.transparency.org.
[9]ibid.

In an attempt to curb bribery in Eastern Europe developers launched Bribespot, an app which allows tracking and reporting of bribes anonymously with a smartphone. It can be used to explore corruption hotspots, get specific information about locations and about average sizes of bribes and provides case studies.

Bill Ristow in his report 'Cash for Coverage: Bribery of Journalists around the World' (2010: 7) relates how Alexandra Wrage, founder and president of TRACE, discovered coverage in India.

> TRACE International, a non-profit association that helps multinational corporations deal with bribery and corruption around the world, wanted publicity for an event in India. It asked for a proposal from a respected local media relations firm. The firm submitted two proposals, but Wrage was confused. They were full of 'oblique language,' and the prices were very different. When she asked the firm's representative why she had received two such different reports, the answer was straightforward. Wrage remembers: the higher-priced proposal 'would provide enough money to pay off journalists to get the stories we wanted'.

Indeed corruption in India is rife and many Indian citizens have had enough of this way of life. The Guardian online[10] reports how two farmers, fed up with constant bribery demands, took it into their own hands to protest. They released three sacks filled with snakes on the floor of a northern Indian tax office.

PR practitioners must behave ethically if they and their clients are to be trusted. And trust is fundamental to any successful communication campaign.

The public is becoming increasingly intolerant of corruption and public relations practitioners should lead the way. 'In a world of enormous transparency, companies that win the reputational race will be those whose moral courage is matched by their moral futurism', observed Rushworth Kidder, President of the Institute for Global Ethics[11]

Task

What are the important issues to consider when constructing a global PR campaign?

IGNORE CULTURAL DIFFERENCES AT YOUR PERIL

Eric Kramer[12] writes: 'In the field of intercultural communication, ignoring real cultural differences is, well, as the word suggests, self-imposed ignorance. Of all fields, intercultural communication demands deep and broad knowledge of specific cultures in order to understand how people from different linguistic and cultural backgrounds actually interact.'

The Global Alliance chair, Daniel Tisch, related how he was one of the few non-Muslims on the speakers' list for the First Global Congress for Muslim Public Relations Practitioners, held in December 2011 in Kuala Lumpur, Malaysia.[13] 'The inclusion of perspectives from both inside and outside Islam underlined one of the key messages of the conference: the need for humanity to bridge a cultural gap that has grown all too large in the last ten years, and the opportunity for communicators to be in the vanguard of that critical cause' (15 December, 2011).

---

[10]www.guardian.co.uk/world/2011/nov/30/india-corruption-protest-snakes-tax-office?intcmp=239
[11]Institute of Business Ethics, 'Celebrating 25 years', 2011
[12]http://erickramer.net/download/papers/Kramer2011-Praface%20for%20Religious%20Misperceptions.pdf, a preface to Croucher, S. & Cronn-Mills, D. (2011) *Religious Misperceptions: the Case of Muslims and Christians in France and Britain*. New York: Hampton Press, pp. vii–xxxii.
[13]www.globalalliancepr.org/website/news/chair-communication-borderless-world

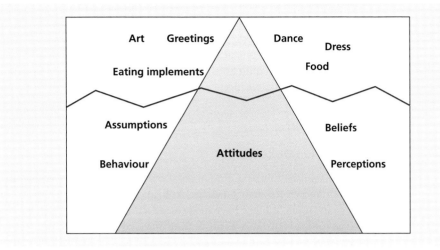

FIGURE 5.4 Iceberg model of cultural practices

In order to be successful in an international context where one is dealing with many different cultures, broad understanding is needed. It can be convenient to have some standards against which judgements can be made and some guidelines of behaviour. Here, the iceberg model can be helpful (Figure 5.4). Typically an iceberg has only 10 per cent of its mass visible while 90 per cent is hidden under the ocean.

The part that is visible displays those cultural practices which can easily be seen and experienced. These include food, music, dance, art, traditions, whether hands are shaken, noses are rubbed or bows taken when greeting colleagues, and many more. Some, such as the way people eat, may even seem rude, unappetising or strange when judged against one's own culture.

The others, the 90 per cent under the country's cultural surface, consist of patterns of behaviour, attitudes, beliefs, assumptions and perceptions. It is these which give the full and detailed picture of the citizens of a country.

Signs, symbols and body language

Each culture has its own rules about proper behaviour which vary from culture to culture: looking people in the eye, or not; saying what one means overtly or talking around the issue; proximity to people when you talk; table etiquette when eating.

In Samoa most meetings with the chiefs and villagers are conducted in mud huts sitting on the floor and it is extremely important not to point your feet at your host.

Some gaffes

- George Bush famously got the V-sign wrong when visiting Australia in the 1990s by turning his palm the wrong way.

- In most of Latin America and West Africa, as well as Greece, Iran, Russia, Sardinia and the south of Italy, the thumbs-up sign is not good and means the same as the middle finger does in the US: 'sit on it and swivel'.

- The O-sign – used by divers – usually has a positive meaning in the UK; but in France it means 'zero' and in some countries is even worse.

- A Japanese audience may close their eyes while listening; they are not being rude.

Colours also symbolise different things. In the South Pacific,[14] white clothes are worn to church, a habit encouraged by the early missionaries. White is regarded as the symbol of a pure

---

[14]www.une.edu.au/chaplaincy/uniting/finding_god/samoan.pdf Church life in Samoa – Lina Tuiavii

heart. However, in certain countries such as China, Vietnam, Korea and India, white is the colour of mourning and death.

In China red is lucky whilst in Japan black is unlucky. Green is considered a special colour in Islam and some colours have tribal associations in parts of Africa.

In order to feel confident in the countries visited, one needs to have a good understanding of local customs and practices.

Language

English is spoken here

Lack of language can be a fundamental obstacle to communicating effectively. The British are not well known for their language skills and, with English being an official language of the European Union, too few have made an effort to master any other.

One company, which was promoting financial thought and opinion across 21 countries, was asked what languages the members of the team spoke. After a long pause, they answered: 'Well, one speaks Australian', adding quickly, 'Thank goodness most of the people we deal with speak English'. That sort of arrogance is still all too prevalent in the UK.

There is an amusing interchange in Mark Twain's *Huckleberry Finn* (Chapter 14) regarding language:

'Why, Huck, doan' de French people talk de same way we does?'

'No, Jim; you couldn't understand a word they said – not a single word.'

'Well, now, I be ding-busted! How do dat come?'

'I don't know; but it's so. I got some of their jabber out of a book. S'pose a man was to come to you and say Polly-voo-franzy – what would you think?'

'I wouldn' think nuff'n; I'd take en bust him over de head – dat is, if he warn't white. I wouldn't 'low no-one to call me dat.'

'Shucks, it ain't calling you anything. It's only saying, do you know how to talk French?'

'Well, den, why couldn't he SAY it?'

'Why, he IS a-saying it. That's a Frenchman's WAY of saying it.'

'Well, it's a blame ridicklous way, en I doan' want to hear no mo' 'bout it. Dey ain' no sense in it.'

English may be spoken worldwide but it does not mean it is the same English. English is the first language in the USA, Canada, New Zealand, South Africa and Australia but many words carry different meanings and colloquialisms differ a great deal.

It is evident what potential pitfalls lie in wait for the unsuspecting.

Lost in translation

A common problem is when people think they understand one another but in fact do not. Many companies do attempt to translate messages to bridge the cultural gap. Sometimes one has to wonder why.

- In Taiwan, for example, Pepsi launched a 'Come alive with Pepsi' campaign which they translated inadvertently as 'Pepsi will bring your ancestors back from the dead'.
- The Skoda car was a laughing stock in Poland as 'szkoda' translates as 'it's a pity'.

- The international business educator David Ricks tells the story of the Igbo people in Nigeria who were taught by Christian missionaries to sing 'O, Come all ye Faithful' (1999: 59). The missionaries thought they had taught them to sing 'Very God, begotten not created'. In fact, tonally it translated into 'God's pig, which is never shared'.

All such examples are fairly lighthearted but there is a far more serious side to communicating in the local language. Although English is one of the most widely spoken languages in the world it would be dangerous to rely upon it when dealing internationally.

In a paper on Behavioural Conflict in 2009, now developed into a book (2011), which has been endorsed by some of the most eminent people in the military, Major General Andrew Mackay and Commander Steve Tatham argue for more language training in the Ministry of Defence. During operations in Bosnia, Iraq and Afghanistan the MoD had to rush personnel through language training courses – a process that in some instances can take years. 'Whilst we recognise it is impossible to retain a corps of global linguists it is possible through proper research to determine these areas of the world where the probability of future conflict or intervention is highest and to properly prepare at least a small seed-corn cadre of individuals', they say.

Finally, learn to speak slowly. If you slow to a pace where you feel you are speaking very slowly, that is the pace at which you should be speaking. It is also the pace at which people are more likely to understand you.

Music

Music is an international language. Little is as immediately evocative and nowadays we are surrounded by it. In the supermarket and shops it is played to encourage us to buy. At certain London underground stations classical music is played to prevent aggressive behaviour. An accordion is immediately evocative of Paris in the 1950s and Spanish guitar transports us to the energetic flamenco of an Andalusian dance hall.

In many countries singing and story telling is an integral part of the leisure time and music can be used to amplify messages, particularly where literacy levels are low.

Research has shown that music can have a very considerable effect and can even change perception. It is well known that moods can be changed by listening to happy or sad songs. Now, Science Daily has reported[15] (2011) that listening to happy or sad music can even change the way we perceive the world. For example, people will recognise happy faces if they are feeling happy themselves.

Music is, moreover, interpreted the same way globally. Research[16] (2009) has shown that the three basic emotions of sadness, happiness and fearfulness in music can be universally recognised.

It can also bridge gaps that might otherwise seem separated by chasms. Internationally renowned pianist Daniel Barenboim and Palestinian intellectual Edward Said created the West-Eastern Divan Orchestra (WEDO) in 1999. The aim is to promote coexistence and intercultural dialogue. The interfaith effort, which brought together Israeli, Palestinian and Arab musicians, has won praise around the world.

They named the orchestra after Johann Wolfgang von Goethe's collection of poems entitled 'West-Eastern Divan', a central work for the evolution of the concept of world culture.

'[The musicians come from] countries where the open ear has been too often replaced by the unsheathed sword, to the detriment of all. An orchestra which . . . shows that people who listen to each other, both musically and in all other ways, can achieve greater things.'[17]

[15]www.sciencedaily.com/releases/2011/04/110427101606.htm
[16]www.sciencedaily.com/releases/2009/03/090319132909.htm
[17]www.west-eastern-divan.org/

Lifestyle and business mores

Just as private and social behaviour are not the same throughout the world, neither is business behaviour. Anyone going on business abroad would do well to learn and understand the basics of business etiquette in that country. Even within Europe this can differ substantially.

Addressing colleagues

The way we greet people is just one difference, which can affect relationships. In the United States and the UK most people are now on first-name terms from the beginning. But in many cultures, such as in Germany, where people are much more formal, and Cyprus, it would be extremely rude to launch immediately into an old friends routine.

Japan is riddled with pitfalls for the inexperienced Westerner from the appearance of the business card, which should look smart, to the way you hold it with two hands, to the bow which follows receipt. And you should never write on it.

Loss of face

Case study
Water Authority of Samoa – introduction of water tariffs

Eva Maclaine – team leader and communication expert

In the South Pacific people do not like to disagree with you. It is considered rude.

Samoa had the highest per capita usage of water in the world, no water tariffs, leaks aplenty and the government had run an advertising campaign claiming 'Water is a Gift from God', thus discouraging any responsible attitude towards this valuable resource.

The task was to devise a public relations programme for the introduction of water tariffs.

In order to determine perceptions and preconceptions about water and its use, several focus groups had been organised with different sectors of the population, all with different standards of education and from different socio-economic groups.

In order to encourage exchange of know-how a local marketing company was engaged and briefed how to carry out the focus groups.

However, in Samoa no one wants to be seen to criticise. Neither did they find it comfortable to contradict the focus group leader who was a national. There was some real hesitancy about teamwork and a fear of doing anything that might challenge superiors.

It was only after carefully leading the discussion, encouraging a sense of safety and explaining the reasons behind the meeting that people slowly began to open up. It took an immense amount of time to get any worthwhile results but in the end and after a lot of groundwork, the groups turned out to be invaluable in shedding light on Samoan perceptions.

Emotion

The emotional levels of people in different countries can play an important role in how meetings develop. In some Mediterranean countries, people can debate very emotionally and can appear to be talking over each other rather than listening – however, conclusions are arrived at.

Food and drink

Press conferences in Eastern Europe are often followed by large, opulent lunches, laid on tables with white tablecloths, overflowing with food and drink. They are lengthy affairs and might take another two to three hours after the business of the day. And in Poland everyone must say thank you to everyone else when leaving the table.

In Korea, on the other hand, custom dictates that you thank the host before starting and after finishing. The most senior position[18] in Korea is at the middle of the table, on the side farthest from the room entrance. The eldest person is always allowed to sit down first and start eating first. As a junior, you are expected to keep your posture correct and should not place your spoon and chopsticks on the table (indicating that you have finished eating) until the eldest has done so. The eldest is also first to leave the table.

If you want to retain a clear head in Russia you may be well advised to plead alcoholism to avoid having to match others drink for drink. You may be allowed to shake the second glass to show you do not want it filled but it is difficult to get away with this for long.

In Samoa, when you visit a family, you do not take flowers but an offering of food such as the much-beloved taro.

Other customs

In Syria family restaurants may refuse to serve all-male groups – there must be a woman with them.

Segregated buses in Israel are causing controversy and women are required to enter through the back doors and sit at the back of the bus. Those who refuse to sit in the back are frequently threatened verbally and physically by the orthodox 'Haredi' men who enforce the system.

In some European countries, for example, Poland, Hungary, France and Italy, chrysanthemums are associated with death and should never be offered if you are invited as a guest to a family.

Some business habits can make working in a foreign country difficult. Attitudes to punctuality for example can set very different tones. In some countries punctuality is very important and considered as professional. Meetings tend to finish on time. In many other countries, though, there is a different culture. Here it may be necessary to rearrange a meeting several times before it actually happens.

It is vital to consider what is acceptable in each market. For instance, My Daily reported in March 2011[19] that fashion retailer H&M decided to cover up their model for the Dubai market. Having appeared in a skimpy little dress in the West she suddenly donned a white T-shirt underneath for the Dubai promotions.

It is well worth investing the time and effort in advance rather than making irreparable mistakes. The Arabic satellite TV channel MBC discovered this to its cost[20] when it aired its version of the reality TV show *Big Brother*. An immediate public outcry ensued in Bahrain when 1,000 people protested and a group of Bahraini MPs threatened to question the information minister on the issue. 'This programme is a threat to Islam. This is entertainment for animals', said 34-year-old teacher Shahnaz Rabi'i, who helped organise the demonstration. The programme was withdrawn after just one week.

Humour

The great value of laughter is that it can overcome negativity and stress. It is worth remembering, however, that humour does not travel and can be dangerous in an international context. It should only be used very carefully. It is easy to misinterpret humour and much of it, such as humorous speech errors, malapropisms and spoonerisms, are virtually impossible to translate.

[18]Dining with elders in Korea – Passport to Korean culture www.scribd.com/doc/24837238/Passport-to-Korean-Culture
[19]www.mydaily.co.uk/2011/03/22/gisele-bundchen-handm-ads-too-racy-for-dubai/?a_dgi=aolshare_twitter
[20]Arab Big Brother show suspended BBC (BBC News Online) Monday, 1 March 2004, 17:41 GMT http://news.bbc
.co.uk/1/hi/world/middle_east/3522897.stm

Jokes broadly fall into the following categories:

- Ethnic jokes within the same ethnic community; for example, Jewish people sharing Jewish jokes. This can be a healthy way to reinforce a sense of common identity.

- Ethnic jokes told between different ethnic communities in a spirit of friendly teasing. This can be positive if both sides are friendly and relaxed enough to celebrate their differences without causing resentment. A great example of this is the Bruno Bozzetto cartoons[21] on Italian behaviour, which can be found on YouTube. He gently prods fun at the way Italians behave in comparison with other European nationals.

- Ethnic jokes told by one ethnic community against another without any feeling of friendship. This is very dangerous as it can verge on racism. The challenge is to differentiate between this and the spirit of friendly teasing.

The role of humour in business is a serious subject now studied in some depth internationally and there is even an International Society for Humor Studies which meets annually to share research and ideas. There is no doubt that humour can ease communication and act as a bonding strategy which helps establish sound relationships.

Comedy can indeed be useful when wanting to challenge perceptions and alter views. The *Washington Post*[22] reported that a group of four American Muslim stand-ups were touring the American Deep South with a highly successful show called *The Muslims Are Coming*. This is being followed by a documentary about Islamophobia in America. They said they were not aiming at the ultra-hardliners: 'We're trying to affect the people in the middle, people with questions, the "persuadables", 'said cast member Negin Farsad, an Iranian American.

Some things are funny inadvertently. Donald Rumsfeld's message that 'There are no knowns' was one such case. 'There are things we know that we know. There are known unknowns. That is to say there are things that we now know we don't know. But there are also unknown unknowns. There are things we do not know we don't know', he said at a press conference at NATO Headquarters, Brussels, Belgium, 6 June, 2002. Although this was reported as a joke it was in fact a very serious comment, which has considerable relevance to good communication for example. But because it was convoluted it assumed comic proportions.

What is humour to one person can be offensive to another. One key to successful humour is that a joke is intelligible to the audience in spite of different cultures. The other is a common view on what is appropriate and acceptable behaviour. For this, one needs to have a sound contextual understanding of the joke. One American failed these tests completely when presenting in China in 2011. Whilst attempting to show the Chinese as adaptable and hard-working, his slides were misconstrued. Suddenly a Chinese woman in the audience jumped up to complain about the false ethnic stereotyping.

It is surprising, however, what does translate and play well internationally. British programmes such as *Father Ted Goes to Italy*, *Monty Python* and *Mr Bean* have, against all probability, done extraordinarily well overseas.

Humour can also be used to promote messages. In France the English are called 'Les Roastbeefs'. When the French, whose emblem is a cockerel, won the rugby match against England on 8 October 2011, within minutes Nike had put an amusing cartoon on Facebook of a cockerel captioned: 'Elevé au Roastbeef' or 'promoted to roast beef'. This cartoon was immensely popular and prompted 161 'likes' and 2,616 'shares' (people forwarding it to friends).

Some golden rules when using humour are:

- It is easy to misinterpret humour – it doesn't travel well.

- What is funny in one language can be insulting in another.

- Research your audiences and understand what is funny to them.

---

[21]www.youtube.com/watch?v=HHWBL9_alKs
[22]28 December 2011

- Do not use humour in presentations and speeches unless you are completely sure of your audience.
- If you decide to use humour make sure it can bring your audience on side and not alienate it.

Task

Think of some ethnic jokes, that are teasing rather than racist. Make a list of customs from other countries – do you know which are different from the UK?

HOFSTEDE'S DIMENSIONS OF CULTURE

Professor Hofstede has contributed a valuable tool with which to consider international communication, called dimensions of culture. A Dutch social psychologist and anthropologist, Geert Hofstede is a pioneer in his research of cross-cultural groups. He demonstrates that national and regional cultural groups influence the behaviour of societies and organisations, and that these are persistent over time.

Looking at how cultures affect the world in which we live he stated: 'Culture is more often a source of conflict than of synergy. Cultural differences are a nuisance at best and often a disaster'.[23]

He believes[24] we tend to have a human instinct that 'deep inside' all people are the same – but they are not. Therefore, if we go into another country and make decisions based on how we operate in our own home country, the chances are we'll make some very bad decisions.

He cites the example of cultural differences in business between the Middle Eastern countries and the Western countries, especially the United States.

When negotiating in Western countries, he says, the objective is to work towards a target of mutual understanding and agreement and 'shake hands' when that agreement is reached – a cultural signal of the end of negotiations and the start of 'working together'.

In Middle Eastern countries much negotiation takes place leading into the 'agreement', signified by shaking hands. However, the deal is not complete in the Middle Eastern culture. In fact, it is a cultural sign that 'serious' negotiations are just beginning.

Five dimensions of culture

Professor Hofstede has developed a validated five-dimension model (Figure 5.5) to explain intercultural differences. They are explained here in brief but there is far more detailed information on his website. [25]

Power Distance Index (PDI) This is how the less powerful members of society accept that power is distributed unequally. Is it a hierarchical society where people are obedient and accept that there is inequality or one where they question authority? In countries with a high score status symbols of power are very important in order to indicate social position and 'communicate' the respect that should be shown.

Individualism (IDV) In individualistic societies people look after themselves and their direct family and tend towards a strong work ethic. They are generally the wealthy countries. In

---

[23]www.cyborlink.com/besite/hofstede.htm
[24]www.geert-hofstede.com/
[25]http://geert-hofstede.com/

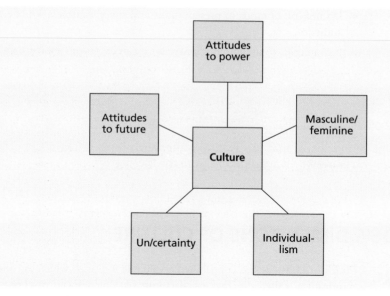

FIGURE 5.5 Hofstede's five dimensions of culture

Source: Geert Hofstede, Gert Jan Hofstede, Michael Minkov, "Cultures and Organizations, Software of the Mind", Third Revised Edition, McGrawHill 2010, ISBN 0-07-166418-1. © Geert Hofstede B.V. quoted with permission

collectivist societies people belong to groups that take care of them in exchange for loyalty; they tend to be the poorer countries.

Masculinity (MAS) Countries with a high score in masculinity enjoy competition, achievement and success; in this instance success is defined by winning or being the best. Countries having low masculinity scores means that the dominant values are caring for others and quality of life. A feminine society is one where caring for others and quality of life are the signs of success. Here standing out from the crowd is not encouraged.

Uncertainty Avoidance Index (UAI) This deals with a society's tolerance for uncertainty and ambiguity. It shows whether people feel uncomfortable in unstructured situations, which are novel and unknown and can therefore be surprising. Those countries preferring certainty tend to minimise such situations by strict laws and rules. The people are also more emotional.

Cultures which accept a lack of certainty are more tolerant of a variety of opinions and have as few rules as possible. They are more phlegmatic and contemplative, and not expected to express emotions.

Long-term Orientation (LTO) People in countries associated with Long-term Orientation believe that truth depends very much on situation, context and time; they tend to be thrifty, like to save and invest, and persevere in achieving results.

Values associated with Short-term Orientation are respect for tradition, fulfilling social obligations, a relatively small propensity to save for the future, and a focus on achieving quick results.

There is a Culture GPS iPhone app, based on the 5-D model of Professor Hofstede, with which you can compare 98 countries and three regions with each other or with your personal profile.

Understanding these traits and modes of behaviour is essential when preparing a public relations strategy if it is to succeed in relating to the publics.

Task

Consider which countries you think fit Hofstede's five dimensions. Where do you think your country fits?

RUNNING A VIRTUAL TEAM

Why and how have virtual teams developed? First, as the world has become smaller and far-flung outposts become more accessible, technology has led the way. It is at the basis of all virtual teams. These days when you can share documents on Googledocs, hang out on Google+ with numerous people and post videos to anyone you wish, it is supremely easy to communicate.

This is not the place to consider the importance of the effects of technology and the internet on communication. Suffice to say that, with 338 million[26] internet users, it affects international communication perhaps even more than communication which is within one country.

As the technology has developed so has our thirst for knowledge and a desire to have 'conversations' with people wherever they are. Distance is no longer a restriction to sharing.

Organisations are, therefore, using this opportunity for numerous reasons. The virtual team can be a team with the same people who meet regularly and discuss a variety of issues or it may be co-opted to coordinate one particular event. For instance, a company might wish to launch a new car for the international market and by gathering their PR teams, possibly with the designers, it will ensure the most appropriate communication strategy. On the other hand, a virtual team may be composed of public relations people who meet on a regular basis to exchange ideas and best practice.

The internet and intranets have made communication easier than before and emails, bulletins, video online chats, Skype and dedicated forums can make sure managers can stay in touch with their team whenever they need to.

The principles and disciplines of running a virtual team are much the same as those of managing any team. Aims, objectives, strategy, target audience and publics all must be identified. The roles and responsibilities of team members must be clarified early on. One needs to nurture a virtual team just as any other. Rapport between members has to be built; a charter should be developed so that members know what is expected of them.

Certain things are more difficult and time is needed to make sure these succeed. For instance, the ages and cultures of the teams can be diverse. It may be more difficult to understand a manager's expectations unless these are clearly spelt out from the outset. The simple courtesies of life such as saying please and thank you are even more important that they might be when one is dealing face to face. Feelings of isolation in team members can be far greater than in 'real' teams. Lack of physical contact, the coffee machine exchange and of face time bring their own difficulties. Lack of focus can be particularly prevalent in virtual teams.

All these challenges have to be countered and new ways of supporting the members must be developed. It is important that the group members all feel an important part of the team. A good manager will help them do just that by facilitating the development of the group and allowing it to form its own identity and personality.

Language within virtual teams can also be problematic. Some may not feel sufficiently confident in the chosen language of the team. There is a false perception that shared language means shared culture.[27] 'Welch, Welch and Marschan-Piekkari (2001: 197) and Usunier (1993) show that . . . individuals can be lured into a false sense of confidence and fail to perceive that they are not culturally close. This can have a negative impact on business communication processes and personal relationships' (Henderson 2005: 75).

Some enterprising communicators try to address this. A young woman, Rebecca Voss, working at an insurance company in the United States dealt regularly with their Northern Irish company. When stumped by a reference to 'at the coalface' in some post-event notes, she decided to put together a list of colloquialisms to make sure of better understanding. The list included better-known sayings as well as more obscure ones such as 'Wind yer neck in!' meaning 'You're joking!'; 'That's stickin out' meaning 'That's great'; and 'I haven't a baldy' meaning 'I don't have a clue' and finally 'Now yer sucken deezel' meaning 'That's a good way of doing that'!

---

[26]China Internet Network Information Center reports, June and November 2009
[27]http://en.wikibooks.org/wiki/Managing_Groups_and_Teams/How_Do_You_Manage_Global_Virtual_Teams%3F

Effective communication must be at the very heart of any virtual team and requires as much thought if not more to ensure that the team is successful and engaged. For example, it is nearly always best to address conflict and confront it head-on, with transparency. Disagreements, if not cleared up very quickly can fester and damage the productivity of the team. It is usually best to pick up a phone to clarify points rather than use email.

Even virtual teams aim to meet if possible and once a year would seem to be the minimum. However, there are other ways of engaging the members. The *Wall Street Journal* reports[28] that the CUNA Mutual Group, a global insurance company, has a virtual cocktail hour for far-flung co-workers and managers to get to know each other!

Finally, trust is one of the key ingredients in a successful virtual team. The members have to trust that their colleagues are able to do the work, that they act honestly and will do what they promise to do and that they have the integrity to support them and stay loyal even 'offline'.

Question

Think of some of the pitfalls and some benefits of running a global virtual office.

Virtual teams can sometimes provide solutions that would not otherwise be available. The following case study reveals how communication was used to win the Georgian propaganda war against the might of the Russian military and gather accolades from the Western press.

Case study
The power of Skype during the Russian invasion of Georgia

Christopher Flores, Senior Communication Consultant, Brussels, Belgium

Challenges and objectives

Roughly 16 years prior to the Russian invasion of Georgia in the summer of 2008, most of the world was unaware of the Georgian civil war that led to over ten thousand deaths and hundreds of thousands of internally displaced persons. In stark contrast, the 2008 Russian invasion was broadcast on every major television network almost round the clock, but what was the difference and how was it done?

During the evening of the first full day of fighting, I was called into the office of the Head of the National Security Council. Joining him in the room was the Prime Minister, the Minister of Foreign Affairs, the Minister of the Interior, the Deputy Minister of the Interior and the senior advisor to President Saakashvili. It was agreed amongst the Georgia cabinet that their strongest weapon was the media.

The Georgians, despite having better training and better equipment, were being overwhelmed by Russia's aerial bombardments and the sheer size of its military forces. The only way to end the conflict quickly would be to capture the full attention of the international community and recruit their involvement in negotiating a ceasefire via the media.

However, our ability to conduct a strong communication operation was easier said than done. Despite being able to garner significant international media coverage for a country of Georgia's size prior to the conflict, many journalists still were unfamiliar with the country and its complex history. Furthermore, the invasion occurred during the summer when many journalists were on holiday and it coincided with the Olympic Games in Beijing.

---

[28]http://online.wsj.com/article/SB10001424052970204524604576611262007838444.html?KEYWORDS=virtual+office

In addition to these obstacles and physical attacks, the Russians, either officially through government centres or indirectly through 'independent' actors, had also launched a cyber-attack against Georgian government websites. Thus the way in which information was exchanged between the Georgian government and its advisors had to be secure in order for our media operations to be effective.

The solution

At the advice of a former senior intelligence officer of a former Soviet republic, Skype was determined to be the most secure and most efficient way to coordinate and share information between several government ministries and advisors in Tbilisi, Brussels, Berlin, New York, Paris, Rome and Washington DC. In fact, Skype was considered far more secure than any other form of Georgian government communication platform.

Skype allowed us to develop several conversation threads or themes to keep those involved updated on the latest events and to exchange thoughts on strategy. Given the various different time zones, this tool proved invaluable as the conversation thread was always saved. Furthermore, the same information could be distributed to the media teams around Europe and the US simultaneously for them to disseminate the information in almost real time.

Being able to distribute information on a regular basis and as quickly as possible played a critical role in our ability to win the information war. While the Russians were focusing on the physical fight, Georgia quickly took the undefended news and information domain.

From the first hours of the conflict, Georgian officials readily made themselves available for media interviews and these were mainly coordinated between the various countries via Skype. In addition to government officials based in Tbilisi, information was shared between the various media bases to engage ambassadors to also serve as media spokespersons and to keep them on message and informed of the latest information from the field.

Beyond supplying government information to journalists, our team was active in ensuring that the broadcast media was receiving the latest information from the news wires. We had a small media monitoring team in Tbilisi that would share the latest wire articles via Skype. We would use this information to send to the major broadcast media, which resulted in our ability to dominate the CNN news ticker.

The result

'Saakashvili might have lost the war against Russia, but, scant consolation perhaps, he is widely seen to have won the propaganda battle. Big bad Russia against plucky little Georgia. Accurate or nonsense, thanks to Misha's Brussels-based PR men, it is the picture that's dominating the world media', proclaimed the *Guardian's* Ian Traynor.

'The PR campaign went into overdrive last week when Georgia found itself on the receiving end of post-Soviet Russia's first ever invasion of another country. Reporters covering the conflict have been showered daily with emails providing news, contact details, mobile phone numbers of officials, video footage, background material, and tele-conference access to Georgians from Saakashvili down. Highly efficient, highly effective, usually punctual.'

During such a crucial and frantic time in Georgian history and with its support teams based in four different time zones and seven different countries, compounded with ongoing cyber-attacks, Skype proved an instrumental tool to coordinate and run an effective and efficient virtual media office. Our ability to share information in real time, keep it securely stored and to hold secure conference calls was paramount to our ability to win the PR war and recruit the involvement of the international community, which eventually led to a ceasefire after only five days of fighting.

Question

This case study is only giving one side of the story in a propaganda war and the Russian viewpoint is that they were defending the rights of South Ossetia, where the Georgians had been putting down a bid for independence, involving many thousands of deaths. What care must you take before making decisions about international conflict?

REFERENCES

Anholt, S. (2000) *Another One Bites the Grass: Making Sense of International Advertising*, John Wiley & Sons

Committee to Protect Journalists (2012) www.cpj.org/killed/europe/russia/murder.php, May

Czarnowski, P. (2003) 'The transition of Polish PR', *IPRA Frontline* 1: 37

Henderson (2005), http://en.wikibooks.org/wiki/Managing_Groups_and_Teams/How_Do_You_Manage_Global_Virtual_Teams%3F

Knapp, K, W. Enninger and A Knapp-Potthopf (1987) *Analyzing Intercultural Communication*, Mouton de Gruyter

Laszyn, A. (2001) 'Poland's PR slowdown', *IPRA Frontline* 1: 16–17

Mackay, A. and S. Tatham (2011) *Behavioural Conflict: Why Understanding People and their Motivations Will Prove Decisive in Future Conflict*, Military Studies Press

Ricks, D. A. (1999) *Blunders in International Business*, 3rd edn, Blackwell

Ristow, D. (2010) 'Cash for coverage: bribery of journalists around the world', Center for International Media Assistance and National Endowment for Democracy, 28 September

Ting-Toomey, S. (1999) *Communicating across Cultures*, The Guilford Press

Tisch, D. (2011) Global Alliance release: 'Communication without borders: one year until Melbourne welcomes the World PR Forum', www.globalalliancepr.org/website/news/communication-without-borders-one-year-until-melbourne-welcomes-world-pr-forum, 22 November

Toth, E. L. and L. Aldoory (2010) 'An in-depth analysis of global public relations education', Department of Communication, University of Maryland, March

Usunier, J.-C. (1993) *International Marketing: a Cultural Approach*, Prentice Hall

Wakefield, R. I. (1996) in H. M. Culbertson and Ni Chen (eds), *International Public Relations – a Comparative Analysis*, Lawrence Erlbaum Associates

Welch, D., L. Welch and R. Marschan-Piekkari (2001) 'The persistent impact of language on global operations', *Prometheus* 19(3): 193–209

White, M. (2009) *International Marketing Blunders: Marketing mistakes made by companies that should have known better*, Atlantic Publishers and Distributors

Wilcox, D. L., P. H. Ault and W. K. Agee (1998) *Public Relations Strategies and Tactics*, Addison Wesley Longman

Wrage, A. (2010) (TRACE International) telephone interview by Bill Ristow with Alexandra Wrage, Annapolis, Maryland, 5 July

Chapter 6
Writing press releases
Paul Noble

Learning outcomes

By the end of this chapter, you will be able to:

- Understand the need for correct and effective language when writing releases
- Appreciate the general style in which releases are written and the need to adapt this for different sectors
- Understand the structure and formatting of a professional press release
- Recognise what print media require in terms of photography
- Understand which features of a release prompt good-quality media coverage
- Appreciate the role of the press release in a social media context

Introduction

If there is one writing task that is associated more than any other with public relations, then it is the humble press release. However, it is difficult to find anything that public relations people do worse than write press releases. More accurately, poor press releases are frequently issued not because the author does not know how to write a good release, but because the clients or managers approving releases insist on issuing marketing copy that they would like to be printed, rather than a neutral and objective story likely to be successful in educating and informing.

A press release is a news story issued by an organisation announcing something they would like to be covered by the media. The key word here is 'news': press releases should only be issued if they contain information on something that is new or different, or at least can be reasonably portrayed as such. This may be a new product, service, or customer; it may be new information such as the results of a survey, success in an award, an achievement by an employee or the effects of a new product or service on a customer.

Newsom and Haynes (2011: 158) are direct in their definition of news for public relations people. 'News is what newspapers and magazines publish and what radio and TV stations broadcast on their news shows. News is not what you think it is or what the company president thinks it is.'

BUILDING INTEREST

It is important to take an objective view. The news must be of interest to those it is targeted at and not just of interest to the organisation issuing it. It may well be that the biggest error in communication is taking the perspective of the sender of the message rather than that of the receiver; it is certainly the case that one of the major mistakes common in press releases is that the content is of interest to the sender and of no interest whatsover to the intended receiver.

The thing to do is to subject it to the 'so what' test. Is it really of interest to anyone other than the organisation issuing it? What would the reaction of a journalist be? Press releases should only be sent to media whose readers, listeners or viewers are interested in the topic of the release. Alongside 'so what' are two other guidelines. First, is the content either new or different (unexpected, counter-intuitive)? Second, a press release can be considered as a bitter pill (the corporate message) which needs to be sugar-coated to make it digestible to the media so they will swallow it. This sugar coating can be considered the creative bridge that links what the issuer wants to say with what journalists consider will interest their audience.

The aim of a press release is to achieve coverage. A press release is a communication between an organisation and its specific target audience (prospects, customers, investors) which uses the media as the vehicle to carry that communication. A press release is not aimed at communicating with the press; it is aimed at communicating via the press. This author remembers many years ago (as a client) being – falsely – reassured by his consultancy's account manager that, although a press release had not received any coverage, journalists would have read it, become more informed about the company, and long-term benefit would therefore accrue – this is not correct.

A press release is a common way of presenting news to a publication in an interesting, succinct and unbiased way. It is quite simply a news story and therefore should be written as such. Almost all the guidelines concerning the writing of press releases (such as summarise the story in the first paragraph, add a 'human' quote, and so on) are guidelines that journalists use when writing a news story.

The overriding purpose of a press release is to persuade journalists that this is a story worth covering or pursuing. You do this by showing them how a news story might be written on this subject. Normally journalists will want to put their own stamp on the piece. However, sometimes a good release will be used as issued (in whole or in part). This is much more likely in the trade and local press than in the national or consumer media.

So, while the first job of a press release is to be noticed, this is pointless unless it then is published – or at least prompts the journalist to write a story based on it. However, it is becoming more common for communicators to comment that they are planning to get less media coverage. An immediate reaction can be one of horror: this is a sentiment that is almost heretical in public relations. What they mean, of course, is that they are planning to sacrifice quantity for quality: less coverage, but better coverage. And when they say better coverage, they mean two things: it is in the right media and it is carrying the right messages.

Journalists have an ambivalent attitude to press releases, as they do to public relations people in general: mainly because most are a waste of time and effort but occasionally they are useful. A press release that gets little or no coverage, coverage in the wrong media or even extensive coverage that does not reflect one or more corporate messages is – quite simply – a waste of time. A press release is the cornerstone of many a PR practitioner's armoury but the sad fact is that the vast majority are wasted.

What makes this more frustrating is that it is actually very simple to write a good, straightforward press release and (importantly) then target it at the right journalists. This chapter gives some guidelines on how to write a good press release.

It should be usable by the media in its entirety and exactly as it is written: it should therefore be written in a style that would be found in a newspaper or magazine. This does not mean that it has to be used as is but it shows the journalists that it works as a news story, even if they choose to develop their own angle.

It must be issued at the right time: it must be issued when the news is at its strongest and most relevant. However, this needs to be tempered by an understanding of how the media operate so that your press release schedule dovetails with the deadlines of the media.

The news must be clear: make sure you are telling only one news story at a time and that the recipient can understand exactly what it is. Another common error is the view that two hooks are better than one, and three are even better. If you have three hooks, then use them for three different releases (or promote them as exclusive angles for key media). Three strong hooks in the same release will confuse and threaten to cancel each other out.

It must gain the journalist's attention immediately: publications and other media outlets receive hundreds of press releases a week. Yours will be just one of them – and you have to maximise its chance of being noticed and read. That is why it is vital to follow the accepted structure (see below) which focuses on the headline and first paragraph; only then will your release stand any chance of being noticed.

It must be written in a suitable style and tone: a news release is written for use by journalists and therefore should be written in a journalistic style. This means no ridiculous claims (for example, the world's leading organisation or the biggest and best product). It has to be factual; any claims must be substantiated. Cut out hype, keep adjectives and adverbs to a minimum, and avoid flowery, emotive language.

Only include information you are happy to see published: all information should be verified and approved by anyone involved. Consider what colleagues and stakeholders would think if they saw your release reproduced verbatim in their favourite publication. If third parties are quoted or mentioned, normal practice is to seek their approval before issuing the release.

Here is an example of a relatively short and simple release, which conveys the news clearly and follows all the rules above. The only weak point is the final paragraph: the release would be stronger if this was slightly more hard-hitting. The language employed is unlikely to be used by the press. It would also have been better if the final two paragraphs (both quotes) were combined.

Mini case study
Marks & Spencer announces details of chairman role

Marks & Spencer Group plc (M&S) today announces that Sir Stuart Rose, currently Executive Chairman, will become Chairman from 31 July 2010 on a salary of £875,000.

Sir Stuart will continue to chair the M&S Board and ensure a smooth transition for Marc Bolland when he joins the company as its new Chief Executive on 1 May 2010.

Sir Stuart will leave the company in March 2011. Headhunters have now been appointed to identify and recruit an independent Chairman.

Sir David Michels, Deputy Chairman of Marks & Spencer, said, 'The Board has set out this process to ensure a smooth transition over the coming months and enable Marc to draw on Stuart's considerable experience.

'We are pleased to be moving into the final stage of our commitment to split the roles and appoint an independent Chairman by March 2011.'

Source: http://corporate.marksandspencer.com/media/press_releases/company/Marks_And_Spencer_Announced_Details_Of_Chairman_Role

CORRECT AND EFFECTIVE LANGUAGE

Public relations practitioners are professional communicators. Although writing is not the only way they communicate with journalists, it is a vital one. No PR practitioner is going to make a successful career in public relations without being an effective (business) writer and being able to advise others accordingly. So, the ability to write accurately and effectively is an essential element in the public relations toolkit.

Naturally, therefore, press releases need to be correct in spelling, grammar and punctuation (but they frequently are not). There are three reasons why this is crucial. First, journalists are – if nothing else – skilled writers and their training will have included writing skills. If they are sent badly written releases, then the issuing organisation will lose credibility and the material may well be ignored. Second, the rules of correct English are not designed to torment us but to aid clarity of communication, and PR people are professional communicators. Finally, the public relations function should be where writing expertise resides; where the organisation goes to for professional writing ability.

One word of warning: press releases should be carefully checked ('proofread') and it is reasonable to use a spellchecker as part of this process. However, it is dangerous to rely on spellcheckers as they will not pick up correctly spelt words in the wrong context. A common problem area is where different words or phrases sound the same (or nearly the same). So attention has to be paid to homophones such as: complementary/complimentary, stationary/stationery and principal/principle. An extreme example resulted in the publication of the correction shown in Figure 6.1 in Australia's *Morning Bulletin* newspaper.

Journalists are inundated with press releases and only give them a quick glance. So it has to be clear at first reading what they are about and what the news angle is. This means they have to be expressed in simple terms. For example, releases for the national and consumer press should be aimed at the averagely intelligent 13-year-old but neither should they be simplistic.

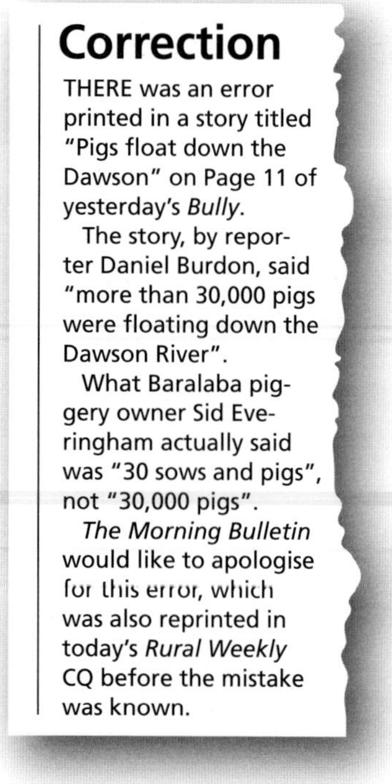

Correction

THERE was an error printed in a story titled "Pigs float down the Dawson" on Page 11 of yesterday's *Bully*.

The story, by reporter Daniel Burdon, said "more than 30,000 pigs were floating down the Dawson River".

What Baralaba piggery owner Sid Everingham actually said was "30 sows and pigs", not "30,000 pigs".

The Morning Bulletin would like to apologise for this error, which was also reprinted in today's *Rural Weekly* CQ before the mistake was known.

FIGURE 6.1 An embarrassing misunderstanding, although the editor was entitled to expect the reporter to check the 30,000 figure
Source: http://languagelog.ldc.upenn.edu/nll/?p=2951

Writing for the technical press

In the trade press, a relatively informed audience is being addressed and a technical press release should be aimed at an 18-year-old technical student: that is, assume a general understanding of basic concepts but not specific product or technical knowledge. A good example is shown:

Example

Major breakthrough in investment casting optimises the manufacturing of high performance parts

Morgan Technical Ceramics, Certech, has pioneered a new flow modelling technique for the design of ceramic cores used in the manufacturing process of high performance parts for the aerospace, automotive and medical markets. The use of the software is a major breakthrough for the investment casting process and will significantly optimise injection moulding of ceramic cores and enable the design of parts with more complex geometries.

While flow simulation software is commonly used throughout the plastics manufacturing industry, to date it has not been used by the ceramics industry in this way.

Morgan Technical Ceramics is the first ceramics company to offer the software simulation as part of its service. The company has been innovating and investing in the software for the past 12 months and is now working closely with its customers to enhance the design and manufacturing process of their products.

By using the software, Morgan Technical Ceramics' specialists are able to accurately predict how the ceramic core cavity will fill. Any areas of stress and potential breakage are highlighted early in the manufacturing process. The design of the core can then be refined to ensure it is filled in a controlled and uniform way, which improves the quality of the finished ceramic core and consequently the metal casting.

The whole process is more efficient than traditional methods because simulation is carried out before any metal is cast, saving precious time and resource.

Through better understanding of the way ceramic flows during injection moulding, engineers can design higher performance parts with more complex geometries, for example, turbine blades for aircraft engines or industrial gas turbines used in power generation. Tolerances of up to +/–0.1 mm can also be achieved.

'This breakthrough in investment casting will enable the design of parts that will exhibit increased performance and we're already pushing boundaries in the aerospace and automotive markets', says Dr Robert Oscroft, Technical Manager, Morgan Technical Ceramics, Certech. 'Our customers can now realise the benefits of flow modelling simulation for the first time and we can offer them full technical engineering solutions and expertise to improve their whole manufacturing process, from design right through to production'.

Source: www.morgantechnicalceramics.com/news_events/news/major-breakthrough-in-investment-casting-optimises-the-manufacturing-of-high-performance-parts/

This release is written in a way that makes it comprehensible to someone without any real technical knowledge, but great care is needed though. A trade magazine editor may have twenty-five years' experience in that sector. Or they may be an equally competent journalist who has moved over from an unrelated title in the same publishing house and will therefore need more background.

There are several additional key points to ensure clear (and therefore effective) use of language.

- Do not underestimate your own intelligence: if you do not understand what you are writing about, then neither will your audience.

- Remember that brevity is a driver of clarity. If it is possible to cut out words without losing any meaning then do so.

- Keep your sentences short. Although variety is important in longer pieces, in a press release, sentences should be no longer than 10 to 15 words.

- Long sentences usually make several points, so your short-term memory is overloaded and you have to re-read it. Long sentences can be shortened by splitting them, cutting out repetition and deleting redundant words: sometimes bullet points can help.

- Keep your words short. Prefer *start* or *begin* to *commence*; *jobs* to *employment opportunities*. Keep your paragraphs short. Have only two or three sentences per paragraph.

- Keep the whole release short. It is frequently difficult to keep the whole press release to one side of A4 but it should be exceptional to exceed two pages. If you really cannot restrain your story to two sides of A4 (one-and-a-half spacing), then either a press release is inappropriate (the story is too complex) or you need to split it into two (a news release and separate product background piece, for example, or are you trying to shoehorn two stories into one release?).

- Keep your sentences logical. This is enabled by short and simple sentences and by keeping related words together.

- Ensure that your grammar and punctuation are right. The basics of grammar help you keep your tenses, plurals and singulars consistent so the reader is not confused. A good command of punctuation also helps the text to be understood quickly at first reading.

- Use the positive form. Negative associations can taint the whole release: if you are promoting an agency for French homes, then stress the benefits of France rather than denigrating the UK.

- Use concrete, specific language. For example, adjectives and adverbs are rare in well-written releases. A more specific noun (or verb) is preferred to a noun (or verb) and qualifying adjective (or adverb). The result is more precise and fewer words are used: so *run quickly* becomes *sprint* and *top rank* becomes *elite*.

- Use the active voice. *Widget plc has launched a new widget* is better than *a new widget has been launched by Widget plc*. The active makes it clear who the 'actor' is and is generally more concise.

- Use reader-friendly words. Write language the reader can understand without pausing to think or having recourse to a dictionary.

- Avoid redundant words and phrases: they hinder clarity rather than enhance it. What is *an 'added' bonus* and what is *a consensus of opinion* if not *a consensus*? The phrase *in terms of* can be deleted without exception (or any loss of meaning).

PRESS RELEASE WRITING STYLE

The style of the press release will vary according to which media sector it is aimed at. The best way to start is to immerse yourself in the publications your company or your clients are targeting. Look at the news pages: examine the style; the sentence length; the vocabulary; the structure of the story; the length of the paragraphs. It is particularly interesting when you find the same story covered by both trades and nationals, or the trade and consumer press. They will take different angles and so should your releases. Here is an example: the heading and first paragraph from two releases announcing the same story, one for the consumer press and the other for the business press. While the consumer release focuses on the five awards, the business release highlights the most relevant award for the business market.

Example

Canon scoops five TIPA awards for the second year running

United Kingdom, Republic of Ireland, 22nd April 2010 – Canon has won five awards from the Technical Image Press Association (TIPA) – Europe's leading photo and imaging press association, for the second year in a row. The awards acknowledge the market-leading quality of Canon's photo and printing products.

Source: www.canon.co.uk/About_Us/Press_Centre/Press_Releases/Consumer_News/News/Canon_scoops_five_TIPA_awards.aspx

Canon's new large format printer scoops TIPA award

LONDON, UK, 22nd April 2010 – Canon's recently launched image PROGRAF iPF6350 was among five TIPA awards the company has won from the Technical Image Press Association (TIPA) – Europe's leading photo and imaging press association. The awards independently honour the most innovative products on the market – thus acknowledging the market-leading quality of Canon's photo and printing products.

Source: www.canon.co.uk/About_Us/Press_Centre/Press_Releases/Business_Solutions_News/1H10/Canon_new_large_format_printer_scoops_TIPA_award.aspx

SELECTING APPROPRIATE WORDS

The first point is to be careful about jargon and clichés. Jargon is a private language that is only appropriate when the audience you are addressing understands it. It is inappropriate to use language that the reader will not understand even though you and your colleagues may do so. For example, there is a phrase in the railway industry ('clock-face' timetable) to describe a timetable where there are trains to particular destinations at the same number of minutes to and past the hour. So you don't need to have a timetable, just to remember that there is a train to your favourite destination at twenty past each hour. So use the phrase 'clock-face timetable' if you are sending a release to the *Railway Gazette*. Use this phrase because the readers understand it – and it's a short phrase that takes a couple of sentences to explain. However, don't use it for the travel page on a national newspaper, as the readers won't understand it.

Clichés are more complex. A cliché is a phrase that has become worn out and emptied of meaning by overuse. It is impossible not to use them: they are too common and can be used to communicate simple ideas economically, particularly in informal social language. Where clear and precise communication is required, guard against clichés doing the work that words of your own choosing may do better. Why talk about a *level playing field* rather than specify that a new regulation should apply to all companies operating in your sector? Why talk about putting something *on the back burner* rather than specify that a decision has been postponed until the new chief executive joins in three months' time?

Superlatives and hype are also to be avoided if for no other reason than that they will not find their way through to a news story. Indeed, they will positively hinder your chances of coverage because they detract from, rather than enhance, the impact of the release.

STRUCTURING A PRESS RELEASE

A press release is written in a journalistic style, promoting an aspect to do with your client or company. In an ideal world, the release would be so well written, so (apparently) independent and so interesting that a publication would simply take your words and use them word for word. However, this is not often the case.

So what does a press release comprise? It follows the 'inverted pyramid' news story rule: it gives the journalist upfront the most important facts of the story and then gradually builds from there, with each paragraph less crucial than the preceding one. By following an inverted triangle format, the most important information goes first and information decreases in importance as the release continues. A journalist or subeditor should be able to cut the release from the bottom upwards, paragraph by paragraph, and the remaining copy should still communicate the story you want to tell.

A journalist should only need to read the headline and first paragraph before deciding whether a press release is newsworthy – or not. When you remember that they receive hundreds of press releases a week, you can see how vital this is.

A press release normally comprises one or two sides of A4 on headed paper (if it's sent as an attachment or posted on a website). If a journalist is interested in a release, it's likely that they will print it out. So take responsibility for how it looks once it is printed out.

If the release runs to more than two sides, condense it. If it's not possible to condense it then it is probably a story that is too complex to be communicated by a press release. In its most simple form, it would be made up as follows.

Heading. The heading must grab the attention: this is your only chance to hook the journalist. The heading should contain the core news in a short, succinct sentence so that the journalist reading it is encouraged to read on . . . There is nothing wrong with using lively language to attract attention but do not play with words to the extent that it's not crystal clear at first reading what the release is about.

Lead paragraph. The first paragraph must contain the bare facts of the story: if it doesn't, the journalist will simply move on to the next release in the inbox. It must contain the six Ws: who is releasing the story; what is the story about; when did it happen; where did it happen; why this is different or important; and how it was achieved. This paragraph should be able to stand by itself without any supporting information and give the gist of the story.

Second and further paragraphs. The next paragraphs should develop the story by adding layers of supporting facts: use the next one, two or three paragraphs to give more information on the news, supporting the first paragraph and expanding on it.

Include one or two quotes. A quote can contain opinion and comment that is more promotional than the body of the release. The quotes should be from relevant people: a representative of someone featured in the release (the customer, the central figure in the news) and/ or the managing director of the organisation issuing the release. They should illuminate the story and add a bit of colour.

Boilerplate or notes for editors. Always finish with background on the organisations mentioned: this is commonly known as the 'boilerplate' and is usually a standard paragraph containing basic facts about the organisation.

The overriding principle should be KISS: keep it short AND simple. Include relevant details needed by the press: this should include the date of issue, the name and contact details of the person available to give more information, and other useful facts such as whether there are photos available. Paragraphs should be short: no more than four sentences, but the ideal is two or three. Sentences should be short and concise: one idea per sentence. If a sentence is over-long, cut it into two. It is imperative that press releases are short and simple because they are very much a one-way form of communication: you are not there to explain the finer points of your announcement when journalists receive your release.

As we have already discussed, the vast majority of journalists assess a release on the basis of the heading and first paragraph only, so that these two elements bear more detailed examination.

HEADINGS

There is more disagreement over press release headings than any other aspect: should they be clever and witty or straight and to the point? As you only have a few seconds to grab a journalist's attention, it is probably the most important part of the release. The heading is dictated by the strongest news thread in the release. So to write a good heading, you need to highlight the news.

It is this author's view that headings should be short, plain and clear. If they are a puzzle, then the release will be ignored because of the pressure of time that journalists operate under. Also, the title of a press release is an odd beast as it is extremely rarely used – even a trade paper using your press release in its entirety is likely to write its own heading. So, the headline of a press release is actually a label telling the journalist what is inside and so should be written with this is mind.

There are always exceptions, of course. Direct Line, the UK insurer, once issued a press release headlined 'Boars drive better than monkeys'. This certainly doesn't immediately alert the reader to what the release is about, but it would have to be a pretty humourless journalist who didn't have a peek at the first paragraph to see what the release was about (it was reporting some internal research on the different claims records of motorists born under different Chinese signs).

Some general points on headings:

- Keep it short: a headline is a summary and attention grabber: 10 words max.

- Keep it simple: find a simple idea that is the central point of the release.

- Use short words: this will help headlines fit the (limited) space available as well as conveying ideas more simply.

- Put in a verb: a verb is an action word that brings a headline to life and gives the impression (correctly?) that something new is happening.

- Only try to be funny or clever as an exception rather than as a rule: subs will write their own headline and if they think a 'funny' headline is appropriate, they will write their own. Sometimes, maybe when you are using a survey to create news from nothing in the tabloids, a 'teaser' headline might be appropriate.

Look at the following release headings:

- London 2012 and BP launch a major new development programme for young people: The London 2012 Young Leaders Programme www.london2012.com/press/media-releases/ 2010/01/london-2012-and-bp-launch-a-major-new-development-progra.php

- Barclays Business announces Seminars with Rene Carayol www.newsroom.barclays.com /Press-releases/Barclays-Business-announces-Seminars-with-Rene-Carayol-6c3.aspx

- Citrix Breaks Virtual Appliance Performance Barrier, Unleashes Cloud Scalability in the Datacenter www.citrix.com/English/NE/news/news.asp?newsID=1865242

Are you still awake? How many of those would you have carried on reading? They are either of the 'what we are doing' school (who cares) or broad, vague statements (so what?).
Now let's look at some better headings:

- Tesco brings solar power to the people www.tescoplc.com/plc/media/pr/pr2010/2010-03-31a/

- Pepsi adds refreshing content to Nokia's Ovi Store www.nokia.com/press/press-releases /showpressrelease?newsid=1408217

- Why you shouldn't eat 'al desko' www.rentokil.co.uk/news/2009-news-archive/news_367420 .html

All three of these headings leave the reader wondering what the release is about and wanting to read on. Unfortunately, they also remove the chance of the publication using these clever words: no self-respecting subeditor would ever use a heading verbatim.

Perhaps the best course to follow is a straight short and snappy heading that provides the facts without being clever:

- AMEC awarded 11-year contract with EDF for new UK nuclear power stations www.edfenergy .com/media-centre/press-news/AMEC-awarded-11-year-contract-with-EDF-for-new-UK-nuclear-power-stations.shtml

- Dell reinforces commitment to cyber security http://content.dell.com/us/en/corp/d/press-releases/10-05-04-dell-cybersecurity.aspx

- Training budgets must be restored say HR professionals www.hays.co.uk/mediacentre/ mc-training-budgets-must-be-restored.aspx

Sometimes press releases have a subheading as well. This should be the exception rather than the rule. It is an admission that the heading alone is not clear. This means either that the story is too complex (and so not suitable for a release) or that the headline is not clear – a cardinal sin for a press release. News stories do not have subheads so the default for a press release should be the same.

FIRST PARAGRAPH

Once you have grabbed the attention with your headline, you need to cement the interest with the first paragraph. This is crucial: it is make or break. It must tell the gist of the story in no more than three sentences and preferably in two.

Without overloading, you should aim to get over the six Ws – as we have already discussed – in the first paragraph:

Who are you talking about?

Why are you writing about it?

What are you writing about?

When did it/will it happen?

Where did it/will it happen?

How did it/will it happen?

And most crucial of all: remember what your job is and always mention your company or client in the first paragraph. BUT avoid the off-putting practice of opening the first sentence with your company's or client's name (it is quite a good idea not to make a mention until the second sentence).

A good guide to whether you have included the necessary information in the first paragraph is to read it in isolation from the rest of the release and ask these questions:

- Does it stand alone?

- Would it work as a short news piece?

- Does it contain the vital pieces of information you want to get over?

Here is a perfect example of a sentence containing all the necessary facts:

In the 11th century [when], Lady Godiva [who] rode [what] naked [how] through the streets of Coventry [where] in a bid to cut taxes [why].

These are the sorts of things you should avoid: too much emphasis on the client or product at the expense of the news; hype and over-inflated claims ('the world's number one', 'the market-leading' etc.). These are complete turn-offs and will consign the release to the bin.

Here are some examples of first paragraphs.

Example 1

Virgin Atlantic is pleased to announce that it will be opening a new customer service operation in Swansea in September 2010. The move will create more than 200 jobs in the area over the next two years. The new customer service centre will run in conjunction with Virgin Atlantic's existing operation in Crawley, West Sussex. Julie Southern, Chief Commercial and Financial Officer, Virgin Atlantic commented: . . .

Source: www.virgin-atlantic.com/en/gb/allaboutus/pressoffice/pressreleases/news/swansea.jsp

Comments

This opening paragraph immediately uses language that is unjournalistic, making it unusable ('is pleased to announce'), it lacks solid information on the 'why': why has this been opened; what exactly will it do, and it leads straight into a quote before it has built the story.

Example 2

The UK's favourite supermarket has launched a solar electricity and hot water service, offering customers the opportunity to generate their own electricity and slash home energy bills at the same time. Customers will actually be paid for the electricity they produce – following the launch of the government Feed-in Tariffs on Thursday 1 April.

Source: www.tescoplc.com/plc/media/pr/pr2010/2010-03-31a/

Comments

This paragraph makes a fatal mistake in that it lacks the vital 'who'. It is actually about Tesco, and the name is mentioned in the heading, but this makes it unusable verbatim as the heading is unlikely to be used. The paragraph does not stand alone: you are left wondering what this is actually about. It needs more explanation to clarify the story. It is poorly constructed: in particular the use of the dash in the second sentence. Finally, what is 'the government Feed-in Tariffs'?

Example 3

Nokia today announced the launch of the Ovi Store football channel featuring exclusive Pepsi content as well as entertainment, apps and information from the world's most recognized football content providers. The channel leverages Ovi Store's global reach to offer Nokia football fans around the globe the easiest place to shop for the most popular and most refreshing mobile football content.

Source: www.nokia.com/press/press-releases/showpressrelease?newsid=1408217

Comments

This follows the rules very well. It contains all the facts needed. The only criticism is the use of the word 'leverages': a simpler word would be preferable.

SPOKESPERSON QUOTE

A quote is a common feature of a press release – and a much abused one. It is a useful way of adding colour and variety to the release, and also gives you the opportunity to say something that would not sit well in the text of the release. What it must not do is go over the top by saying 'this is the most wonderful thing since sliced bread'.

When issuing photographs, ensure that they are well captioned. As well as sending out photographs with press releases, build up a photographic library of relevant people, products, and even buildings to respond to enquiries and for general illustrative purposes.

A few pointers on good – and bad – photos

- Look at the publication you are aiming at – what sort of photos do they use?
- Photographs should either illustrate a point or be eye-catching to the journalist (and therefore the reader).
- Avoid using those brochure shots unless the publication is suitable.
- Avoid the typical head-and-shoulders shots of senior people. Try to put them somewhere interesting; find an interesting pose; make them look good (it is always possible!).
- Avoid a 'grin and grip' handshake photo to accompany any sort of agreement release – a complete turn-off!
- Be careful if your release is being sent out internationally – think about cultural implications (see Chapters 1 and 5)

Here are a couple of examples of good photographs to go with press releases. The first is an excellent 'stunt', while the second example is a story that is so strong it doesn't need any more help.

Mini case study

Confused.com is a leading price-comparison website in the UK and many of its users are interested in car insurance. In early 2010 (after heavy snowfalls), research undertaken by the website identified a particular road (Somerville Road) in the town of Worcester as having generated one of the highest numbers of accident claims in the UK. So Confused.com decided to protect the local residents by bubble-wrapping the entire street: everything from garden fences and ornaments to cars and postboxes got covered. See Figure 6.2 and for further details go to www.confused.com/accidentavenue.

FIGURE 6.2 It's a wrap: Somerville Road, Worcester protected by Confused.com
Source: Michael Blann/Gelty

Mini case study

Another, more strategic, approach has gained widespread international coverage. The 'best job in the world' was the theme of a worldwide campaign to promote the islands of Australia's Great Barrier Reef. The newly created post was as Tourism Queensland's Island Caretaker and more than 34,000 people applied – in the process generating media coverage that reached approximately 3 billion people across the globe. See Figure 6.3 and for more details see: http://youtu.be/SI-rsong4xs.

FIGURE 6.3 Aerial view of the Great Barrier Reef, location of the 'best job in the world'
Source: cool chap/Fotolia.com

WHEN NOT TO USE A PRESS RELEASE

Given the volume of press releases some companies (and PR consultancies) issue, you would be forgiven for thinking they were the only way of getting press coverage. There are plenty of alternatives and plenty of occasions when there are other approaches to getting your story reported.

Complexity. The best press releases are short and succinct. They do not suit a message that is relatively subtle and/or complex. Provided it is of interest, this might best be handled by meeting face-to-face.

Demonstration. There are occasions when the only way to appreciate a new product or service is by trying it out or seeing it demonstrated. Car manufacturers issue plenty of releases but test drives and motor shows are key elements of their relationships with journalists.

Special features. Many publications plan topics they are going to examine in depth well in advance and let the world know (usually on the net) what those topics are. This gives you an opportunity to provide comments to feature writers or even to submit an article.

Opinion pieces. Virtually all publications from the *Financial Times* down will print opinion pieces provided they are generic comment on current issues from an informed source.

Case study
Sixty seconds with Neal Butterworth, Editor-in-Chief, *Bournemouth Daily Echo*

Less is more: releases should be not more than 100 words, with contact details and supported by a brilliant picture (preferably no more than 3 Mb)

Well-written press releases are a godsend to busy news editors

The same journalist deals with print and web versions

Material for print and web is similar but (because of search engine optimisation) headlines are different

Develop relationships with individual reporters

Get the 'package' (e.g. including supporting materials) to the right person

Journalists hate emails that require a receipt – they normally delete them

Don't ring journalists to see whether they have received your press release. If you have developed the right relationship with the journalist, you won't need to!

The main competition of a local paper (with an associated website) is TV and radio

Case study
Ann Handley's tips for successful tweets

Social media news site Mashable reports journalist Ann Handley reporting that all she needed to know about Twitter she learned at journalism school 20 years earlier. She goes on to list some of the lessons she learnt as an undergraduate that now inform her tweeting.

Make every word count: space is limited online and offline but it's more difficult than you think to be concise.

Keep it simple: the best news stories are clear and simple, but keep it professional by avoiding the liberal use of abbreviations.

Provide context: news reporters provide some background on any particular new story; with Twitter offer context by using keywords and hash tags.

Lead with the good stuff: the 'inverted pyramid' style places the most important information in the first paragraph of a press release; the same approach is used in a tweet with the key elements, and then linking to the rest of the story.

Write killer headlines: headlines 'sell' a news story or a blog post either because they say precisely what's on offer or because they're clever or funny.

Graphics expand on the story: a good visual complements a news story; a picture on Twitter adds impact.

People make things interesting: news stories favour a human angle; on Twitter talk to people in a conversational tone.

Consider the reader: a lot of time is spent coming up with the right angle for a news story; so more time thinking about what to tweet, than actually tweeting.

Source: Based on http://mashable.com/2009/06/05/twitter-journalism-school/

So, much of the advice (but not all) on writing releases for social media echoes the points made when talking about traditional press releases. For example, these suggestions concerning social media press releases are based on advice from ehow.com:

- Be informal. The traditional-style press release is typically formal in style and structure. Formality is unsuitable for social media and the audiences it addresses. Material that is clearly self-promotion will be rejected.

- Grab attention. The headline is the key element for grabbing attention. Headlines should be short to match the online reader's attention span.

- Get your focus right. Announcements will only make an impact if presented in terms that are relevant to the target audience.

- Use the right language. Press releases should be written in friendly, interesting and accessible language.

- Create value. Creating value for your readers in your press release will engage their interest and fuel its spread across the social media community.

- Keep it brief and to the point. An online reader will typically scan an article or release using its heading, subheading and captions before actually reading it.

Search engine optimisation (SEO)

There are, however, some key points of difference that need to be addressed. These concern 'media-rich' releases and the pressures associated with SEO.

Press releases are becoming an important part of online visibility and SEO has therefore become an issue they need to address. Increasingly press releases are using keyword techniques to enable them to be picked up by online news sites and by search engines. This not only increases their visibility, it also drives more traffic to your website. Brown (2009: 56) states: 'the type of language that we use in our written output needs to consider the use of terms that are more likely to be used when our audiences are using search engines'.

In short, it is becoming more common for target audiences to access press releases directly through search engines and release distribution services. This is putting pressure on public relations practitioners to make their press releases search-engine-friendly. This is fine – but only up to a point. As with web copy, for example, the press release still needs to be a good press release once it is found. There is no point in SEO dominating the text to such an extent that once accessed, the release is rejected as it is no longer an effective release. As Brown (2009: 80) states: 'There is a great danger that as we start to optimize our copy with keywords we forget the most important thing: the copy still needs to be well written and interesting.'

Constraints related to relying upon search engines

Here are just a few points that are pertinent in the context of this tension between optimisation and a good release (with thanks to Daryl Wilcox Publishing):

- An 'SEO' press release still has to deliver news. The crucial difference is that you also need to include keywords or phrases that will be used in a relevant search. The big battle is between optimising your release by including your keywords and phrases without sacrificing readability, meaning and news impact.

- Your keywords should be determined by the words or phrases your target audience will use in their searches rather than what you want them to hear.

- Embedded links add power to your releases: they increase their SEO value significantly. However, use them judiciously to avoid alienating readers or driving them away too often.

The web now opens your press releases up to a far wider audience: they will not just be read by journalists but also prospects, customers, shareholders and other stakeholders. So, this makes it even more important that your releases communicate your news and corporate messages clearly and succinctly.

Media-rich releases

The social media release (SMR) is defined as 'a press release that is posted on the web and done so in such a way that will improve the likelihood of content being disseminated' (Brown 2009: 126).

As with all releases, content is king, and in a social media environment this means considering multimedia content such as video, audio and images that can easily be shared. The traditional structure of the release is not abandoned but links to additional content are provided. This could include photography, MP3 files or podcast links with relevant sound bites, graphics (market information, for example) and video such as a talking head or product demonstration.

There is an important health warning here. A media-rich release may well be attractive to hard-pressed journalists editing content for both their print offering and the newspaper's online presence but only if the content is suitable and relevant. Including a podcast that is a corporate plug only vaguely related to the main content of the release will only serve to antagonise rather than delight.

Brown (2009) explains that SMRs are different from traditional releases posted on the web. They are not emailed out but have their own presence on the web and are discovered or journalists are invited to view them. They contain links to other social media, and have searchable content, and might include the multimedia content outlines above. Figure 6.4 is an example of an SMR template.

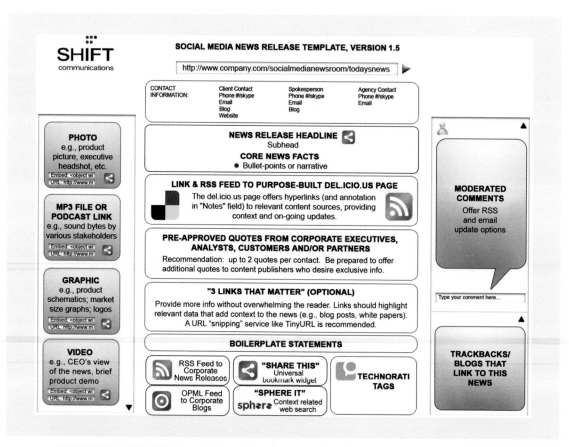

FIGURE 6.4 This SMR template provides plenty of ideas for adding additional 'richness'
Source: www.shiftcomm.com/downloads/smr_v1.5.pdf

SUMMARY AND LEARNING POINTS

A press release must contain something new and be of relevance to the audience: always subject it to the 'so what' test.

The aim of issuing a press release is to get it published: it therefore has to be written in a way that makes it usable in its entirety by a journalist, demonstrating its use as a news story.

Journalists are inundated with press releases so you need to do everything possible to get yours noticed and to avoid alienating the recipient. Headings and first paragraphs, as well as correct and clear language, are crucial in ensuring it gets more than a cursory glance.

There are a number of techniques that can add impact and news value to your release, including statistics, quotes, photos and hooks onto current issues.

A press release is not the only weapon in your armoury. Use with care and only when other devices, such as features, press visits, exclusives and tours, have been ruled out.

A press release is only as good as the recipient list it is sent to. The most carefully written press release will not generate pertinent and worthwhile coverage unless it is sent to the relevant media.

Press releases now need to function in cyberspace and this brings a completely new dimension to the way they are written and distributed.

Exercise 1

You have been asked to write a press release (for the trade press) on behalf of Schlumberger. These are the notes you have made following a telephone briefing. If you feel that you need additional information (this is unlikely to be extensive) then use your common sense to make up further details as if you have had a further conversation with Marie-Pierre DuPont.

Planet Card is the first professional training programme dedicated to smartcards, to be launched in June.

Schlumberger has the technical know-how; now training expertise has been added. For example, one of the partners is Learning Tree International (a well-known international training organisation). Previously (and this is what competitors are doing now) the training has been provided by product managers who have the technical knowledge but not necessarily the training expertise.

Up till now training has been provided in Montrouge, Paris. Under Planet Card, worldwide, it will be delivered at any location where there is the demand. Certainly, Austin, Texas in the USA, where Schlumberger has a technical centre. Asia is another area likely to be an early adopter. First sessions in January. Tailored to local needs.

Not just restricted to customers, any potential business partner who wants it. Average length of courses is 2 or 3 days. Type of demand will vary: in USA and Asia basic smartcard training, in Europe more technical because people know more about smartcards.

Will cover all smartcard product areas and applications/markets (particularly e-purse and loyalty). First training courses: Cyberflex (industry's first Java-based smartcard) and Activa (new-generation SIM toolkit-compatible smartcard for mobiles). Likely application areas of interest: electronic purses and loyalty schemes.

Planet Card Training Manager is Marie-Pierre DuPont, who wants to help business partners get developments to market quicker.

Schlumberger is an international technical company selling products and services designed to improve the productivity of its customers. The company operates in more than 100 countries and employs 65,000 people across the globe.

Schlumberger's Smart Cards & Terminals division is in the vanguard of smartcard developments. A smartcard is the size of a credit card and is embedded with an integrated circuit chip. The chip both stores information and protects it from unauthorised access so the card can be used for applications such as an electronic purse. A smartcard can be used anywhere and everywhere a reader terminal is installed. Schlumberger believes that smartcards will have a major impact on our daily lives: all communications, transportation, banking, retail, health care and network applications being smartcard-based.

Exercise 2

Your task is to write a press release on behalf of ASDA, commenting on the findings of the PMP, using the information below.

ASDA was the first supermarket to introduce a food nutritional labelling system (2009). It comprised a traffic light system using green, amber and red to indicate low, medium and high levels of fats, sugars, salt, saturated fats and calories, plus more detailed guideline daily amount (GDA). This followed pressure from government and the Food Standards Agency (FSA) to give consumers more information on sugar, fat and salt as well as calorific values.

The FSA at the time preferred the so-called 'traffic light' labelling system, which uses green, amber and red to indicate low, medium and high levels. Food manufacturers claimed this was too crude and preferred a more complex system that lists the amount of each nutrient in grams and the percentage of the GDA this represents. ASDA developed a hybrid system that is based on the traffic light approach but also provides the more detailed GDA information for those who appreciate it.

Other supermarkets followed with their own schemes but none was as comprehensive as ASDA's, with both the traffic lights and GDA.

The FSA set up an independent panel (Project Management Panel – PMP) in 2009 to look at the impact of front-of-pack (FOP) nutritional labelling on shopping behaviour. This report has now been published and has stated that a single scheme is needed, and one using a combination of traffic lights and GDA is the strongest, which is the same as the scheme launched by ASDA. The FSA has now said it will take forward these findings.

ASDA's Corporate Affairs Director is very keen to use these findings to create coverage for ASDA, positioning it as a market leader in food labelling.

Sources: FSA and ASDA press releases

Answer 1
Schlumberger launches worldwide smartcard training programme

Smartcard market benefits from unique combination of technical expertise and professional instruction

Schlumberger has launched the first professional training programme dedicated to smartcards. This innovative scheme, called Planet Card, combines Schlumberger's in-depth knowledge of smartcard technology and applications with the professional expertise of independent training organisations. Available worldwide, but adapted to meet local needs, Planet Card will be rolled out from September this year.

Current smartcard training schemes are based on the technical expertise of product managers. Now Schlumberger has teamed up with highly skilled international educators such as Learning Tree International to provide a quality training portfolio covering all aspects of smartcard products and applications. A typical course lasts two to three days.

Initially, courses will be offered at Schlumberger's Paris headquarters and its technical centre in Austin, Texas. However, they will be run at any international location where there is sufficient demand. Importantly, they will also be tailored to geographical requirements. For example, demand for basic smart card training is anticipated from the United States and Asia, while more sophisticated programmes are likely to be required in the more established European smart-card market.

Planet Card encompasses both product-based and market-specific courses. Early examples will be based on existing product-based programmes covering innovations such as the Cyberflex, the industry's first Java-based smartcard, and Activa, a leading example of new-generation SIM toolkit-compatible cards for mobile phone applications. E-purse and loyalty are two of the application areas that are receiving early attention.

Marie-Pierre DuPont, Schlumberger's Planet Card training manager, explained the background to the launch of Planet Card: 'Smartcards are emerging as a new standard form of portable computing device. They represent an open platform for software developers on which a host of commercial applications can be developed. Our aim is to equip existing and potential business partners with the knowledge and expertise to ensure that these applications are brought to market quickly and successfully.'

Answer 2
Consumers prefer ASDA's food labelling system

Independent consumer research commissioned by the Food Standards Agency (FSA) has confirmed that ASDA leads the field in front-of-pack (FOP) food nutrition labelling. ASDA uses the 'traffic light' approach backed up by information on Guideline Daily Amounts (GDAs). The FSA has endorsed the ASDA system and suggested it is rolled out across the food industry

ASDA introduced the new combined labelling system in July 2007, ahead of all other supermarkets. It uses distinct traffic light colours to highlight low, medium and high levels of sugar, fat, salt, saturated fats and calories in each product. The product labels also give the precise amount of each nutrient in grams per serving and the percentage of the GDA this represents.

The independent Project Management Panel (PMP) was established by the FSA in 2007 to evaluate FOP nutritional labelling. It has now concluded that a universal FOP scheme would be most helpful for shoppers, as different labelling systems cause difficulties for consumers. In addition, the balance of evidence demonstrated that ASDA's was the most robust approach for helping consumers to make healthier choices when buying food.

ASDA's Paul Kelly, Corporate Affairs Director, commented: 'We welcome these findings and see them as confirmation that our approach is the simplest and clearest. We therefore urge major food retailers and manufacturers to conclude this debate, listen to customers, and commit to our combined labelling scheme.'

FURTHER READING

For a series of white papers on writing press releases and associated topics, go to www.dwpub.com/whitepapers.php

For the latest on research into media relations and other public relations topics, go to www.instituteforpr.org/research/

For white papers discussing social and traditional media, go to www.vocus.com/wp/

For views on a wide range of public relations issues including annual international research entitled 'Media myths and realities', go to www.ketchumperspectives.com/current/

For more on how to write social media press releases, go to www.ehow.com/how_4449904_write-social-media-press-release.html#ixzz0wCqeFEEw

For a lively commentary on all things PR, go to www.prmoment.com/

REFERENCES

Brown, R. (2009) *Public Relations and the Social Web*, Kogan Page

Newsom, D. and J. Haynes (2011) *Public Relations Writing*, 9th edn, Wadsworth

Chapter 7
Communicating by objectives
Planning and executing the public relations campaign

Ronél Rensburg

Learning outcomes

By the end of this chapter, you should be able to:

- Define and describe public relations campaign strategy and tactics
- Contextualise public relations planning and management
- Understand the differences between campaigns, programmes and social movements
- Describe the various elements that make up public relations planning, development, implementation and management
- Plan a public relations campaign or programme on your own, using the communication by objectives (CBO) model

Introduction

Although public relations is strategic in nature, practical logistics and implementation thereof are just as important for public relations efforts to be effective and successful. There are local and global issues that need to be addressed through strategic, but also technically sound, communication.

This chapter will investigate the planning and management of public relations campaigns. The engagement of organisations with their various publics creates the setting for the planning, management and implementation of a public relations campaign or programme as one of the most pivotal functions of the public relations professional, public relations consultant or communication manager. This is so because the public relations campaign combines strategic planning and input with technical know-how.

The chapter will cover the following issues:

- The differences between strategy and planning
- Public relations planning and management
- The environment and social circumstances of campaigns
- The organisation; the public relations or communication planner; the message; the media; the target audiences or publics; the effects and effectiveness; and feedback as role players in public relations campaigns
- Types of campaign
- Objectives of campaigns
- Stages of effective campaigns
- The Communication by Objectives (CBO) model for public relations campaign planning and management as an emphasis that Communication by Objectives is aligned to Management by Objectives and therefore an important functional area of management

Mini case study
Martin Williams launches human trafficking awareness campaign at World Cup

Following is a brief case study that illustrates the power of succinct and effective communication management and public relations and what outcome these can achieve. As you read through the case think about the public relations campaign objectives and stages involved.

The Soccer World Cup was hosted by South Africa during June and July 2010. Many campaigns and programmes were launched to coincide with this event. One such campaign was 'The Not For Sale Campaign draws attention at year's biggest sporting event' (Minneapolis, June 10/PRNewswire).

When 400,000 soccer fans converge in South Africa this June and July for the World Soccer Cup, many of them will become familiar with the work of Martin Williams Advertising. The agency is launching a new campaign in conjunction with the Not For Sale Campaign, an anti-human-trafficking non-profit campaign that aims to draw soccer fans' attention to the issue of modern-day slavery. Using both traditional and non-traditional media, the campaign will capitalise on the crowds attracted by the largest sporting event of the year to highlight human trafficking issues in both South Africa and the world.

The agency's new 'Red Card' campaign utilises a well-known soccer icon to draw the attention of World Cup fans. In soccer, the red card signifies that a player has committed a most serious offence, and Martin Williams has adapted this symbol to call attention to modern-day slavery as the most serious offence against humanity. The agency's plan calls for street teams dressed as soccer referees to attend World Cup events and distribute Red Cards to visitors. The reverse sides of the cards will be printed with a range of headlines, including 'The youngest pro footballer signed at 14; which is old if you're a sex slave' and 'Child slaves outnumber pro footballers. Makes you wonder what our favourite pastime really is'. Each card includes the message 'Stop Offences Against Children'.

The Not For Sale Campaign estimates that there are 30 million slaves in the world today, more than at the height of the transatlantic slave trade. Of this group, 50 per cent are under the age of 18, a key factor in the World Cup campaign's emphasis on children. The Red Card campaign will also be adapted for flyers, stickers, posters and billboards. Ten million flyers will be distributed through South Africa's Pep Retail Stores, and 30,000 flyers will be distributed to local students by the Save the World Foundation.

'Human trafficking is an issue all over the world, and the eyes of the world will be on South Africa during this sporting event', said David Batstone, founder of the Not For Sale Campaign. 'This campaign will be a powerful tool in helping us capture the attention of World Cup fans and raise awareness of modern-day slavery.'

About the Not for Sale Campaign

The Not for Sale Campaign is an international abolitionist movement of students, entrepreneurs, artists, and others. It aims to educate and mobilise through the innovation and implementation of open-source activism. Inside the United States, the campaign identifies trafficking rings and collaborates with local law enforcement and community groups to shut them down and provide support for the victims. Internationally, the campaign partners with poorly resourced abolitionist groups to enhance their capacity.

Source: adapted from Martin Williams Advertising 2010

The tangible outcome of communication or public relations efforts is usually public relations campaigns or programmes. Public relations *planning* entails planning of unstructured, informal communication. This means initiating communication for the sake of beginning a communication process (Windahl et al. 1993) or conversation. Public relations *management* is the process of monitoring the planned communication from its initiation, through the *implementation* phase, up to the post-implementation or *evaluation* phase (Rensburg 1996: 41).

THE ELEMENTS OF PUBLIC RELATIONS PLANNING AND MANAGEMENT[1]

There are certain important elements that underlie the processes of public relations planning and management. These elements are essential for any communication process and can also be utilised in public relations planning and management. These elements are now discussed and illustrated by using examples under the following headings:

- The environment or given circumstances
- The organisation
- The public relations or communication planner
- The message
- The medium
- The publics
- The effects and effectiveness
- Feedback as role players in public relations campaigns.

The environment or given circumstances

Understanding the environment or the circumstances surrounding issues is very important in communicating with publics. The environment is the background or 'setting' in which communication takes place and public relations campaigns are delivered. The environment (religious, political, social, economical, natural, intercultural, gender) can change rapidly and publics (target markets, recipients, destinations, the public in general) need timely communication to address these changes that might impact on their lives and operations. The role of *environmental scanning* is a very important research tool in the hands of public relations professionals as they plan and execute their campaigns. Today, many publics are living and working in multicultural environments across the world. It is also the task of the public relations professional to be fully aware of what is current in the world. There are a variety of global issues that serve the initiation of public relations campaigns, and that will touch all of our lives, like international terrorism and global warming.

[1]Extracts on pp. 159–72 from *Public Relations: African Perspectives*, 2nd ed., Heinemann Publishers (Pty) Ltd, 2009 (Rensburg, R. S. and Kant, M. C. 2009).

Question

Can you think of any other surrounding circumstances or issues out of the environment that can become initiators for public relations campaigns?

The organisation

The communicator or initiator of the public relations message or campaign is usually an organisation, group or institution that the public relations professional or consultant represents. The organisation periodically wishes to or needs to express some meaningful idea to the publics by the utilisation of communication. Here the organisation can fulfil a variety of roles (Westley and MacLean 1957; Rensburg 1996). The organisation can have an *advocacy role* by striving to influence publics in the environment, directly or indirectly. A *channel role* has a less purposeful character. Its objective is to provide publics with information and to act as intermediary between the organisation and the publics. A *behaviour role* is held by the publics, for example readers, listeners, viewers and the public in general, who can become active communicators by acting on the information they receive from the organisation. (See Chapter 3 for more on publics.) In the explosion of today's social networks and media, publics of organisations become very powerful as they send their messages across the globe in cyberspace. The following example might illustrate these roles: the Department of Health in a country launches a 'Citizens stand united against HIV/Aids' communication effort involving the mass media, government in general and other channels of communication. Clearly, in this case, the Department of Health plays an *advocacy role*. Using the mass and social media (a *channel role*) the Department of Health also transmits the information. The publics (the citizens) who receive the communication assume a *behavioural role*.

Question

Can you think of any similar situation where an organisation had been the initiator of a public relations campaign and where these roles were fulfilled?

The public relations or communication planner

This is an important role and is usually played by the public relations professional, consultant or communication manager on behalf of the organisation. In an initiating role, the public relations professional is normally working for the organisation – formulating the organisation's message to publics. The public relations professional is regarded as a communication planner, as the real source of what is being expressed by the organisation. In a time of crisis (like a mining accident) in an organisation, the public relations professional will put the organisational communication message together and convey it to all relevant publics of the organisation – both internal and external.

Question

Can you think of more examples of the roles of public relations professionals as communication planners? (See Chapter 2.)

The message

The communication content that is put together and transmitted in the communication process is called the *message*. This message can be overtly expressed or it can have an underlying (or covert) meaning. The message of any communication or public relations effort embodies the meaning attributed to the content by those publics who receive the message. The message, while existing on its own, may be the property of the organisation, the public relations professional and the publics it intends to reach. An example might be to plan an organisational message about new human resources developments in the organisation.

Question

Can you plan a message for an organisation or a cause that expresses the overt and the underlying (covert) meaning of the communication?

The medium

The media are the channels through which the communication messages of the organisation reach the publics. *Medium* and *channel* are often used interchangeably in communication, although there is a technical distinction between the two concepts. Channel, in this context, denotes the physical means of carrying a signal (O'Sullivan et al. 1983: 31–2). It therefore has little to do with meaning, but rather refers to the capacity to carry information. A medium, in the public relations planning and management context, is an intermediate agency that enables communication to take place through the use of one or more channels (O'Sullivan et al. 1983: 134). Usually the term is used synonymously with mass media, but people may also take on the role of medium.

The recent explosion in the development of electronic communication technology has also seen the entrance of social media (Facebook, Twitter, Myspace, Second Life etc.) – social networking as well as cellphone message usages. Publics are now becoming recipients, authors and editors of their own communication messages.

In the developing world context there is a distinction between social media and mainstream *conventional* mass media (film, radio, television, outdoor, print, electronic and transportation) and *unconventional* media (including group communication such as rural television, roadshows and industrial and community theatre). In Africa there are also traditional media, folk media or '*oramedia*' (Jefkins and Ugboajah 1986) which are based on the indigenous culture produced and consumed by members of a group. Unlike the mass media, which reach many publics at a time but mainly have a cognitive influence (knowledge, awareness and interest) oramedia reach only a few people at a time, but can be an effective relay chain to the mass media. Oramedia have visible cultural features through which social relationships and a world view are defined and maintained. They take on many forms and are rich in symbolism. Oramedia include ceremonial socialising, rumours, oratory, poetry, music, singing and dancing, charms and insignia, marketplace gossip, praise singing and many others.

Question

If you have to plan a message about greening your immediate environment, which media or channels will you use?

The publics

The publics may be defined in this context as people who attend to the particular prepared message content. The public relations professional, as communication planner, must realise when planning communication material that the publics may often be a heterogeneous audience – from different religious, ethnic, subcultural and cultural settings. In the national and global contexts of communication, the communication environment is usually made up of publics that are largely heterogeneous and geographically dispersed. These may cause difficulties in public relations planning, management and implementation (Rensburg 1996: 44).

Question

Think about being a public relations consultant. You are asked to develop a message about an environmental disaster in your immediate community. Who will the publics be?

Effects and effectiveness

When dealing with communication content and public relations efforts it is necessary to distinguish between campaign *effects* and *effectiveness*. Public relations effects can be described as consequences of a communication process – circumstances that would not have occurred without the presence or intervention of some other circumstances (Anderson and Meyer 1988: 161). Public relations effectiveness is an outcome of objectives fulfilment. A public relations professional, finding that a communication action has generated only meagre results, might argue that this campaign was not 'effective'.

Question

How would you determine – as a public relations professional – that your public relations or communication campaign had been effective and successful?

Feedback as role players in public relations campaigns

There is no doubt that *feedback* is an important element in any communication process. Feedback is a response on the part of the publics to a public relations professional's communication. Feedback is reactions that are transmitted back to, and actually reach, the organisation. For the public relations professional, feedback on his or her communication efforts is important, providing a tool for interpreting and understanding the outcome of these efforts better.

Feedforward, however, is information about publics and their possible reactions that is gathered by a public relations professional prior to initiating communication with them (Rogers 1973). It is true that in planned communication the more one knows beforehand about the target audience, or publics, the greater the chances are for effective communication. Hornik (1988) has indicated the need for feedforward in developing countries' agriculture development work, where government agents acting as communication planners are often insensitive to the needs of farmers. Feedforward may also encompass active public relations campaigns by giving hints as to the messages that will follow. For example, the flying of a trial balloon (or researching possible reactions) before an official announcement of a drastic reduction in the general speed limit could provide a measure of the strength of the opposition to such a measure. Feedforward can therefore be viewed as an activity that enables a professional, as communication planner, to formulate a comprehensive background, which can be used to plan and design a public relations strategy (Rensburg 1996: 45).

Question

Explain how you would handle feedforward and feedback in a major public relations campaign.

The above are essential elements in public relations planning and management and are concepts that will occur as we move throughout this chapter.

CAMPAIGNS, PROGRAMMES AND SOCIAL MOVEMENTS

Before the public relations campaign can be described in more detail, it is necessary to distinguish between campaigns, programmes and social movements since, although they may have many similarities, there are degrees of difference between them.

The public relations professional or consultant should ideally have an ongoing relationship with organisations, clients and publics. There should be continuous *programmes* for all publics. A *campaign* that continues over a long period of time is therefore called a public relations programme.

A *social movement* can be defined as an ideological, issue- or cause-oriented campaign or movement (Larson 1986: 201). The African National Congress (ANC) in South Africa as well as the IRA (Irish Republican Army) in Ireland had been ideological movements before they evolved into political parties. Many activist activities are organised in ideological or social movements rather than programmes or campaigns.

Organisations can have a variety of campaigns – from marketing campaigns, advertising campaigns and corporate identity campaigns to public relations and reputation management campaigns. Planning, implementing and managing the public relations campaign is one of the public relations professional's most important strategic as well as technical (tactical) functions.

Most changes in attitude, behaviour, belief or action are not the result of a single communication message. In many instances, where people or institutions change their attitudes or behaviour, the change is the result of their being exposed to a lot of data, a series of messages, or the effect of combined messages. This is called a campaign.

Objectives of campaigns

According to Rensburg (1996: 55) and Rensburg and Cant (2009) campaigns may have different general objectives (outcomes or effects). A campaign can be planned that merely wants to *inform* target publics about an issue or to *create awareness* about an issue or cause, for example to inform voters about the venues in their areas where they should register as voters for the local elections. This would also create awareness about the upcoming elections. In addition a campaign can seek to *persuade* publics to change their attitudes, for example a campaign may seek to persuade voters that the local elections 'are even more important than the national elections'. Campaigns can also urge publics to act – their objective is to make publics *behave* in certain ways. For example, a campaign could say 'Take action against HIV/Aids now!' A campaign's objective may also be to *educate*, for example a voter education campaign before the country's actual elections. It is also possible, according to Rensburg (1996:55), for a campaign to include all these objectives – to inform, to create awareness, to persuade, to urge publics to act and to educate – presenting them in various phases over a period of time.

The above are *general objectives*. Individual campaigns may also have *specific objectives* – objectives set out by communication planners for a particular situation or campaign.

Types of campaign

According to Larson (1986: 201) there are three kinds of movement, programme or campaign. They are:

- the politically oriented campaign
- the product- or service-oriented campaign
- the ideological, issue- or cause-related campaign.

Newsom et al. (1993: 474–5) add to the above and differentiate between six types of public relations campaign:

- The *public awareness campaign* that makes people aware of something.
- The *information along with awareness campaign* that includes not only awareness, but also information about something.
- The *public education campaign* that educates or 'teaches' the publics about something.
- *Campaigns* that *reinforce the attitudes and behaviour* of those who are in agreement with the organisation's position. All these publics may need is a reminder of shared values.
- *Campaigns* that *have to change or attempt to change the attitudes* of those who do not agree with the organisation's position, for example activist groups that disagree with how the organisation conducts its business in the environment.
- *Behaviour modification campaigns* which convince publics, for example, that they ought to wear their seatbelts or that drunk driving is not in their or society's best interests.

Each of these campaigns attempts to motivate different levels of behaviour, which is the sole reason for conducting campaigns. Behaviour is the outcome that campaigns seek – not necessarily the thinking or feeling or even social interaction that precedes the behaviour. These are merely the means to an end. (See also the discussion regarding objectives of campaigns; the types of campaign align perfectly with those objectives.)

Stages of effective campaigns

A campaign is not just a series of messages, all dealing with the same issue. Nor is it a debate over an issue. Campaigns are developmental in nature. They move from stage to stage. They have a beginning, a middle and an end. They neither run on the same level and at the same pitch from beginning to end, nor do they always have the same strategy. Instead, campaigns grow and change and adapt to the response by the publics and the emergence of new issues. They use different methods and lures. If one method does not succeed after a period of time, another is developed and tried. As the mood of the publics develops, the mood of the message of the campaign also develops and changes. If campaigns are to succeed, they must create a sense of the dramatic in their publics. Campaigns need to depict their cause as one of historic magnitude. Then they need to invite publics to join and share in the great cause in some real or symbolic way. Campaigns also need to convince publics they should align or identify themselves with the organisation, cause or idea being promoted.

There are, according to Larson (1986), five functional stages of development in all campaigns. They are discussed below.

Identification

An organisation, product, service or idea must develop identification. It must design identifying symbols (for example logos, emblems, corporate colours, insignia) to encourage public buy-in and recognition. Slogans also assist identification and frequently become a corporate heritage if they are catchy enough. In addition jingles, uniforms, salutes and all manners of campaign paraphernalia (for example corporate gifts) assist in establishing name and purpose identification.

Legitimacy

The second functional stage is to establish legitimacy. Organisations can demonstrate legitimacy in several ways. They can show they care about the environment, for example, by communicating their intention to take care of the surrounding environment and the community. In idea campaigns large numbers of participants or amounts of money are frequently used to demonstrate the legitimacy of a particular idea or cause. The participants are usually known supporters.

Participation

In the participation stage the communication planners seek to involve previously uncommitted persons. There are many techniques for doing this. Some include effort by participants, whilst others involve minimal, or only symbolic, involvement. The wearing or display of a red bow on a jacket lapel illustrates 'symbolic' support for the fight against HIV/Aids or the pink ribbons representing the awareness of breast cancer month. Requesting motorists to switch on their lights at a particular time to show solidarity in welcoming foreign delegates to a particular country can be a symbolic gesture. The effects of these gestures are to increase commitment to a cause or an idea.

Penetration

This stage can be described as having 'made it'. The organisation, idea, cause, product or service has been successful enough to establish a meaningful share of the market or constituency, or a meaningful 'presence' in the environment. In idea- or cause-oriented campaigns, penetration is achieved when those in power find that they are hearing about the campaign frequently enough that they must do something about it. A recent example in South Africa has been the Treatment Action Campaign (TAC) and the debate surrounding the anti-Aids, anti-retroviral drugs. Politicians and supporters of the dissident view that HIV does not cause Aids and that Aids can be cured by eating beetroot and garlic, were compelled to pay attention to those campaigners who felt strongly that anti-retroviral drugs had to be given to people with Aids. Another example is the launch of a counter-campaign, as attempted a few years ago by President Robert Mugabe of Zimbabwe. At the beginning of 2002, during the general elections in Zimbabwe, President Mugabe's objective was to fight the imposition of possible sanctions against Zimbabwe by the international community, which doubted that the elections were conducted in a free and fair manner. He lobbied the international community against the sanctions and appointed a public relations consultancy, Cohen & Woods International, to assist him in fighting against the imposition of sanctions.

Distribution

In the final stage of development – distribution – the campaign or movement succeeds and becomes institutionalised. The communication planners of the campaign, programme or movement, having eventually achieved the control that they sought, must now live up to their promises in some way. They must show the target publics that some action or change will occur. Implementation of the campaign ideas must take place and plans of action are usually suggested. These plans of action must align with the promises made in the campaign and with the objectives spelled out in the campaign.

A serious problem is that campaign planners – and the organisations, causes, people and issues that they represent - do not always live up to their promises, for example, land is not distributed, drugs cannot be supplied or legislation cannot be passed in the promised format. The targeted publics then usually become cynical about the campaign and about the organisations and communicators involved.

Defining the public relations campaign

It has already been stated that there are many types of campaign and, although all campaigns have some similarities in their definitions, there are important differences. The purpose of this chapter is to concentrate on the public relations campaign, which is the initial tangible product of the public relations planning process. The term 'communication campaign' is also often used. Of course there are many different definitions for a communication or public relations campaign. Generally the term 'campaign' means 'a connected series of operations designed to bring about a particular result' (Kendall 1992). For the purposes of this chapter we borrow from the definition devised by Rogers and Storey (1987: 817):

> [Public relations] campaigns are purposive attempts to inform, persuade or motivate behaviour changes in a relatively well-defined and large audience, generally for benefits to the individual and/or society at large, typically within a given time period, by means of organised communication activities involving mass media and often complemented by interpersonal support.

If we examine the above definition of a public relations campaign more closely, we can see that it contains four basic elements:

- A public relations campaign is *purposive* – general and specific outcomes are intended.
- It is aimed at *various diverse publics* that usually make up a large audience.
- It occurs during a *given time period*, which may range from a few weeks (for example, it involves traffic information concerning an upcoming long weekend) to many years (for example, it deals with the fight against breast cancer).
- A public relations campaign involves an *organised set of communication activities*, for example, environmental scanning or research, message production, distribution and evaluation.

Public relations campaigns may include supportive communication that deals with family planning, Aids prevention, general primary health care, nature conservation, voter registration and education, organisational diversity and employment equity. The target publics of the public relations campaign may be urban or rural, from the developed or developing world, the whole population, employees in an organisation. The effects or outcomes sought for the public relations campaign may range from increasing literacy to acquiring votes, from preventing drug abuse to promoting road safety and from changing eating habits to transforming a social or political structure.

The criteria for public relations campaign effectiveness

The following are criteria that might contribute to communication or public relations campaign effectiveness or success. They have been drawn from various literature reviews on campaigns (Rogers and Storey 1987; Rice and Atkin 1989).

The role of the mass media and social media

The mass media are important for creating awareness and knowledge and for stimulating publics to participate in the campaign process. However, it is unlikely that more ambitious effects such as behavioural change might occur by using the mass media as a message vehicle on their own.

The recently developed variety of social media can also have an immense impact on public relations campaigns and their messages and can be more likely to influence hard-line publics.

The role of interpersonal communication

Interpersonal communication, particularly through peer groups and social networks, is instrumental in attitude and behaviour change and in the maintenance of such change.

Characteristics of communicator, communication planner and medium

The *credibility, reliability, legitimacy* and *believability* of the communicator, communication planner and medium are extremely important and can influence the outcome of a public relations campaign. The more credible, reliable, believable and legitimate the source and communicator, and the more believable the medium, the more effective the campaign will be.

Formative evaluation

Both public relations campaigns and messages need to be evaluated to make sure they fit media habits, public dispositions and the availability of resources. For example, if bicycle riding in a particular area is promoted as a viable exercise option, communication planners must ensure that the supply of bicycles is capable of handling increased demand, and that the public relations effort is promoted through all possible communication channels available.

Campaign appeals

Public relations campaigns must be specific rather than general to appeal to the values of publics. Campaign appeals or campaign approaches are the ways in which a campaign decides to communicate about a certain organisation, product, service, cause, person or issue. For example, message appeals in an HIV/Aids campaign could emphasise the danger to the individual rather than referring to abstract national health standards.

Preventive behaviour

Long-term prevention goals are difficult to achieve because rewards are often delayed and uncertain (for example, wearing safety belts in a vehicle). As a result delayed benefits must be related to immediate ones as far as possible.

Timeliness, comparability and accessibility

Public relations campaign messages must be timely and culturally acceptable and the channels through which they are transmitted must be accessible to all the target publics. Rogers (1973) refers to cues to action as critical events that may spur a change in attitude or even behavioural change. For example, after an accident, an injured person might be more disposed to adopt the practice of wearing safety belts

Public relations campaign effectiveness is a key factor in planned communication. It is measured in relation to the objectives for the campaign, set out by the public relations professional as communication planner. These objectives should be in line with established norms and values (McQuail 1987). However, these norms and values might not be universally accepted. If the norms on which a campaign is based reflect the communicator's or communication planner's point of view rather than the target public's point of view, the campaign is not likely to be effective. An example is family planning, which is a positive value in the developed world but, in many developing countries, birth control campaigns encounter considerable opposition from religious, social and cultural groups.

The communicator or organisation in a campaign is usually a collective, striving to appear as sympathetic, as authoritative and as credible as possible to the target publics. The nature of the relationship between communicator and publics is crucial in a public relations campaign. If the organisation as communicator ignores the needs, values, interests and communication potential of the publics, or if the receiving publics do not attend to and understand the message of the organisation, it is likely that the public relations campaign will fail.

Source: Rensburg and Kant (2009), pp. 196–205

Step 17: Test the communication

Before the communication campaign is presented it should be tested. Testing of the campaign (sample testing by experts, researchers or the communicator) is essential to ensure that the encoding is correct and that all publics are reached.

Delivery stage

Step 18: Deliver the communication

This is the last stage of the campaign that a communicator can control before the publics receive the communication and start the decoding and interpretation process. It is important, therefore, that public relations professionals know as much as possible about the different presentation techniques and are able to make use of them as and when they are needed. These techniques may include speech or personal presentation, written communication through the printed media, audio-visual and electronic communication, or a combination of all of these.

Feedback stage

Step 19: Arrange for feedback

Feedback is the information that the communicator acquires from the publics once they have received the public relations campaign, and from which the communicator can determine the measure of success (the eventual attitudinal or behavioural change of the publics) that has been achieved in terms of the objectives set. In this case, of course, also the measure of improving the environment. There are a number of ways to receive feedback: through direct observation, through research – for example the use of questionnaires, through marked changes in attitude and behaviour, through voluntary comments, through support for the campaign and through expert evaluation.

Step 20: Evaluate effectiveness

After receiving feedback from the publics the communicator is in a position to evaluate the public relations campaign efforts.

Step 21: Stop or repeat

After evaluating the success (or lack thereof) of the campaign the communicator must decide on future action: that is, whether to stop or repeat the campaign, and how to correct possible mistakes in the communication.

Source: Rensburg and Kant (2009), pp. 207, 208–210; adapted from Fourie (1982)

The CBO model is one of many models that can be used in the planning of a communication campaign. Although it is a detailed model, it might be criticised for being too elaborate and lengthy. It is, however, sufficient for moving through the various steps and stages of campaign planning.

Case study
The status of civic and voter education in Zambia

Background

The Electoral Commission of Zambia under Article 76 of the Constitution has the following Constitutional functions:

- To supervise the registration of voters and review the voters registers/roll
- To conduct the Presidential and Parliamentary elections
- To review the boundaries of the constituencies into which Zambia is divided for the purpose of election to the National Assembly.

In addition to the Constitutional functions the Commission has the following Statutory functions to perform:

- To supervise a referendum (Referendum Act CAP14)
- To conduct and supervise the Local Government Elections (Local Government Elections Act CAP 282)
- Formulation and review of Electoral General Regulations
- The Commission may perform any other statutory function that the National Assembly may call upon it to undertake.

The Electoral Commission of Zambia is not mandated by legislation to conduct voter education. However, due to the high levels of voter apathy, especially in by-elections leading to the 2001 elections, the Commission took an initiative to carry out voter education administratively by establishing a committee called the National Voter Education Committee (NVEC).

The establishment of Committees is provided for under the Electoral Commissions Act No. 24 of 1996 section 9 and it allows the Commission to establish Committees that it considers appropriate for a certain function. The NVEC, which was established in May 2001 is charged with the responsibility of spearheading a national, non-partisan voter education programme to sensitise the electorate on the importance of exercising their right to vote.

The NVEC comprises 11 non-governmental organisations (NGOs) and is chaired by a representative from one of the member NGOs. The Commission acts as a secretariat providing technical, financial and other support. The committee has similar structures at district level in all the 72 districts of the country. In order to enhance capacity and to strengthen voter education activities the Commission and NVEC members with the help of Consultants from University of Zambia, Curriculum Development Centre and Anti-Corruption Commission of Zambia came up with a syllabus and manual for voter education. The Commission was also privileged to have expertise from the Electoral Institute of Southern Africa (EISA) that also had input into the voter education curriculum.

Problem statement

There was a high level of voter apathy during the by-elections leading to the 2001 election. This led the Electoral Commission of Zambia to establish the committee called the National Voter Education Committee (NVEC) in May 2001, to sensitise the electorates on the importance of exercising their right to vote.

Objectives

- To sensitise the electorates on the importance of exercising their right to vote.
- To increase the number of registered voters.

Method

Voter education activities

The Commission's efforts of carrying out voter education activities are supplemented by the use of Zambia information Services, a multi-faceted public media organisation. The role that NVEC plays in the electoral process cannot be over-emphasised.

The NVEC helps in identifying appropriate strategies and programmes to improve voter turnout. It also helps to build and maintain voter confidence through the dissemination of relevant information at every stage of the electoral process.

Since the Committee was formed, it has embarked on various activities throughout the country to educate the public on the need to vote, the importance of their vote and the right for a voter to vote for a candidate of his/her choice other than being influenced by favours or gifts from candidates. The Committee also widely publicises the requirements for one to register as a voter and requirements to vote, especially in the pre-election period prior to general elections and during by-elections. The team conducted more voter education campaigns during the publication and collection of voters' cards, when people were required to verify their particulars in the voters' register and collect their voters' cards. See Result below for the outcome.

During the elections NVEC was again deployed throughout the country to encourage those who had registered as voters to exercise their right to vote. The Committee also realises the need for gender balance in the electoral process. It encourages women's independent participation in voting for candidates of their choice without being influenced by anyone, for example, their spouses.

During the campaigns the Committee also ensures that it makes the electorate aware of corrupt practices and educates them on electoral offences.

Status of voter education

The team, alongside Zambia Information Services, periodically conducts voter education during by-elections using the same mechanisms that are used for major elections, such as the mobile public address system, drama groups, posters, brochures, and flyers. Voter education activities and material are disseminated in English and the seven main local languages.

Although a great amount of effort in voter education is confined to the commission and NGOs at the moment, it is worth noting that political parties as major publics are being encouraged to carry out voter education among their members and the electorate. For example, parties are expected to conduct awareness on the importance of their members to register as voters and to exercise their right to vote.

It is envisaged that with the help of donor funding to supplement the Commission's voter education budget for future elections, voter education efforts could be doubled to even include door-to-door campaigns and other activities in which the Commission has fallen short in the past.

It is the wish of the Commission to carry out continuous voter education but this has not been possible due to inadequate funding. However, it is hoped that funding for voter education will improve especially if it is legally recognised as a function of the Electoral Commission. To this effect, the Commission together with other publics recommended to the electoral Reform Technical Committee (a body that was reviewing existing electoral laws and regulations with a view to amendments) to legally empower the Commission to conduct voter education. The Commission has also recently recruited a Voter Education and Training Manager who will run a fully fledged Voter Education Unit in liaison with Elections and Public Relations Departments.

Result

The Committee embarked on a massive voter education campaign for the registration of voters exercise before the 2001 tripartite elections. The campaign saw an increase in the number of registered voters. From a targeted 4.3 million eligible voters, 2.6 million votes were captured as compared to about 2.2 million that were captured during the 1996 voter registration. There is an increase of 400,000 registered voters that is, an 18 per cent increase. Of the targeted eligible voters, 60.4 per cent registered, that is more than half of the eligible voters.

Lessons learned

Conclusively, voter education has proved to play a key role in the capturing of a large number of potential voters, which is one of the key factors in the successful conduct of elections. Therefore, it is ideal that countries adopt or enhance their voter education programmes to promote wider participation in elections by the electorate.

Source: Electoral Commission of Zambia, adapted from Odedele (2008)

CONCLUSION

This chapter provided a description of the following:

- the context of communication planning and management
- the different elements of communication planning and management
- the degrees of difference among campaigns, programmes and social movements
- the communication by objectives (CBO) model for campaign planning and management
- a variety of case studies to illustrate how public relations campaigns are planned, executed and evaluated.

Questions for self-evaluation

1. You are a public relations professional in a large organisation. Your organisation decides to launch a campaign to illustrate its social responsibility towards civil society. The organisation asks you and your department to assist in a country-wide 'Campaign against indiscipline and crime'. Plan such a campaign for your organisation, using the communication by objectives (CBO) model described in this chapter.

2. Use the communication by objectives (CBO) model of campaign planning to evaluate the case below. (Note: this case is summarised and it will be your task to apply the steps of the CBO model to it.) This is also an awareness campaign. What would you do to broaden the communication to have behavioural changes as result?

Kick Polio Out of Africa campaign comes to a close
Football signed by Desmond Tutu receives a rousing welcome at Rotary International Convention in Montreal

CAPETOWN, South Africa, 24 June, 2010 – African Press Organisation (APO)

Rotary's promise to kick polio out of Africa and the world took centre stage as a football signed by Nobel Peace Prize Laureate Archbishop Desmond Tutu and dignitaries from more than 20 African nations received a rousing welcome at the humanitarian organisation's annual convention, which was held in Montreal, June 20–23.

'Polio eradication is not optional – it is an obligation', said Marie-Iréne Richmond-Ahoua, Rotary's National Polio Plus Committee Chair and Outreach Advisor at United Nations Operation in Ivory Coast, as she presented the ball on stage to thunderous applause to Rotary International President John Kenny. 'We must commit to overcoming the remaining obstacles and free Africa, Southeast Asia, and the world from this crippling disease, which ruins the lives of children. As an African woman and mother, I will not tolerate it.'

The arrival of the football culminates Rotary's Kick Polio Out of Africa Campaign – a four-month, Pan African public awareness drive tapping the continent's excitement over the 2010 World Cup and mobilising the public for massive immunisation rounds this spring targeting more than 100 million African children under the age of five. The ball passed through 23 polio-affected countries en route to Montrèal. The Kick-Out finale event was held in Alexandria, on June 12. Egyptian National footballer Islam El-Shater kicked the ball toward the Mediterranean Sea – symbolically kicking polio out of the continent. The journey is being underwritten by DHL Express. A virtual version of the ball (www.kick-poliooutofafrica.org/) was launched in May and has gathered nearly 10,000 online signatures thus far.

After the 2010 World Cup, the signatures will be formally presented to the other spearheading partners of the Global Polio Eradication Initiative: the World Health Organization, UNICEF, and the US Centers for Disease Control and Prevention. 'While most of the world is polio-free, it still threatens children in parts of Africa, Asia and the Middle East', said Rotary International President John Kenny. 'Kick Polio Out of Africa shows the tremendous resolve of the global community to come together to fight this disease. Rotary and its partners are committed to kicking polio out of Africa – and indeed – out of existence forever.'

When former President Nelson Mandela launched the Kick Polio Out of Africa campaign originally in 1996, almost all countries in Africa were still suffering from polio. Today, polio eradication sits at a critical juncture. Across Africa, 10 of the 15 previously polio-free countries re-infected in 2009 have successfully stopped their outbreaks. Nowhere is progress more evident than in Nigeria – the last remaining polio endemic country on the continent – where case numbers have plummeted by 99 per cent, from 312 cases at this time last year, to three cases in 2010.

In his keynote address at the Rotary Convention on June 22, Bruce Aylward, director of the Global Polio Eradication Initiative at the World Health Organization (WHO), encouraged the thousands of Rotary members in attendance to share the 'terrific news' that polio is on the run, and that Rotary's vision of a polio-free world is within sight. 'The stakes are now much higher, because in the past 12 months you have proved, without a doubt, that polio can be eradicated. The world has also learned the full consequences of failure', said Aylward, referring to a current polio outbreak in Tajikistan which is now showing signs of stopping.

Rotary's Kick Polio Out of Africa campaign organiser June Webber echoed Aylward's message in Cape Town. 'During the last 12 months, the world has witnessed what Africans can do when they get determined to do so. Football is a team sport – a unifying global force, much like the Global Polio Eradication Initiative (GPEI) which has so many players.'

The polio-eradication initiative is facing a US $1.3 billion funding shortfall over the next three years, according to WHO. Calling for support from donor countries, footballers, and fans from the 32 countries represented at the 2010 FIFA Cup, Webber said, 'We need your help to raise awareness and the much needed funds to finish the job. This World Cup is not just about the game. This World Cup presents a strong image of a united Africa to the world – and the profound power of the African Ubuntu spirit.'

On February 23, when the Kick Polio Out of Africa awareness campaign was launched, the Victoria & Alfred Waterfront in Cape Town and the Pyramid of Khafre, the second largest of the ancient Egyptian pyramids of Giza, provided a dramatic backdrop for an equally dramatic message: **End Polio Now**. Those words – *En Finir Avec la Polio* (in French) – were projected onto the exterior of Bonsecours Market in Old Montrèal to celebrate the ball's arrival and re-affirm Rotary's determination to end this crippling childhood disease once and for all. Beginning in 1985, when polio paralysed more than 350,000 children in 125 countries every year, eradication has been Rotary's top philanthropic goal. Since then, polio cases have been slashed by 99 per cent worldwide, with fewer than 1,700 cases in 2009. Just four countries remain polio-endemic: Nigeria, Afghanistan, India and Pakistan. However, other nations remain at risk for infections 'imported' from the endemic countries. As the volunteer arm and top private sector contributor in the polio eradication initiative, Rotary has contributed more than $900 million and countless volunteer hours to immunise more than two billion children in 122 countries. To see the football's journey, go to http://kickpoliooutofafrica.wordpress.com/. Rotary is an organisation of business and professional leaders united worldwide to provide humanitarian service and help to build goodwill and peace in the world. It is comprised of 1.2 million members working in over 33,000 clubs in more than 200 countries and geographical areas. Rotary members initiate community projects that address many of today's most critical issues, such as poverty, disease and illiteracy.

Distributed by the African Press Organization on behalf of Rotary International.

Source: adapted from Rotary International and the African Press Association (APO), June 2010

REFERENCES

African Press Organization (APO) (2010) *Kick Polio Out of Africa Campaign*. Montreal: Rotary International, June

Anderson, J. A. and T. P. Meyer (1988) *Mediated Communication: a Social Action Perspective*, Newbury Park, California: Sage

Backer, T. E., E. M. Rogers and P. Sopory (1992) *Designing Health Communication Campaigns: What Works?* Newbury Park, California: Sage

Bizcommunity.com, 30 March 2008

Cutlip, S. M., A. H. Center and G. M. Broom (1985) *Effective Public Relations*, 6th ed, Englewood Cliffs, New Jersey: Prentice-Hall

Davis, A. (2007) *Mastering Public Relations*, 2nd edn, Basingstoke: Palgrave Macmillan

Fourie, H. P. (1982) *Communication by Objectives*, 2nd edn, Johannesburg: McGraw-Hill

Hendrix, J. A (1992) *Public Relations Cases*, 2nd edn, Belmont, California: Wadsworth

Hornik, R. C. (1988) *Development Communication: Information, Agriculture and Nutrition in the Third World*, New York: Longman

Jefkins, F. (1982) *Public Relations*, Plymouth: Macdonald

Jefkins, F. and F. Ugboajah (1986) *Communication in Industrialising Countries*, Hong Kong: Macmillan

Johnson, G., A. Langley, M. Melin, and R. Whittington (2007) *Strategy as Practice: Research Directions and Resources*, Cambridge: Cambridge University Press

Kendall, R. (1992) *Public Relations Campaign Strategies: Planning for Implementation*, New York: HarperCollins Publishers

Larson, C. U. (1986) *Persuasion: Reception and Responsibility*, Belmont, California: Wadsworth

McQuail, D. (1987) *Mass Communication Theory: an Introduction*, Beverly Hills, California: Sage

Mersham, G. M., R. S. Rensburg and J.C. Skinner (1995) *Public Relations, Development and Social Investment: a Southern African Perspective*, Pretoria: Van Schaik

Newsom, D., A. Scott and J. Van Slyke Turk (1993) *This Is PR. The Realities of Public Relations*, 5th edn, Belmont, California: Wadsworth

Newswire (2010) *Human Trafficking Awareness Campaign*, Johannesburg: Martin Williams Advertising, 10 June

Odedele, S. (2008) *Evolution of Public Relations and Communication Management in Africa: Case Studies of Countries in Transition*, 2nd ed, IPR: USA

Oliver, S. (2001) *Public Relations Strategy*, London: Kogan Page

O'Sullivan, T., J. Hartley, D. Saunders and J. Fiske (1983) *Key Concepts in Communication*, London: Methuen

Rensburg, R.S. (ed). (1996) *Introduction to Communication: Communication Planning and Management*, Course Book 4, Cape Town: Juta

Rensburg, R. S. and G. C. Angelopulo (1995) *Effective Communication Campaigns*, Johannesburg: Southern

Rensburg, R. S. and M. Cant (eds) (2009) *Public Relations: African Perspectives*, 2nd edn, Sandton: Heinemann

Rice, R. E. and C. Atkin (eds) (1989) *Public Communication Campaigns*, 2nd edn, Newbury Park, California: Sage

Robinson, S., W. Githing and N. Paulus (2001) 'The last rites', *Time Atlantic* 158(23): 70–2

Rogers, E. M. (1973) *Communication Strategies for Family Planning*, New York: The Free Press

Rogers, E. M and J. D. Storey (1987) 'Communication campaigns', in *Handbook of Communication Science*, C. R. Berger and C. H. Chaffee (eds), Newbury Park, California: Sage

Skinner, C. and L. Von Essen (1995) *Handbook of Public Relations*, 4th edn, Johannesburg: Southern

Van der Meiden, A. and G. Fauconnier (1982) *Profiel en professie: inleiding in de theorievorming van public relations*, Leiden: Stenfert Kroese

Westley, B. and M. MacLean (1957) 'A conceptual model for mass communication research', *Journalism Quarterly* 27: 383–90

Windahl, S. and B. Signitzer with J. T. Olson (1993) *Using Communication Theory. An Introduction to Planned Communication*, London: Sage

Chapter 8
Crisis management

Sue Wolstenholme

Learning outcomes

By the end of this chapter you should be able to:

- Understand more about the importance of reputation
- Realise that there is danger and opportunity in every crisis
- Develop further your appreciation of issues management and its role in preventing or mitigating a crisis
- Identify the origins of crises and some of the different types that can happen
- Appreciate the dangers and opportunities offered by the World Wide Web and social media
- Identify a crisis-prone organisation
- Write a crisis plan

Introduction

This is intended to be a practical chapter, underpinned by knowledge and a range of experiences offered by case studies. It will illustrate the roles of reputation and issues management and ask you to look into your memory of events and to explore the internet for evidence on the ways that crises have been handled, and consider how they might have been differently approached and what impact your changes could have had on the outcomes.

There is also a practical guide to making a plan and adjusting it according to the circumstances.

In the best-run organisations life will, occasionally, trip up the flow of everyday smooth running and potentially put a great deal at risk, including the staff, the buildings, business continuity and a well-established, highly regarded reputation.

In most cases of untoward incidents, all that is often required is a meeting involving the chief executive, the most relevant senior team members and the head of communication, to sort out:

- a plan to deal with the problem,

- fully inform all concerned through all appropriate channels and
- write a statement for the news media.

However, sometimes much more is needed and practising for much more can teach an organisation a lot about itself and improve its preparedness to be under the spotlight.

Natural disasters, accidental or deliberate contamination incidents, sudden acts of violence or malevolence, terrorism, damaging rumours or all kinds of scandals can not only rock the foundations of the organisation's smooth running, any one of them could destroy a carefully developed reputation that might have taken years to establish.

Whether the organisation is an innocent victim or the main guilty party, the news and social media and their main audiences in the court of public opinion, will decide upon its fate not entirely by cause and blame but more so by reporting how, once the lights go on, it behaves in reaction to the situation.

Most organisations have a plan for dealing with threats and interruptions to operations and they should have assessed the likely causes of problems with staff, buildings and equipment – but too few spend enough time accounting for the risks to their reputations.

As Iago advises Othello:

Good name in man and woman, dear My Lord,
Is the immediate jewel of their souls;
He that steals my purse steals trash […],
But he that filches from me my good name
Robs me of that which not enriches him,
And makes me poor indeed.

Loss of reputation is seen as the biggest threat to business. Contrast this with the finding that only 22% of companies have a formal strategy in place to manage brand and reputation risk, and the complicated nature of this risk and the enormity of the challenge become apparent. (PricewaterhouseCoopers 2000)

Weiji is the Chinese character for crisis and it means danger and opportunity.

For public relations practitioners the greatest danger that a crisis represents is to their organisation's reputation and the opportunity, which must be exploited, therefore, is for the crisis to be managed as an example to promote the character of the organisation.

Many organisations feel the frustration of being misunderstood and under-appreciated but the problem lies with the fact that, when good things happen only a few people (usually those involved) take any notice, but when something appears to have gone wrong, the world and her dog pause on their way past to have a good look.

That is the main reason why it is so important to, not only do the right thing, but be open enough to be seen and heard to be doing the right thing.

Crisis management is about working to a plan, which will have been devised and practised with a team within an organisation, so that everyone in the organisation knows what to do and how to behave and what to say.

With all that has been read so far it should now be clear that reputation is dependent on trust, which in turn relies upon the truth being portrayed. Therefore the public relations or communication lead for an organisation will have worked with them to ensure that, should a crisis occur the opportunity can be easily taken as their character has already been established to be a good one.

As Professor Stanley Fischer, the Governor of the Bank of Israel, said to David Frost, 'What you do with a crisis depends on what you did beforehand – on what shape you're in' *(Frost over the World*, Al Jazeera, 14 May 2012). It's too late for your reputation at that time to put your organisation into good shape when the crisis hits, but the wake-up call might make it a good place to start for the future.

If all the relationships that an organisation needs to function well have been properly managed and maintained, there will be a large number of allies who can be called upon to help or provide endorsements for the good name of the organisation. The list of key publics needed for your plan, needs to be added to appropriately and used as a checklist regularly, to make sure that they have all been kept informed during normal running, involved and consulted in times of change and invited to share in the celebrations when things have gone well. Good relationships provide the foundations for forgiveness when mistakes are made and for the building of new futures when situations demand radical action. If it is put into a personal frame, as so often helps when thinking about relationships for work, it might make more sense.

When a trusted friend says something out of turn or makes an error of judgement the offence or hurt is soon dissipated by the clear evidence of their own horror at their actions and their well-meant apologies. If, on the other hand, they behave in a cavalier or uncaring way towards you, despite the obvious hurt that you feel, you reappraise that friendship. As was explained in Chapter 3, at a societal level you might withdraw your permission for that person's association with you and end the friendship altogether – not because of what they have done but because of the way they have behaved towards you as a result.

Mini case study
Nairobi fire

In February 2009 a huge fire broke out in the centre of Nairobi. The city came to a standstill and there was great confusion. A large Nakumat supermarket was on fire and large numbers of anxious people, looking for relatives, had to be controlled by riot police outside. At the end of the day there were 47 people missing and it transpired that the shop's security people had locked the doors to prevent people from stealing from them.

In many countries that kind of behaviour could result in a charge of corporate manslaughter.

Source: Sue Wolstenholme

At a meeting of PR practitioners interested in crisis management, in Nairobi later that year, a number of questions were posed about the Nakumat fire.

Q. What had the company done since? **A.** Gas bottles were no longer kept inside the shop and the security staff were wearing fire officer badges

Q. Had they apologised? **A.** No, not at all.

Q. Did any of the clients of the audience members still supply them? **A.** Yes, they all did.

Q. Did any of the audience still shop there or were there any boycotting Nakumat, as far as they knew? **A.** Everyone still used the store and did not know of anyone who didn't.

Question

Do you think that they needed to learn about crisis management in Nairobi in 2009?

Maybe not, but they wanted to change things and saw crisis management as a possible way to show how things could be different, which, done well, it is.

ISSUES MANAGEMENT

The Institute for Crisis Management publishes surveys and reports annually and they always find that most crisis situations for business, NGOs and public-sector organisations are foreseeable, with more of them smouldering rather than happening suddenly. In 2011 the figures were as shown in Figure 8.1.

This figure demonstrates that a well-run issues management group has a role to play in averting most crises (see Chapter 3).

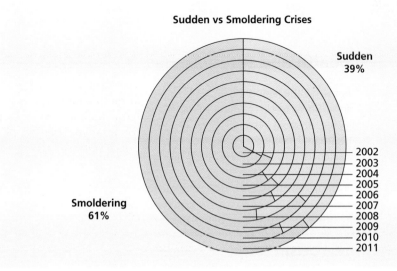

FIGURE 8.1 A crisis is not always sudden
Source: Annual ICM Crisis Report Vol. 21 No.1, May, p. 2 (Institute for Crisis Management 2011), Figure Sudden vs Smoldering Crises

Crises can come from many directions, including:

Service failure

Satisfaction is the difference between expectation and experience, and when publics' expectations are not met it can lead to a crisis for the employer or service provider. (See the case study on Heathrow Terminal 5 below.)

Contamination (accidental or deliberate)

Accidents do happen but regular risk assessments should minimise them and issues management should minimise their impact. (Look up on the internet for case studies on Perrier, which was handled differently in different countries and is worth comparing for the various outcomes; South West Water in Cornwall, where tap water became contaminated with aluminium; and Coca-Cola, makers of Desani, where they had already upset the British public by selling them tap water and soon afterwards had a contamination incident and so had to recall all their products. Coca-Cola no longer sells Desani in the UK.) Deliberate attacks on products or services can also be carried out by disgruntled staff or ex-staff members as well as by campaigners seeking publicity (look up Tylenol, a Johnson & Johnson product, which had to be urgently recalled, though the crisis was handled very well).

Natural disaster

Look up some natural disasters that you remember and consider who contributed to helping and came out of them well and who was criticised and therefore suffered as a result. (You may find the earthquake and tsunami in Japan, Boscastle's flood in Cornwall, Haiti's earthquake, lots of snow and the eruption of Icelandic volcano Eyjafjallajökull.)

Task

List all of those named in each case and find evidence on the internet for the immediate impact on their reputations.

Health and safety issues

In the UK the tabloid news media enjoy making fun of regulators at local council and national government levels (often pointing to the wrong organisations) when they find stories of people's enjoyment being restricted in the name of health and safety – often proclaiming that 'It's health and safety gone mad'. (Look up conkers, that innocent British schoolyard pursuit, and also check on a search engine for accidents on school trips; at work, especially on building sites and in clubs and dance halls; and see how quick those same news media are to condemn and cry foul.) On the other hand, some examples of why it has become difficult to do the right thing can be found at: www.dailyrecord.co.uk/news/editors-choice/2008/11/20/the-crazy-world-of-health-and-safety-rules-86908-20909703/

Terrorism

While terrorists are almost unanimously held up to account for their actions, their victims are also often put in the frame for criticism as well. (See example of Pan Am later in this chapter.) Also look up coverage of the 7 July 2005 bombings in London and consider how Transport for London came across or how the attacks in Mumbai on 27 November 2008 reflected upon the Indian authorities.

Scandals

There are plenty of examples involving money (MP's expenses in the UK www.guardian.co.uk/politics/mps-expenses, Bernard Madoff www.guardian.co.uk/business/bernard-madoff and Asil Nadir www.telegraph.co.uk/news/uknews/crime/9032865/Asil-Nadir-raided-146m-from-Polly-Pecks-accounts.html – white-collar crime is rated as the biggest cause of crisis in the US. Others involve sex, Dominique Strauss-Kahn, head of the IMF, 15 May 2012, who lost the chance to become the President of France, www.belfasttelegraph.co.uk/news/world-news/strausskahn-faces-new-rape-probe-16162014.html and Bill Clinton, who was the president of the USA, www.guardian.co.uk/world/2012/feb/12/clinton-allies-monica-lewinsky-affair.

BUSINESS CRISES

Focusing on business, the Institute of Crisis Management analyses trends and types of crises every year. Figure 8.2 shows how issues management might have foreseen and prevented behaviours, within all types of organisations, which were allowed to drift and become crises. Executives and managers are responsible for at least half of all crises, on average, while employees are credited with causing 32% and outside forces triggered the remaining 18%, on average, during the past ten years. The percentage in 2011 was the same as 2010.

Task

Have a look at Table 8.1. What reasons could there be for the slow but perceptible rise in whistle-blowing? Might social media be helping people to find their voice? This could be an excellent research study, to be done with whistle-blowers.

Figure 8.3 indicates the types of industries in the US that were most prone to suffer a crisis in 2011. Shipbuilding and repair came into the list in 2010 for the first time because of the Deepwater Horizon drilling rig. For more information go to: www.guardian.co.uk/environment/bp-oil-spill

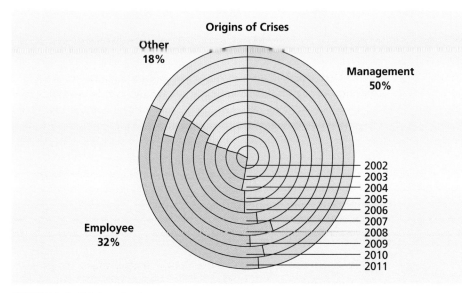

FIGURE 8.2 Origins of crises
Source: Annual ICM Crisis Report Vol. 21 No.1, May, p. 3 (Institute for Crisis Management 2011), Figure Origins of Crises

TABLE 8.1 Crisis categories compared 1990–2011 (% of total crises each year)

	1990	2009	2010	2011
Facility damage	5.5	7.0	11.0	8.0
Casualty accidents	4.8	11.0	10.0	9.0
Environmental	7.8	2.0	3.0	1.0
Class action lawsuits	2.2	7.0	7.0	7.0
Consumer activism	2.8	9.0	5.0	5.0
Defects and recalls	5.4	8.0	6.0	5.0
Discrimination	3.3	3.0	3.0	3.0
Executive dismissal	1.3	1.0	1.0	1.0
Financial damages	4.2	5.0	6.0	8.0
Hostile takeover	2.6	0.0	0.0	0.0
Labor disputes	10.3	8.0	8.0	8.0
Mismanagement	24.1	16.0	8.0	11.0
Sexual harassment	0.4	1.0	2.0	2.0
Whistle blowers	1.1	1.0	2.0	3.0
White collar crime	20.4	18.0	20.0	19.0
Workplace violence	3.8	4.0	9.0	10.0

Source: Annual ICM Crisis Report Vol. 21 No.1, May, p. 2 (Institute for Crisis Management 2011)

Most crisis-prone industries in 2011

1. *Air transport industry
2. *Pharmaceutical companies
3. *Petroleum and natural gas
4. *Banking
5. *Security brokers and dealers
6. Electric utilities
7. *Automobile industry
8. Telecommunications
9. *Shipbuilding and repair
10. *Software

*In top ten previous year (ranked by percentage of database)

FIGURE 8.3 The most crisis-prone industries in 2011
Source: Annual ICM Crisis Report Vol. 21 No.1, May, p. 3 (Institute for Crisis Management 2011)

Case study
A case for a thorough risk assessment before stepping out into the public gaze

British Airways would have booked a stand at the Conservative Party Conference in 1997, soon after launching their new tail fins, to attract the media attention that would be involved when Margaret Thatcher, then the UK Prime Minister, visited them there. However, they should have researched the risks more fully. Senior politicians and members of royal families are always closely guarded on visits and their PR people carefully risk-assess the people they will be meeting, the premises and all aspects of their appearance there to make sure that their reputations will be safe. The host is even asked to supply details of news coverage from the previous year, to indicate any issues that could cause embarrassment. Sadly the hosts often don't take the same care.

In 1986 Mrs Thatcher attacked British Rail and others for serving French mineral water and during her time as Britain's Prime Minister, she became a fearsome defender of flying the British flag against imports.

In 1997, British Airways spent £60 million having their tail fins, where they had previously displayed the colours of the Union flag, painted to appear more cosmopolitan. As

Mrs Thatcher shows her disapproval
Source: Chris Wood/Fast News Pix/TopFoto

soon as Mrs Thatcher came on to the stand, she took a handkerchief from her handbag and covered up the newly designed tail fin. Her action became the next day's front page story.

Question

Were they wise to involve Mrs Thatcher during this sensitive launch phase?

It must be remembered that the majority of VIPs, whether royals, politicians or rock stars, will be coming to visit you for their reputation's sake, rather than yours, and they will not shrink from embarrassing you for the sake of their headline.

THE INTERNET

The internet has added to the areas where PR people must be vigilant, as a crisis can blow up so quickly, without an organisation realising. If you're not there, where you are being discussed, you cannot address the situation properly.

Case study
London Fire Brigade discovers the importance of Twitter

When London Fire Brigade was contacted by the news media, about a terrorist bomb at Liverpool Street Station late on 8 July 2010, they were puzzled. Tenders were there fighting a fire in the Burger King restaurant but they knew nothing about a bomb. LFB had no presence on Twitter at the time and, had they been following it, they would have seen a number of posts from travellers, 1,000 of whom had been evacuated from the station without knowing what was going on. They tweeted that it was probably a bomb and posted pictures of the flames, and the news media picked them up, believed the story and got in touch for further information. Even when the situation became clear they could do nothing as they had no presence on Twitter and so they couldn't join the conversation that was raging there.

LFB is on Twitter now, they have over 26,000 followers and they have won awards for their Twitter feed. This not only reduces the possibility of rumour and misinformation, it reduces fires too, as described in a news release from them in November 2011:

Strictly Come Dancing, X Factor *and Twitter helped make last November 5 the quietest on record for the capital's firefighters, according to a new report being published next month.*

According to the report from the London Fire Brigade, the number of Bonfire Night call-outs firefighters received this year fell sharply after 7 pm, when Strictly Come Dancing *started. Often, the number of fires on Bonfire Night continues to rise until at least 8 pm and remains high well into the evening. However, with November 5 falling on a Saturday this year, fires peaked between 6 pm and 7 pm before dropping by around a third. The number of Bonfire Night blazes stayed low for the rest of the night, resulting in the quietest Guy Fawkes Night on record.*

The report puts the drop in fires down to a triple whammy of factors that saw people curtail their usual Bonfire Night plans. Strictly Come Dancing *and* X Factor *meant more people stayed inside to watch TV or finished their celebrations early. The London Fire Brigade's live Tweetathon, where it tweeted live to thousands of people about every Bonfire Night fire, also encouraged people who were celebrating to stay safe.*

For example, one tweet read, 'If you're going inside to watch #xfactor, please make sure your bonfire is completely out', and another, 'If you've had a couple of cheeky #bonfirenight beers please don't be tempted to light a firework (or bonfire), booze + fireworks = bad idea.'

London Fire Brigade's twitter messages were seen by millions of people as The X Factor *and Philip Schofield tweeted their millions of followers about the @londonfire Tweetathon.*

Overall, firefighters went to 154 fires on November 5 this year, down 12 per cent on the previous year, making 2011 the quietest Bonfire Night in London since records began.

Ron Dobson, Commissioner of the London Fire Brigade, said:

Bonfire Night is traditionally the busiest night of the year for firefighters up and down the country but this year was different. With Strictly *and the* X Factor *encouraging people to stay inside and the London Fire Brigade highlighting the dangers of Bonfire Night live via Twitter, people were much more likely to stay safe.*

We know that young people, celebrating with their friends, are amongst those most likely to have fires on Bonfire Night. Our Tweetathon was a great way of communicating with young people who might not otherwise think about fire safety.

Source: The London Fire Brigade (http://www.london-fire.gov.uk/news/959D0744117C4DDC9D4FCD43F25A9849_PR2931.asp, Strictly the quietest Bonfire Night on record, say firefighters, 26 December 2011)

One negative tweet can be read by many millions within a few minutes of its having been posted, through retweets. It can also be read and addressed by an alert public relations person and turned into a positive message, which might also be retweeted to millions of followers.

Case study
Hudson River, 15 January 2009

Source: Brendan McDermid/Reuters

A tweet: 'A US Airways plane bound for Charlotte just crashed into the Hudson River after aborting its takeoff from LaGuardia Airport. It's still sitting in the river, slowly sinking with people standing on the wings being rescued by ferries.' This was reported by the news media extensively. www.guardian.co.uk/world/2009/jan/16/us-airways-plane-crash-lands-on-hudson.

The American Airline's senior management were at a meeting when the crash occurred and heard about it when a family member of the chief executive called to say they'd seen it on the news. They had some trouble believing it at first, but a member of the public had photographed it and sent it to Twitter, and it was on television before anyone had reported it officially.

As Steve Earl and Stephen Waddington wrote in their book *Brand Anarchy* about the impact of social media on crisis management: 'Principally the impact is two-fold: speed and participation. Technology enables a crisis to be communicated at breakneck speed and social media enables anyone to comment on it' (2012: 09). See Chapter 3, for a discussion of the speed with which citizens used social media to add weight in number to their revolutions in the Arab world.

With such easy access to the web, organisations need to be using issues management to keep closely aware of any grudges or concerns that their employees, customers, neighbours or suppliers might be feeling as communication can be so powerful. As Steve John and Stuart Thomson wrote about the World Wide Web: 'Capitalism and corporations are under more pressure now than at any time since the Great Depression' (John and Thomson 2003: 1).

Look up how an attack orchestrated by Greenpeace against Nestlé through YouTube and Facebook: (www.marketingvox.com/greenpeace-attacks-nestle-via-facebook-some-tips-if-it-happens-to-you-046515/) went through a stand-off and an embarrassing climbdown to result in a partnership that was hailed 'a model for sustainability', www.triplepundit.com/2012/05/nestle-greenpeace-sourcing-of-palm-oil/. The Marketing Vox page has some useful tips for dealing with such attacks, including:

> Social media has become an excellent vehicle for customers – or highly engaged and visible protestors – to talk to companies and vice versa. Given the nature of social media, companies are not so easily able to brush off critics with platitudes or press releases. With that in mind, companies that have a social media presence need to have a plan ready to put into action should, or rather when, they are on the receiving end of complaints – complaints that can quickly go viral no matter how minor.

BEING CRISIS-PRONE

Ian Mitroff and Thierry Pauchant, discussed by Regester and Larkin (2010: 163), talked about how some organisations can be more crisis-prone than others. This is another point for the issues management group to be aware of as they learn about attitudes from and towards their organisations. They put the most vulnerable under two headings, the destructive – exploitative, uncaring or 'little to be done' types – and the tragic – understand the need to change but just don't seem to be able to, culturally or in resource terms. This second type could apply to public-sector or NGO concerns, where funding may be short and not often at their behest.

To this list I would add the arrogant, who don't feel the need to explain and will not allow their PR people to 'tell them they are wrong'.

Task

Consider these three types of crisis-prone organisations and look at the case studies in Chapter 3 (Brent Spar) and in this chapter (BA, Arla Foods and Pan Am). What types of organisations would you consider Shell, British Airways, Arla Foods and Pan Am to have been at the time of the crises discussed?

One of the best defences against a crisis is a well-managed reputation. Where there is a high level of trust and appreciation already established and an organisation admits its fault, there is likely to be forgiveness for mistakes and the impacts of accidents and crises will be mitigated.

Case study
A good reputation earns forgiveness

In 1994 Unilever brought out a new washing powder which they boasted would eat dirt and stains. It contained special ingredients for the purpose but they proved to be more hungry than had been accounted for and very soon after the launch people were complaining that parts of their clothes had been eaten as well, with holes appearing after washing. Unilever did not just rely upon Persil's previous good name but they were quick to recall the product, compensate all the customers and apologise profusely for the mistake. They were quickly forgiven and did not suffer as a consequence, with the supermarkets saving the shelf spaces for their replacement products.

Sir Michael Perry, the chairman, admitted the episode had been a disaster. 'It is the greatest marketing set-back we've seen', he said. 'Something was clearly not noticed somewhere but the key is that we don't make these mistakes again.' Lessons had been learned and internal processes reviewed (Cope 1995).

For more on Persil Power and other examples of business crises, check: www.bbc.co.uk/blogs/tv/2011/05/evan-davis-business-nightmares.shtml

Unilever's mistakes were made even more public by their main competitor, Procter & Gamble, the makers of Ariel, which had the biggest share of the market for stain removal at the time. One organisation's crisis is always their competition's opportunity.

THE PLAN

Whether it is called crisis communication, response management, untoward incident handling or whatever feels the most appropriate to fully focus minds on its importance, the plan must be developed, refreshed and agreed at least once a year and it should involve representatives from across the organisation, the key publics and the emergency services. Legal advisers and insurers need to be told about the plan and your intentions for managing it. If the lawyers and others are ignored, they might turn up on the day and want to run things very differently.

The plan should include:

- How you will decide whether to close or carry on?
- Assessing the level of the incident and its likely impacts
- The team
- Practice day report
- An audit of resources or facilities needed
- Contact cascade
- Checklists.

To close or carry on?

Before anything else a decision has to be taken as to whether to close the school, company or service, close some parts of it or carry on as normal. It could be seen as a mark of respect if there have been fatalities or it might be unsafe or unwise to keep open for a number of reasons. As closing can cause problems for many people in many areas, it will not be done lightly. Whatever the decision and the reasons for it, it must be communicated immediately to all of the key publics who will be affected.

Assessing the level

The first task, if it is suspected or certain that something has happened that might attract media or public attention, is to assess at what level the interest might be. The director or head of the public relations function should be leading the assessment and considering at what level to place it, as in Table 8.2.

TABLE 8.2 Assessing the level of the crisis

Level	Extent of interest	Features	Likely to involve	Story might for
1	International	Involves people from other countries and/or has unusual or particularly newsworthy aspects, such as violent crime or scandal	Royals/VIPs and key publics' attention	One to two weeks or more
2	National	Involves something unusual such as violent crime or scandal	VIP and key publics' attention	One or two weeks
3	National	Fits a current news theme, such as problems like this at a similar organisation elsewhere in society or that ties in with a national political agenda	Key publics' attention, including national politicians	Few days nationally but possibly a week locally
4	National	Comes at the end of a current news theme, such as problems of this type at similar organisations elsewhere in society at large that ties in with a local political agenda	Key publics' attention, including local politicians	One day nationally but possibly a few locally
5	Local	Local human interest	Only those involved	One day

The table does not show the whole picture by any means and it should be altered and added to by the team as they work through scenarios during the practices or when incidents elsewhere are observed.

Through issues management (see Chapter 3) media or environment scanning, the public relations, communication or marketing department should have information on the likely reactions of the news and social media players and the key publics in relation to incidents that have affected others. They should also be monitoring the national scene closely to be aware of current news themes and political agendas, which could be brought to their door if the story, which might otherwise be insignificant, fits those agendas.

The team and its roles

There are few organisations with enough qualified people to do their reputation justice on a day-to-day basis, but when an incident occurs that turns the full spotlight of attention on it, there is no organisation that has enough resource, within its public relations, communication or marketing teams to cope. The team on these occasions needs to be added to from other areas. While the incident or the size of the organisation might not warrant a separate person for every one of the roles described below, every one of the tasks needs to be considered and carried out as it is seen to be necessary.

If the interest extends internationally the team will have to be much larger as the news media and relatives could be calling day and night. Therefore there should be enough people to cover two or three shifts and each team should include trained people to adequately cover the following roles.

Leader

A senior, qualified communication or public relations person. The leader will: advise the chief executive and any other spokesperson to be involved; liaise with HR, legal advisers and emergency services where appropriate; prepare the key messages and briefings; direct the team; chair news conferences; handle any VIP visitors and keep in contact with those key people or opinion formers, who might not attend but will want to be kept up to date. VIPs will tend to want the news media to cover their visit and this must be controlled carefully to avoid the risk of your crisis becoming someone else's opportunity. They (or their people) will need to be closely briefed and any tour or meeting, that they will want to take part in, must be managed by the team leader. The team leader must, in line with the organisation's normal media handling protocols and in consultation with the chief executive, sign off all written communications about the incident. The normal protocols should also state that all news media or public enquiries must be routed through the team leader, who will then brief the spokesperson. The team leader will, in consultation with the chief executive, immediately write a media statement containing key facts about the organisation and all the known details of the incident (subject to liaison with the police press officer, if a crime has been committed) which will be updated as soon as reliable information becomes known. They will also create question-and-answer sheets with which to prepare or rehearse the spokespeople for interviews and news conferences.

For a major incident or crisis, a timetable of regular announcements or briefings must be drawn up, communicated and kept to, even if it is to say that no more information is available. If a vacuum forms or a gap is left, speculation will thrive, which will put the organisation on the back foot, reacting to rumour when it should be informing.

One voice

It is essential that messages must be consistent, open and honest and therefore the fewer people involved in their writing or delivering, the stronger they will be. It is also important that the messages must be few and always clearly reflect what the organisation stands for. In other words, they must communicate that the organisation has the best interests of the staff, customers and the local community at heart. If a crime has been committed no messages, statements and releases must attempt to give any details about it as this must be left entirely to the police.

Spokespeople

They will, after consultation with the team leader, give interviews, talk to relatives and be the guides for any visiting VIPs. Not only must the designated spokespeople take part in the whole team-training day but they must also be media-trained. If there are any deaths or serious crime issues to be discussed it should be the most senior member of staff or board of directors, available at the time, who is interviewed. If the incident is serious and the chief executive and/or the chair is known to be in the country and is not in evidence within as short a time as possible, it will be taken as being cavalier and uncaring, which will be instantly damaging for the organisation's reputation.

While delivering the agreed messages, the spokesperson must be genuinely concerned about the situation, accept responsibility for it (but not blame, unless they know they are to blame), apologise and explain what has happened as far as they know and what is going to happen next, to find out more and move towards resolving the incident or, when it is at an end, preventing its recurrence. They must never speculate about what might have happened, make defensive excuses, blame anybody else, offer to resign or over-promise.

It might be necessary to provide relatives support if people have been killed or injured. They will deal with all enquiries from and make contact with relatives and possibly set up a room where they could wait comfortably and be supplied with refreshments (in the event of an incident in the wider community involving staff, customers or students for example). The relatives, even more importantly than the news media, must not be left to guess or speculate about what has happened. Their support person must gather their questions and organise for people to answer them, explain the situation or just talk to them while more information is sought.

Internal and external relations

These will be responsible for ensuring that the organisation and the wider community are kept fully informed. They will handle calls according to briefings from the team leader, coordinate offers of help and log all enquiries. They will also ensure that relevant key publics, as directed by the team leader, are kept fully informed. As offers of help might arrive from various quarters the team leader will create a briefing as to how they are to be handled.

Some incidents might need more help than the team can provide and that should be coordinated with HR, the emergency services, the security or estates department or others, as appropriate, who will be mindful of any child protection or health and safety issues that might arise.

Media relations

These will deal with calls, ensure they are answered promptly, in accordance with briefings from the team leader, and organise news conferences. As with the relatives, there must be no time or room for speculation and the news media will also require a room (not close to the relatives room) with catering and regular spokespeople, reports and if appropriate, under level 1 (see Table 8.2), twice daily news conferences. The news media can be extremely helpful at times of crisis and they should be regarded as such. All news media channels, including message boards, must be monitored and every mention of the organisation or the incident logged for evaluation. Any misinformation or misrepresentations must be highlighted and addressed, immediately after consultation with the team leader.

Social media person

This might be the same as the media relations person.

They will ensure that the website and all social media channels are kept fully up to date with information going out, and that others are monitored for any questions or issues arising that must be addressed as soon as reliable information is available.

Messengers

Where the site (or sites) is spread out and to keep the relatives, news media and VIPs apart, until the leader might decide to bring some of them together, there will need to be messengers, ideally based in each area and keeping in regular email contact with questions and issues for their coordinator to address according to their briefing notes.

Note takers

As each call or question comes in they need to be recorded along with any action taken to deal with them. This not only provides a full record for the eventual debrief but it also helps to ensure that every call and question is answered and answered again as the incident unfolds and more reliable information comes to hand. The notes will also be invaluable for future training; any FOI[1] requests on the incident and to give the communication department a good record of who (especially key publics like journalists or politicians) was interested and how their interest was expressed, handled and later used.

Other considerations

During the incident the team will need to be regularly fed and watered, replaced and sent home to rest when necessary. Therefore a catering manager must also be part of the team.

There must be appropriate resources for accessing social media, emailing and using mobile phones from the rooms identified and it helps to know where on the site the best signal can be

---

[1]FOI refers to the Freedom of Information Act, which exists in a number of countries, including the UK, to promote transparency. Under the terms of the Act, all of the publicly funded sector (e.g. government offices, schools, hospitals and universities) is bound to answer questions from any source, within reason and on any subject. The Act is used a great deal by the news media when they are investigating stories.

found for a satellite truck, which is also safely within cabling distance of a power supply. Also the room where the core team and the news media are working should have a whiteboard, on to which information will be posted at regular intervals. Therefore a senior IT and/or perhaps an estates person should also be part of the team.

Some parts of the site might have to be sealed off and everyone coming into the site carefully screened – therefore a senior member of the security staff should also be part of the team.

The switchboard

This will need to have a full list of the contact details of everyone in the team so that they, or a substitute, can be contacted and brought in without delay. They should know that all media calls should go to the media coordinator and should also be aware that the news media might pose as staff or others, so all calls must be screened carefully. Therefore someone from the switchboard should also be part of the team.

As it may well be necessary to arrange for counselling, personnel or volunteer support, a senior member of the HR department must also be part of the team.

Outside help?

If you know that you will not be able to muster and train enough people from within your staff body for your needs it is wise to secure help from outside in advance of their being needed. If you are a public sector organisation or an NGO it might be possible to work with others, such as the NHS, the local council or a college, but it is vital that they come and train with your team, so that everyone knows their roles and time will not be wasted as people jockey for positions.

You might feel safer having secured the services of a public relations consultancy with expertise in this area – however, there are some cautionary points to consider. You need to see evidence of work done by them before and be able to check the impact that they have had, during a crisis situation, on their clients' reputations. They too should be involved with training in the organisation, which they might offer to set up and lead, but ask for an outline of the day first to ensure that everything is covered.

The training or practice day

As well as everyone in the team, the team leader should also invite a local journalist in to help and advise with the training – to literally be the news media and put the spokespeople through their paces. As the day is an excellent team- or relationship-building opportunity it is a good idea to involve a journalist who does not seem to understand what the organisation is about (rather than being your best friend already) as it is a good way for them to see you doing your best to do the right thing.

It will also be necessary to have some 'extras' to be relatives, VIPs and possibly wounded staff members, depending upon your scenario.

Although a level 1 incident is the least likely it should be trained for (but not in real time) and then the rest is much more straightforward.

The scenario to be used should only be known to the team leader or a separate facilitator, who will take the team through it in real time, giving out information sheets as the day and the incident unfold.

Desk-top exercises can also be held to test communication channels, develop checklists and identify the need for specific skills on the team.

Reports on practices or training should be added to the plan for information on any issues identified.

Audit resources and facilities

All equipment needed (notebooks, tablet computer, laptops or smartphones, name and role badges, tabards, etc.) must be kept somewhere that is easily accessible. A plan of the site, with rooms clearly marked for their suitability, must also be easily accessible along with the plan. The rooms needed, as well as those for the relatives and news media, must also include one for the core team to operate and communicate from and another for holding news conferences. News conferences should be staged in a room with doors at the front and back, so that those being interviewed can leave without having to walk through the journalists, who will very likely delay them from getting back to work. The plan should also show the best places for satellite trucks.

In the same room there should also be some information folders or CDs, containing useful information about the organsiation, which can be given to journalists to keep them informed while they wait for the team to find out what is happening. This can include site plans, staffing charts, administrative and other offices, public receptions, factory floors, storerooms and whatever might be appropriate to the situation that will give the news media the feeling that you are concerned about their need for information. These files or CDs must be kept up to date, along with the training, the composition of the team and the media training of the spokespeople.

Cascade call-out list

The cascade call-out list must also be checked regularly to ensure that all contact details are present and up to date. The CEO must be called first, followed by the team leader and the first team shift on the list. All members of the team should also hold a list of contact details for each other and others they may need to call.

Plan summary

Your plan should contain:

- The questions that need to be asked to help the chief executive and the team leader decide which level they are dealing with. It is useful to devise some questions with the team during practices.
- The lists of each shift of team members and their up-to-date contact details.
- The organisation's mission statement and/or vision and/or values to be referred to for key messages which, despite the incident, must still reflect what the organisation stands for.
- The list of key publics and contact details for channels to them.
- All site plans with key rooms identified.

Checklists

These are written first for quick reference in every eventuality. They are only guidelines as every case has differences and will need specific attention. Record the dates on the lists, when the information is checked for currency and when any training or practising is undertaken, with the names of those who attended.

You will need a full list of partners and publics – with contact details.

Messages for interviews, websites, tweets and blogs

- Inform all internal publics first
- Best delivered by the most senior member of staff available (who has, hopefully been media-trained)
- Never say 'no comment'
- Always put people before money
- Tell the truth at all times

- Stress the seriousness and the concern felt
- Take responsibility (but not blame, unless it is appropriate) and apologise
- Never speculate
- Never blame or criticise an organisation or an individual (such as the government, the unions, the staff, the competition)
- Never make defensive excuses
- Be aware of data protection issues relating to staff
- Check with parents or relatives before discussing an individual, especially in the event of a fatality
- Stress support for staff and if appropriate for the police, counselling and emergency services
- If provision has had to be stopped provide details of alternatives and working with partners to maintain provision elsewhere
- Stress the positive, the achievements and the vital role that the organisation plays in the local community – socially and economically.

It will be back!

You will be glad that you kept detailed notes of any incident because in all likelihood it will be back. The news media publicly revisit your most difficult times on anniversaries (these will pop up on their screens to remind them) during any resulting inquests or legal cases, when reports are published, if anything like it happens elsewhere. Whenever your organisation is mentioned you run the risk of it all coming out again 'this is the charity which . . . . Therefore it is even more important to handle all relationships well and create a good memory of your behaviour on the day!

Case study
Heathrow Terminal 5

Terminal 5 at London's Heathrow Airport was planned for 20 years at a cost of £4.3bn.

On the day it opened for business, in March 2008, after much excited expectation had been raised, there was utter chaos. Passengers said no one was on hand to help and there were no announcements or information on monitors and websites.

By 5.30 am on the first day, 200 passengers had queued for information on cancelled flights, with only two of the twenty-six information desks open to help.

On the operational side, there were technical errors, mechanical failures and little system testing, so that the baggage handling system, which had been designed to handle 12,000 bags per hour, did not work. Bags piled up and seven flights had to leave with no bags on board. Arriving passengers had to wait up to two and a half hours to collect their bags.

Also, adding far more to the technical issues was the fact that staff were poorly trained, morale was low and goodwill had long since evaporated.

Staff (and a large number of passengers) were up to two hours late as the signage for car parking was not clear and could not be followed.

On the management side, it was widely reported that there was arrogance, complacency, poor communication and a refusal to listen to staff and technical experts during the run-up to the opening. When British Airways (BA) and British Airports Authority executives finally emerged, they misjudged the mood badly by mentioning 'teething problems' associated with a 'bedding-down period'. Eventually, a full day after the fiasco, BA's spokesperson admitted that the opening was 'not our finest hour'. He offered a 'promise to do better', walked away from the news media and was filmed going through closing doors, which were locked behind him.

As the BBC reported:

> By the end of T5's first traumatic day, a total of 34 flights had been cancelled and hundreds of passengers had been left stranded, waiting either for a flight or even for their bags.
>
> By Saturday, BA said at least 15,000 bags were stranded at Heathrow – with one source telling the BBC that the number may have been closer to 20,000.
>
> While the airline says it is working to clear the bag backlog, how long it will take for BA to work off the negative publicity caused by the fiasco remains to be seen.

Source: BBC, 28 March 2008

Source: London News Pictures/Rex Features

Question

What would you list as being vital to risk assessing an opening, like Terminal 5, to reduce the possibility of a crisis?

Case study
Sometimes a crisis can hit a company doing everything well

Arla Foods is a cooperative of dairy farmers based in Denmark. Their annual report for 2004/5 mentioned plans for developments in Arab countries such as: 'prioritize the area through significant investment and a doubling of production in Saudi Arabia over the next five years'.

It would have been thought that coming from a small country like Denmark would definitely be a plus when selling in the Middle East.

In September 2005 cartoons featuring the Prophet Mohammed and associating him with terrorism, appeared in the Danish newspaper, *Jyllands-Posten*. It is against the Islamic faith to depict the Prophet in any way. Forty years of building the company in the Middle East came to a halt in five days. A boycott of all Arla products was called for across all Muslim countries.

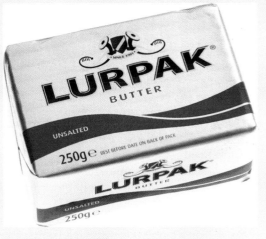

Although an apology was demanded, Anders Fogh Rasmussen (Denmark's prime minister) explained that freedom of speech was under firm protection in his country and any complaints should be handled in court. Arla's products were removed from shelves in over 50,000 stores and their competitors were quick to fill them.

Not surprisingly (and it would not be considered a typical kind of crisis as listed above), political boycott was not in the emergency plan. The cost to the company was €70 million (450m DKK) in 2006 and 300 million litres of milk had to be sold or used elsewhere.

Source: © Chris Harris/Alamy

Arla managed the struggle in the Middle East by extensive communication towards all involved publics – they took a stand at a Gulf food exhibition in Dubai and spoke to as many people as possible, distancing themselves from the actions of the independent newspaper. They kept in regular contact with local staff in Saudi Arabia, business partners abroad, politicians in their home country, media in both environments, and journalists as well as other mediators who could have had a possible impact on business relations.

They published a full-page advertisement in 25 Arabic newspapers on 20 March 2006, stating:

> *Arla Foods wishes to be distanced from the actions of Jyllands-Posten in choosing to print caricatures of the Prophet Mohammed. We do not share their reasons for doing it and we understand and respect your reaction . . . . The time that we have spent in your world has taught us that justice and tolerance are fundamental values of Islam . . . We hope that you will reconsider your reaction to our company.*

The advertisement caused an adverse reaction in Denmark, where until then, the people had been supportive of the company. A campaign against them was launched because of their support for repressive regimes but the impact was low.

An additional means of regaining trust was the demonstration of their corporate social responsibility. The company funded a number of humanitarian projects and created a cooperation agreement with the Red Cross for a programme in Darfur.

On 3 April 2006 the International Committee for the Support of the Prophet officially brought the boycott to an end by distributing a news release announcing that they appreciated Arla's reaction and their declaration against the cartoons. It was made clear that the boycott was only lifted against Arla (Lego and Ecco shoes were also involved) as they had apologised and sponsored projects for the needy.

Arla's products were back on the shelves of over 3,000 shops by 6 April 2006.

About 16 months after the boycott was launched, the company showed the first records of improvement. Astrid Nielsen, Director of Communication, told the author: 'We're approaching the normal amount of sales. I think by the end of 2007 we will be back on 2005 levels.' And they were.

Question

Consider the turning points for this crisis for Arla. What did they do that worked?

It is not having a crisis which causes the reputation damage but the way that an organisation behaves once problems arise and attention is focused upon them. As Ian Mitroff and Thierry Pauchant explained: 'How people react to crises provides one of the most powerful windows, if not the most powerful window, into the souls of people and their institutions' (2010 : 163).

Case study

As can be seen above, the air transport industry is one of the most crisis-prone. Within three weeks of each other, there were two serious plane crashes in the UK.

Pan Am flight 103

On 21 December 1988 Pan Am flight 103 exploded in mid-air, and came down on the town of Lockerbie, in Scotland, killing everybody on board and eleven people in the town. The explosion was caused by a terrorist bomb, which had been loaded on board in Frankfurt Airport.

The company tried to move any blame for lapses in security to the US government agencies, which had been thought to have received warnings about a potential bomb. Pan Am was fined for security failures and faced lawsuits from 100 families of passengers on the flight for $300 million. Pan Am representatives did not visit the site during the aftermath or give interviews.

As an iconic brand they were felt by many to be too strong a target for terrorists and their business suffered.

While not directly to blame for the bomb, their reputation suffered enormously and they went bankrupt in January 1991.

Pan Am flight 103 in Lockerbie
Source: BrynColton/Getty Images

British Midland at Kegworth

On 8 January 1989 at 8.25 p.m. the British Midland flight from London to Belfast crashed onto the embankment of the M1 motorway at Kegworth. Of the 126 on board, 47 were killed, 74 were seriously injured and 5 had minor injuries. One of the engines was failing and so an emergency landing was attempted at East Midlands Airport, at the top of the embankment, 900 metres away from the crash. The pilots shut down the wrong engine, giving them little chance of landing safely.

The British Midland crash at Kegworth
Source: David Hartley/Rex Features

The Chairman of British Midland was quickly at the scene and, although clearly upset, he was immediately available to give interviews to the news media. He was sorry, he was devastated and he promised to find out what had happened and tell all. At that point he did not know what had happened, and so soon after the Lockerbie crash, he refused to speculate.

An honest, clearly caring and speedy response from the top of the organisation was well received. Payments were made to relatives and victims and there was no attempt made to avoid the blame or shirk responsibility.

British Midland was named airline of the year the following year and in 1991 Michael Bishop was knighted.

Two very different outcomes. Where blame was not clear, in Pan Am's case, they suffered. Where blame was clear, in British Midland's case, but a very human reaction was given, they were forgiven.

These two cases are not black and white and cannot be used to prove anything or even to suggest that the chairmen's behaviour made all the difference. There are possibly cultural issues, the scale of the incidents was very different and one was just before Christmas.

However, Michael Bishop's reaction was widely appreciated, which definitely helped to build his company's reputation.

REFERENCES

Annual ICM Crisis Report, www.crisisexperts.com

Cope, N. (1995) *The Independent*, 22 February

Earl, S. and S. Waddington (2012) *Brand Anarchy*, Bloomsbury

John, S. and S. Thomson (2003) *New Activism and the Corporate Response*, Palgrave Macmillan

Mitroff, I. and T. Pauchant (1990) *We're so Big Nothing Can Happen to Us*, Birch Lane Press

Regester, M. and J. Larkin (2010) *Risk Issues and Crisis Management*, Kogan Page

Part 3
Reconceptualising PR

Chapter 9
The Stockholm Accords
Toni Muzi Falconi and Sven Hamrefors

Learning outcomes

By the end of this chapter you should be able to:

- See how much has to go into a process to build an understanding of a subject in an international context
- Have an understanding of value chains and value networks
- Realise the importance of innovation
- Recognise the impact of different leadership and communication styles
- Appreciate different ways in which people behave in relation to information
- Understand how chaos theory can help the communicator's effectiveness
- Know how a communicator can become a leader
- Know what are agreed to be the core concepts of a modern public relations profession
- Understand some of the reputation problems that PR itself has
- Be ready to enter the debate with your own thoughts and ideas, gleaned from other parts of the book, which may counter some of the findings here, as well as from your own knowledge and experience.

Introduction

This chapter, although coming at the end, is not a postscript to the book, in fact it is an ante-script, looking ahead to where a student might take their interests and to where a practitioner might further develop as a professional. Using the ongoing development of the Stockholm Accords to create an internationally agreed platform for the promotion of professional public relations, the chapter outlines the history behind the Accords, details their process and gives an example of one of the theoretical approaches that gave rise to them. It goes on to list the outcomes of the process. The whole is not for examination at the level for which this book is intended but to act as a signpost for future exploration. The concepts will feel challenging for a beginner but the hope is that they will also be both inspirational and aspirational, indicating much of what has yet to be studied and understood before a communicator or public relations practitioner can take their place as part of the leadership of their organisation.

In the fall of 1964, aged 23, the author of this part of the chapter[1] found himself at a 3M Company HQ meeting in Saint Paul (Minnesota) with some ten other international relations practitioners.

An elderly and then just retired William McKnight, legendary founder of what is even today an evergreen success story of a truly 'communicative' global company (can the reader think of any other major multinational that has survived and blossomed for a century without going through at least one major crisis?), walks in the room unannounced and amicably mutters,

'Hey John, who are all these people in the room?'

John Verstraete (at the time senior vice-president for global public relations) stands up and says,

'Bill, these are your public relations people around the world.'

McKnight shakes his head, raises hand to chin, searches in his beard and suggests:

'Yeah! Sure . . . Though maybe, before improving our image, they should worry about improving the image of their profession!'

In October 2006, in New Delhi (India), Harold Burson addressed the ICCO[2] conference and expressed the utmost urgency for a public relations programme for public relations.

It's like the cobbler's children, he said.[3]

Alas! An ongoing challenge each of us seasoned professionals has faced hundreds of times, in schools, colleges, universities, society at large, companies, governments, non-profits . . .

In 2002, sixteen national associations of professionals in public relations formed the Global Alliance for Public Relations and Communication Management.[4]

As of this writing, November 2011, the member associations have since become 29, representing some 160,000 practitioners, a bare 5–7% of the estimated total number of practitioners in the world.

Yet, no other single organisation has a more global representation of the profession.

In November 2009, the Global Alliance Executive Board met in Lugano (Switzerland) and, on proposal by its immediate past Chair, John Paluszek, approved and actively contributed to the project of a collaborative process designed to prepare, draft and subsequently discuss at the June 2010 World Public Relations Forum in Stockholm, a 'brief' to the global public relations profession for a two-year advocacy programme to argue, with locally selected and more relevant stakeholder groups in every part of the world, the areas of most value that public relations brings to society and organisations.

This, of course, is bearing well in mind the 'generic principles and specific applications' paradigm which implies an inescapable correlation between the two poles of that paradigm, and a very detailed analysis of the communicative infrastructure of each specific territory.[5]

---

[1]An Italian national, then in his very first days at work in public relations for the 3M Company in Italy, following a two-year employee communication job at Stanic, a joint venture between 3M and the Standard Oil Company of New Jersey.

[2]The International Association of National Public Relations Consulting Company associations (www.iccopr.com/)

[3]http://haroldburson.com/pdf/2006-10-05%20The%20Cobblers%20Children.pdf

[4]www.globalalliancepr.org/content/1/1/homepage

[5]www.prconversations.com/index.php/2008/11/facing-this-historic-discontinuity-two-recently-developed-certainties-for-out-profession-generic-principles-and-specific-applications-and-stakeholder-relationship-management/

Thus we have a public relations programme for public relations as well as an update of the 1978 Mexico Statement.[6]

A response to Harold Burson's call or to William McKnight's suggestion. . . .

The 'brief'[7] intends to highlight in a succinct document those areas in which public relations contribute today most value to organisations and society – accompanied by all the necessary supporting materials and by a suggested method to evaluate and measure the effectiveness of the effort.

The assignment to coordinate the effort was given to this author, one of the founders of the Global Alliance (GA) and its first Chair (2002/3).

After six months and with the active contribution of some 120 senior global professionals and academics from more than 30 countries, the brief was approved by the 400-plus participants from more than 20 nations and by another 400 participants who closely followed the video-streaming service and Twittered all the way through the two-day discussion at the Forum in Stockholm on 14 –15 June 2010.[8]

This part of the chapter intends to:

(a) describe the process adopted to draft and approve the 'brief';
(b) explain the contents of the 'brief';
(c) elaborate on the implementation of the programme, whose assessment is based on an agreed upon evaluation and measurement mechanism.

As the programme is currently in process, its actual results will be reported at the next World Public Relations Forum, to be held in October 2012 in Melbourne (Australia). Yet an ongoing reporting of its day-to-day progress in all areas of the world can be monitored and commented on on the Global Alliance's website.

THE RATIONALE

A 2005 paper[9] by this author, published by the Institute for Public Relations, reported that in the world there are anywhere from 2.5 to 4 million public relations professionals employing more than 50% of their time in assisting private, public and social organisations to improve the quality of relationships with their stakeholders.

The number varies significantly according to the different possible interpretations of the term 'public relations professionals'.

As public relations is mostly a labour-intensive activity (rather than a mostly capital-intensive activity such as, for example, advertising) that paper argued that its economic impact would better be measured by adapting suggested guidelines normally related to other professions, instead of simply mirroring the traditional methods used by the advertising industry.

This implies, in a given territory, (a) an estimate of the number of practising professionals; (b) attributing a sum to represent their gross annual spend to each organisation; (c) the adoption of an added-value multiplier anywhere between 1.5 to 3.0, according to the actual value perceived.

By and large, that paper indicated an annual 400 billion dollar economic impact of the public relations profession worldwide.

---

[6]It is the art and social science of analysing trends, predicting their consequences, counselling organisational leaders and implementing programmes of action which will serve both the organisation's and the public interest (1978)
[7]www.globalalliancepr.org/content/1/495/with-accords-moves-into-the-future/ and www.globalalliancepr.org/content/1/493/global-alliance-endorses-stockholm-accords-world-forum/
[8]www.wprf2010.se/
[9]www.instituteforpr.org/research_single/how_big_is_public_relations/

In September 2008 Euprera[10] (the European Association for Education and Research in Public Relations) sanctioned, at its annual congress in Milan, the ongoing and accelerated institutionalisation of the public relations function in organisations worldwide.[11]

The annual GAP (generally accepted practices)[12] study by the University of Southern California's Annenberg School of Communication in the USA, and the annual European Communication Monitor[13] conducted by Euprera and the EACD[14] (European Association of Communication Directors), have recently confirmed and consolidated that public relations has become more and more relevant to the success of any organisation.

For this simple reason – and well beyond its growing practices, believed by many to be ethically questionable – the profession is increasingly criticised by social, economic, political, media and management groups, and its inherent ambiguity draws growing activist and regulatory concerns, mostly since the public at large is not often made aware of its methods and processes, as these mostly refer to stakeholder relationships and to third-party (opinion leaders, media) endorsement practices.

Furthermore, while a 1946–96 study of how public relations was perceived in American popular culture concludes that PR practitioners were generally portrayed as 'nice to know' but substantially irrelevant;[15] a similar 1996–2008 study indicates to the contrary that PR people are portrayed as mean, powerful and mostly operating in support of the interests of huge and sometimes 'shady' organisations.[16]

The paradox is that as the profession attracts a growing number of young people, while organisations increasingly value its contribution to their success, societal criticism intensifies.

Thus, the need arose for a reconceptualisation and a call to action for the more aware and concerned members of the global professional community to argue and advocate their profession's societal and organisational value: a public relations programme for public relations.

This reconceptualisation must address new concepts and adopt sustainable processes related to how organisations, private, public and social, seek to create value and enhance their licence to operate.

The process

The first thoughts for this effort, which has never been attempted (as far as the author knows) by any other profession on a worldwide scale, went to some of the more recent developments supplied by the global body of knowledge, the most notable coming from Sweden and South Africa.

Professor Sven Hamrefors from Sweden's Malarden University, has recently completed a comprehensive five-year research effort[17] into Sweden's most effective organisations on behalf of the Swedish Public Relations Association.[18] His report on this work is published in full here, as it has been so important to the development of the Accords.

VALUE CHAINS AND NETWORKS

There is an ongoing change in the prerequisites for organisations to act in the economic system. The traditional way of organising value creation has been the value chain. The logic of the value chain is that several actors gradually refine a product or service in a simple chain: A

---

[10]www.euprera.org/
[11]www.prconversations.com/index.php/2010/06/free-book-download-institutionalising-public-relations-and-corporate-communication/
[12]http://annenberg.usc.edu/CentersandPrograms/ResearchCenters/SPRC/PrevGAP.aspx
[13]www.communicationmonitor.eu/
[14]www.eacd-online.eu/
[15]K. Miller, 'PR in film and fiction, 1930–1995', *Journal of Public Relations Research*, 11(1) 3–28.
[16]Carol Ames, 'PR goes to the movies: public relations in selected films, 1996 to 2008', *Public Relations Review* 36(2): 164–70.
[17]www.sverigesinformationsforening.se/in-english/research-statistics/business-effective-communication.aspx
[18]www.sverigesinformationsforening.se/in-english/

does something for B who does something for C and so on. Due to the increased possibilities for information exchange and the increased demand for knowledge input into the refinement process, these value chains become more complex and turn into value networks (Normann and Ramírez 1993).

Business in value networks is more difficult to manage than business in value chains. Uncertainty increases, speed increases, actors become more replaceable. Some actors in the network will be better at initiating opportunities for value creation; they will create what is usually referred to as 'first-mover advantage'. They are more innovative than the others and will be identified as being the ones creating opportunities for others to create value. Other actors will take already existing opportunities; they will create what is referred to as 'second-mover advantage'. First-movers will be given more power by the other actors in the network; second-movers will be more replaceable than first-movers.

It is difficult to be efficient in the position of first-mover. It requires the ability to:

- Identify the potential for an opportunity of a certain position very early
- Innovate interesting concepts that will be perceived as promising to the network
- Handle multiple resources to create value exceeding expectations.

COMMUNICATIVE LEADERSHIP

Previously, in history, it has usually been more profitable and secure to go for second-mover advantages. However, in an environment of value networks it becomes more important to develop a first-mover advantage. This puts strain on the leadership of the organisation. It must develop a strong *ideological leadership* as well as a *contextual leadership*. Even though these roles relate to the modern world there are historical examples from the political arena. Two types of leadership, by referring to a few examples from history, will be illustrated below. Three good examples of how a focused, ideological and communicative leadership style has worked in conjunction with a leadership style that takes care of the broader perspective will be given.

Case studies from history

Elizabeth I and Sir Francis Walsingham

When Queen Elizabeth I took the throne, she transformed England from an isolated island nation into a political superpower. She had the ability to keep discipline among her subjects in England but as she expanded her sphere of power to encompass an English empire, she had a problem keeping such a heterogeneous group of subjects in check. As a result, she wanted to develop a complementary leadership to her own – one that could control and create multiple relationships in a heterogeneous network. This became an opportunity for Sir Francis Walsingham to develop England's intelligence agency. He worked thoroughly and systematically. In fact, the efficiency of British intelligence authorities today, such as MI5 and MI6, are based to a large extent on the foundation laid by Walsingham hundreds of years ago.

Louis XIII and Cardinal Richelieu

Louis XIII, king of France, had similar imperialistic aspirations to Elizabeth I but his problems were to be found at home. The political climate in France was unstable, which made it difficult for the king to use his resources to build an effective empire. This became an opportunity for Cardinal Richelieu to redirect the rules of the political game in France. Part of that process entailed improving order; certain functions which he enacted can be witnessed today in France, such as the practice of ministerial rule.

Gustavus Adolfus and Axel Oxenstierna

Swedish King Gustavus Adolfus had the intention to make Europe Protestant. At the time, Sweden was a relatively homogeneous culture, but as other countries were incorporated into the Swedish empire, Gustavus Adolfus began to have problems much like the ones Elizabeth I experienced that led to administrative disorder. In order to ease communication in the new network environment that Sweden had created, the king ordered Axel Oxenstierna to develop an administrative system based on communicative efficiency, parts of which are intact to this day.

The cases above are positive examples of how an ideological leadership style can be complemented by leadership that is focused on making communication more effective in a broader context. In contrast, we can look at a less successful example: Hitler and Goebbels.

Adolf Hitler and Joseph Goebbels

Hitler wished to create a vast German empire that would last for a thousand years. To that end, he set up a war machine that surpassed anything the world had witnessed before. Hitler's operative efficiency was excellent; his problems concerned perception. He asserted an ideology that put one type of person in the centre, calling them 'Aryans'. The problem with Aryans is that they are a fictional race. There is absolutely no possibility to determine under objective criteria who is an Aryan and who is not. As such, it was difficult for people to relate to the Nazi ideology. Another problem Hitler had was that he wasn't particularly sensitive when he created networks. As a result, those who were subjected to invasion from Germany felt run over, literally. This created all sorts of movements of resistance that were difficult for the Germans to cope with. In this situation, Hitler needed someone who could supply communication in a broader context. This became Joseph Goebbels's job; he was very adept at communication techniques and the propaganda products he created are in many ways unequalled in history. However, this led nowhere; Hitler's thousand-year plan only resulted in 13 years of misery.

These examples show that entering a network situation requires development of two types of communicative leadership. One is *ideological* and positions the organisation clearly on the map. This type of leadership defines and communicates the direct role of the organisation in its value-creating position and develops direct relationships with the partners with whom the organisation creates value. Ideological leadership is a task for the highest levels of leadership and should therefore personify the ideology of the organisation. Subsequently, ideological leadership develops primarily in relation to the direct partners with whom one creates value, but it could also be made known to a broader audience in order to further reinforce the position of the organisation. For this reason, one finds an increasing number of examples of organisations with leaders who personify the ideology the organisation stands for. Ingvar Kamprad (IKANO), Richard Branson (Virgin) and Michael O'Leary (Ryanair), to name a few.

The other form of leadership that organisations must develop can be termed *contextual*. The task here is to deal with the complex relationships that organisations depend on in various ways. For this reason, the central responsibility for this type of leadership is to develop the organisation's communicative capacity on all levels. This type of contextual leadership is practised on the broader and weaker relationships in the value network in order to support the organisation's position in various dimensions.

This latter role in the leadership is an opportunity that many communicators have identified. As a matter of fact communicators are the one group of professionals most suitable to take this role, under the condition that they acquire the necessary knowledge and abilities.

COMMUNICATORS' COMPETENCIES

A basic competency of a contextual leader is to understand how people function cognitively in their perception- and perspective-making.

dedicated to perspective-making. Usually these processes are based upon the concept of dialogue. The communicator must understand that the effectiveness of a dialogue process is dependent on how it is designed, who is invited and how the results are communicated into the organisation. (See Chapter 1 for more on dialogue.) Another very important aspect of the social interaction is the use of words in the organisation. Communicators are often active in the development of words and concepts aimed at inspiring progress and development. In many organisations, however, the effect is not so progressive. Instead, these kinds of words may have a conservative or even a stagnating effect.

Finally, a very important aspect of the social interaction is to develop intrinsic motivation. As this kind of motivation is based upon a balance between perceived demand and perceived proficiency it opens up a great variety of how to communicate demand into the organisation and how to communicate new opportunities. The communicator has the mission to contribute to an organisational context where there is a balanced situation suitable for the development of personal flow and how to implement changes in the situation in order to increase competency by challenging the personal flow.

Environmental relationships

The fourth knowledge area relates to the relationships that the organisation has with its environment. This has three aspects. One is to understand what is going on out there, a second is to influence the environment in an efficient way and the third is to establish effective processes for knowledge exchange.

The first, to understand the environment, is about the communicator as responsible for dedicated processes for business intelligence. As organisations have an inclination to depend upon particular channels, there is a need for functions challenging those dependencies. In the medieval kingdom the King, who very often was a despot, did not want anyone to challenge his perspective. In fact it could be very dangerous to try to do that. The King, however, needed someone to challenge him. This created the role of the jester. His job was to whisper in the King's ear what the King needed to know but did not want to know. This is exactly the role of the communicator being responsible for business intelligence. It implies suitable mandate to do this and having access to suitable resources.

The second, to influence the environment, is about what is commonly referred to as 'lobbying'. It is a difficult area in itself and requires knowledge of institutional theory. Often lobbying is conducted in political environments with different issues emerging, growing and disappearing within various arenas. In order to cope with this complexity the communicator must be aware of the dynamics of these arenas and find ways to handle them. As the complexity is also influenced by the lobbying itself, the outcome of such activities is very uncertain. Thus, the knowledge of how to influence political parallel processes is important for the communicator to develop.

The third area, to exchange knowledge in the value network, is a knowledge area that has lately become important as the knowledge intensity and the speed of knowledge growth are increasing in most businesses. In order to cope with this area the communicator must participate in building a 'knowledge exchange culture' in the organisation (Teigland and Hamrefors, 2005). It requires effective transparency, good scouting for knowledge networks, efficient entrance into the networks and intelligent strategies for knowledge exchange.

Question

How might these further thoughts on relationship development and environmental scanning add to the approach to issues management in Chapter 3?

Skills

In this research project there has also been distilled a notion of four major skills related to the knowledge areas described above. They are described here as four sub-roles that together constitute the role of the communicator as leader, system designer, mediator, coach and influencer.

For communicators these roles will have different levels of importance in different situations. Usually they are always relevant, but they differ in importance.

System designer

This role is focused on the communicator as participating in the design of processes and structures in the organisation. It contains the skill to integrate the communication of holistic aspects into the processes, to foster initiatives and improvisation and to secure relevant knowledge supply to the processes.

Mediator

Communicators often see themselves as carrying messages from a source to a receiver. This role is, however, upgraded to a higher level as the communicator becomes active in the leadership of the organisation. Instead of only transferring messages the role becomes focused on creating shared understanding or sense-making. Thus, the role is not only to transfer interpretations but to create meaning. This requires skills in negotiation and persuasion. The mediator is the one who is mastering the social game of how people come to share understanding, facilitating cooperation. Often this requires working through others. Therefore, the foundation for this role is to understand the social dynamics of the organisation. The role as mediator requires knowledge of the language of the other professions. In many cases it is about mediating in a situation of conflict of interests.

Coach

The role as coach is about the communicator working as teacher to develop the communication skills of others. This is usually a very demanding task as managers often believe themselves to be better communicators than they actually are. So, teaching people the 'noble art of communication' often meets resistance. Therefore the incentive for new development and local initiatives must be fostered. In this kind of structure middle management has a very important role as communicator of local perspectives as well as general perspectives.

In Volvo AB the communication function has been active in the development of middle managers as communicators. This company has developed a method of measuring the communication efficiency of each middle manager linked to a continuous programme for development of communication skills. It has been running for many years, and measurements show that it has contributed substantially to the development of organisational effectiveness (Nordblom and Hamrefors 2007).

Influencer

The role as influencer is perhaps the most spectacular one of the four. It means that the communicator acts to change people's minds. Successful communicators work very actively to change people's minds to the extent that they change reality. Thus, influence of this kind should not have a destructive purpose, but should rather be focused on conveying incentives for people to really change their reality in a positive direction.

This role requires that the communicator can handle social processes elegantly, facilitating conceptual conveyance (Baagoe and Hamrefors 2006).

Role integration

In reality a role played by a communicator, as contextual leader, must be a combination of all four sub-roles. At the end of the day, the success of his or her aspiration to participate in the leadership of the organisation is dependent upon their knowledge of the four areas described above and the use of this knowledge in the manifestation of a situated role as a combination of the system designer, mediator, coach and influencer.

THEORY

During the development of the project there have been many suggestions for applicable theories in social science, in the search for an explanatory foundation. Some theories explain parts of the knowledge that have been created. For example, institutional theory gives some explanation of the foundation of lobbying processes, socio-cognitive theories may be helpful in understanding social interaction. But none of them tie it all together. None but one – based upon the knowledge that has been created in this project it has been possible to relate it all to one specific theory, namely classical chaos theory.

Chaos theory was originally developed in physics. It says that progressive change in a system occurs in the area where order meets and interacts with chaos. If a system is dominated by order it may change but this change is only an extrapolation of the present state of affairs. So, it will be totally predictable. If a system, however, is dominated by chaos it may also change but in a random manner and it will be impossible to predict and will not seem progressive. Thus, when order interacts with chaos the change taking place will be progressive but not predictable.

Chaos theory has been introduced to social system thinking, for example by Marion (1999). In social systems chaos theory is applicable because of the nature of human cognition. As described earlier in this chapter, humans have cognitively an inclination to seek confirming information based upon the content of memory structure. But humans also have an inclination to seek new information based upon embedded curiosity. Thus, a context must satisfy the need for both confirmation and surprises in a balanced way.

The traditional way of organising is to communicate very clearly what people should do but not very much how they should think. Most management tools are designed for this purpose: budgets, directives, plans, quality control and so on. This management philosophy has a long tradition that can be traced back to Frederick Taylor and how his theories were implemented by Henry Ford. It has proven to be successful in a world where it is possible to build boundaries between the organisation and its environment. In an environment where value networks dominate the stage, this way of organising may create organisations that are easy to lead, but at the expense of less external effectiveness. Thus, internal efficiency may be facilitated, but external effectiveness may be jeopardised.

The conclusion is that the purpose of communication in an organisation is to establish and develop the communicative ability of the organisation rather than only be dealing with traditional communication activities. The communicative ability shall strengthen the conceptual foundation of the organisation and at the same time stimulate the variability in activities. Thus, the communicator, as a contextual leader together with an ideological leadership is in charge of the work to make people think in a similar way but to act differently.

SCURRILOUS PORTRAITS

The role of the communicator as a leader, as described above, is based on the assumption that the organisation has an intention to become an active player in the value creation networks. If the company does not succeed in doing this it will be difficult for the communicator to find a leadership platform. I have identified various, less effective, roles that the communicator may take in this case and I have chosen to give these roles metaphorical labels.

The 'waiter'

This is a role of being a servant in the organisation. It is born out of the prerequisite that the organisation is unable to leave its own planning economics perspective. In this case the attention to the rest of the world becomes very much like scanning in principle. The focus is internal but people falsely believe they understand their environment. In this case the organisation builds up immunity to deviating signals from the environment. This will put pressure on the communicator to serve confirming information to the rest of the organisation. If the organisation has also developed an internal political game, which is common in this situation, the role of the 'waiter' may be extended to the role of 'master of ceremonies'. So the mission of the communicator is not only to communicate confirming information but also to support confirming rituals. In this way the communicator will be another actor conserving the organisation in its role of being the 'unsinkable vessel' like the *Titanic* and it will end in disaster.

The 'useful idiot'

In this case the power in the organisation is located in very few hands, usually only one pair – the dictator becomes isolated. It will lead to a reduced ability to understand the holistic aspect of the organisational context and then the communicator will be used as someone to sacrifice in order to protect the sovereignty of the leaders. In its worst version this role could be labelled as 'the useful idiot'. This label was minted by Stalin and is used for abusing people for your own purpose. This role is really tragic and becomes actually totally counter-productive for the development of the organisation.

The 'firefighter'

If the organisation is unable to manage the turbulence in the network, the environmental forces will fully hit the organisation. Instead of developing an exchange relationship with the environment the organisation will become a victim of its environment. Often this imperfection is due to the lack of an ideological base and one crisis is followed by another. Certainly the communicator plays a very important role in this case, but in the long run it is counter-productive as the ideological base is missing and the organisation will be unable to learn from its mistakes. In the worst case this culture of crisis may be addictive and the organisation will be initiating its own crises.

'Don Quixote'

In this case the imperfection lies within the communicator. He or she is mainly focused on specific actions and is not interested in measures that fall outside conventional communication work. He or she also has a belief that the management of planned and controlled communication processes will lead to participation in the leadership of the organisation. That will not happen, and instead of changing strategies the communicator increases the effort to create results and tries to find ways of showing them, for example by developing ways of measuring the effect of communication. Instead of being promoted to leader the communicator will remain a manager of certain communication processes.

There must be certain prerequisites for the communicator to become a leader in the organisation and it is up to the person in question to take appropriate initiatives to do so.

CONCLUSION

From the reasoning presented above it is possible to draw the conclusion that there are especially favourable prerequisites for the communicator to act as a leader in the organisation as it moves into a complex and expansive business environment.

In this kind of environment the business activities of the organisation must be based upon a strong ideology nourishing a strong position in the value network. It is the role of the top management to define this ideology and it needs its complementary role mastering the networks. This is a role that is tailor-made for the communicator and by developing the activities I have mentioned above the communicator may develop their position in the leadership of the organisation. But this role will never be given, it must be taken.

RETURNING TO THE STOCKHOLM ACCORDS

Professor Hamrefors refers to the accelerating global network society and to the 'value network' concept that describes how organisational value is found in the quality of the relationships exchanged between members of many fuzzy and immaterial networks (internal and external), as well as in the quality of the relationships between the different value networks.

Thus, contrary to (or in extension of) the traditional concept of the value chain, elaborated in the late 1970s by Harvard Professor Michael Porter, where value is created in a linear and mostly material process, this more recent Scandinavian line of thought attributes the creation of value mostly to the quality of relationships.

Professor Mervyn King, a South African corporate lawyer turned Supreme Court Justice, corporate governance counsel to the World Bank and the United Nations, Professor at the University of Pretoria and more recently Chair of the Global Reporting Initiative,[20] had just issued his King 3 Report that immediately attracted the attention of the corporate governance community worldwide.

Amongst other substantial innovations, the King 3 Report[21] dedicates a specific chapter (Chapter 8) to the governance of stakeholder relationships, and affirms that the board of elected officials of any public, private or social organisation is ultimately and directly responsible for developing and implementing policies and programmes aimed at sustaining planned and effective relationships with the organisation's principal stakeholder groups.

As a consequence, board decisions related to which stakeholder interests the organisation should privilege when in conflict, need to be 'situational' and to become a permanent topic of all board meetings.

Clearly this implies the adoption of a full stakeholder governance model and substantially changes the role of the organisation's PR practitioner: the manager normally in the best condition to listen to stakeholder groups, understand their expectations and interpret them, so that the board may make informed decisions for implementation by management.

These two more recent developments (coupled with other recent contributions from the Arthur Page Society,[22] the Public Relations Society of America,[23] the Institute for Public Relations;[24] plus the global stakeholder relationship governance[25] integration with the generic principles and specific applications paradigm[26] of public relations) led to a first and early outline. This was accompanied by a statement of intentions signed by the chair of the Global Alliance, that was sent to some 120 professionals, scholars and educators from 42 countries, inviting them to participate in a two-phase cooperative process by adopting the Cisco Webex Connexia synchronous video-conferencing platform, which was set for 10 February and for 8 March 2010.

---

[20]www.globalreporting.org/Home The globally recognised standards authority for non financial reporting.
[21]www.auditor.co.za/Portals/23/king%20111%20saica.pdf
[22]www.awpagesociety.com/images/uploads/2007AuthenticEnterprise.pdf
[23]www.prsa.org/Intelligence/BusinessCase/?utm_source=home_page&utm_medium=left_nav&utm_campaign=businesscase
[24]www.instituteforpr.com/
[25]www.instituteforpr.org/ipr_info/global_stakeholder_relationship_governance/
[26]www.prconversations.com/index.php/2008/11/facing-this-historic-discontinuity-two-recently-developed-certainties-for-out-profession-generic-principles-and-specific-applications-and-stakeholder-relationship-management/

In the two-week interval between the two video-conferences, participants were separated in six working groups, focused on selected areas of interest, to continue the discussion and complete a redraft of the first outline, validate the redraft during the second video-conference and then, finally, approving a first draft of the document to be posted for comments and suggestions on the World Public Relations Forum website.

The selection of the invitees followed three indicators:

- half professionals (from companies and agencies) and half scholars and educators;
- representation of as many countries as possible and all continents;
- individuals expected to be reactive, interested and available for the effort.

The very first outline of the accords included six areas of value creation: governance, management, sustainability, marketing, and internal and external communication.

Forty-two of the initial invitees participated to the first-two hour video-conference, half of them spoke directly by commenting and suggesting changes and/or made other approaches.

Towards the end of this first effort six volunteer group coordinators[27] were indicated and each participant volunteered to be included in at least one of the six working groups for the following two weeks. The role of the groups was to exchange comments, materials and information and redraft the brief related to that area. Some 80 exchanges between group coordinators and participants were concluded in the allocated time.

The coordinator then drafted a text, which was sent to all selected invitees, including those who had not replied to the first call, requiring them to comment and inviting them to participate in the second video-conference call.

There was general agreement that while the section devoted to marketing, which participants acknowledge is going through a radical conceptual overhaul, had not been able to produce significant added value more than what is generally and commonly understood.

On the contrary, the issue of the alignment of internal and external communication, instead, ended up deserving a section on its own.

Also, a lively discussion dwelt on whether the governance and management areas should not be integrated into one, and subsequently, whether the sustainability area should not also join that group. At the end (of the whole effort) it was decided to keep sustainability, governance and management (in that order) under the first half of the brief, illustrating the societal and organisational value of public relations, while the internal and external communication and the alignment of the two were to belong to the other half of the brief, illustrating the operational value of public relations.

The second video conference call saw the participation of 52 invitees, half of whom were new, while the other half had also participated in the earlier one.

After another two hours of lively discussion, agreement was reached that the coordinator would edit a first draft of the document, send it to all participants of either of the two sessions and ask them to respond with variations and suggestions in the following week.

During this first phase some 80 modifications where introduced, roughly half of a linguistic nature and the other half more of a content nature, in so far as the two may differ.

In the meantime, all cases, studies, links and papers referred to during the discussion were collected and added to the accompanying materials.

The coordinator also prepared a glossary describing, to the best of his knowledge and interpretation, the intended sense of some of the more relevant and relatively new concepts being used in the brief.

The reactions to the first draft by its early contributors were critical more of the language than of the content.

---

[27]Dan Tisch (Canada), Estelle De Beer (South Africa), Anne Gregory (UK), Peder Jonnson (Sweden), Annette Martelle (Canada), Joao Duarte (Portugal)

Possibly the most significant innovation focused on the actual format of each of the six selected areas: a quick statement of the situation, a quick statement of how the communicative organisation acts in that situation, followed by a call to action to the public relations professional succinctly enumerating the ways she or he brings value to the organisation and society.

The first draft of the Stockholm Accords at this point was ready to be posted for the global professional community to comment on on the World Public Relations Forum website for an open and non-moderated discussion.

In the period between the end of March and the end of May, some 60 comments were registered which led to the editing and subsequent posting of a second draft in early June.

Once more, in this first round of the 'open comments' many concentrated on the language aspect, but this time from two different perspectives: a purely linguistic one, as before, but also a more intellectual reference to concepts which were believed by some to be irrelevant, or even counter-productive.

A few of these comments, which in the meantime had also naturally migrated to other blogs which, in turn, generated further interesting and enriching points of view, were explicitly critical, even violently so, while all others were instead positive and in full support.

As much as numbers may seem relevant in this case, 5 were critical and the other 55 generally or very specifically supportive.

The most explicitly critical comments came from a couple of professionals who actually questioned the two initial concepts of the exercise:

1. the stakeholder governance model of the organisation and its implications for public relations;

2. the communicative organisation's role in today's network society and value networks.

Their arguments, occasionally supported by brilliant rhetoric, were not fully integrated into the final outcome, as the vast majority of contributions clearly supported those two inceptions of the process, if not in the relevant sense of attributing to the entire process the role of a proper and operational 'brief', but rather the appearance of a 'manifesto' as if sculpted in stone.

The point here is the speed of change and the likelihood that any statement, no matter how valid, may not be sustainable in a couple of years, when the next World Public Relations Forum is due to take place.

So, the fiercest criticisms, where intelligently thought out, actually became, according to the coordinator, pivotal in devising an ongoing and rewarding outreach programme[28] for the Global Alliance and its members: the Stockholm Accords would need to be revisited, reconceptualised, reformulated every two years, so that the global public relations community may look forward to an ongoing framework and a periodical brief for advocating its value to organisations and society to its stakeholders in every corner of the world.

Amongst the many comments and discussions it was somewhat surprising to register that none were related to the section dedicated to the evaluation and measurement of the effort.

This was surprising for at least two reasons:

(a) for many years now this issue has been at the top of the agenda of many of the more senior professionals and scholars but in this case attracted no comments;

(b) the whole 'brief' is clearly based on a paradigm which not only explicitly indicates in its very contents that public relations professionals need always to evaluate and measure the effectiveness of their activities but even more so, in the accompanying documents, they clearly spell out a suggested research approach to be applied by each adopter in the Accords' implementation process.

[28]This of course is only an idea of the coordinator which will require discussion and decision by the Global Alliance Board.

It is not easy to rationally explain this exclusion of the suggested before-and-after evaluation research from the discussion.

There are two possible options:

(a) the suggested research method is unclear, or was simply ignored by contributors as embarrassingly inconsistent;
(b) research is evidently not, as often claimed, a real priority for the profession, even at its highest levels of expression.

In the hope that the first option is the correct one, this author will now try to better explain the suggested method.

The method indicates that each would-be actor should keep in mind the following major performance indicators:

(a) the quality of the contents of the Accords and of its source (the actor);
(b) the relative dynamic of stakeholder perceptions of the profession compared to those of other management functions and professions;
(c) the growth in integration of public relations (or similar expressions) into management university curricula;
(d) the appointment of public relations professionals into organisational dominant coalitions;
(e) the improved portrayal of the profession in business and general mainstream and digital media.

The last three indicators mostly imply desk analysis comparing the situation in a given territory before and after the process and can be directly performed by the actor. The first three necessarily need an active listening, before and after, of samples of the selected stakeholder groups the actor decides to advocate during the process.

As for the quality of the contents, prevailing literature agrees that at least three sub-indicators may be used to assess the effectiveness of a given communicative content: the credibility of the source, the credibility of the content, the familiarity of the content.

As for the relevant dynamics of stakeholder perceptions of the profession, it seems relevant and coherent to the whole advocacy effort, to compare the dynamics of the reputation of public relations vis-á-vis other professions (legal, accounting, medical) as well as other management functions (human resources, marketing, finance).

If one imagines, for example, a professional association deciding to implement the Accords, it is important to:

(a) analyse the current levels of integration of public relations into management university curricula;
(b) identify the number of public relations practitioners belonging to the dominant coalitions within organisations (from private, public and social sectors);
(c) interpret the current portrayal of the profession in business and general mainstream and digital media;
(d) select, on the basis of the specific knowledge of its own territory, which of the six themes of the Accords can best be the subject of positive advocacy in a two-year period, and with which of the many potential stakeholder groups this effort is best to be directed through a conscious and planned advocacy programme.

As the prevailing mantra says, research *is* important and effective public relations *is* based on research.

According to the substance of the Stockholm Accords, listening to stakeholders before organisational decisions are taken is, by itself, a highly relevant part of communication, if only one stops to ponder the etymology of the term.

The contents

There are many underlying and (relatively new) themes in all Accords areas which require careful horizontal analysis.

1. The Accords acknowledge that the mere speed of organisational and societal change across the globe is such that no single conceptual framework may appropriately highlight how, when and where public relations brings more value to society and to organisations of all sorts, if not for a short time frame of less than 3 years. Then the situation will need to be revisited and adjourned accordingly.

2. The Accords acknowledge that research for any effective public relations programme is essential before, during and after. This has always been true, but now more than ever.

   Research also implies that any form of effective communication programme include listening as its structural component, which means gathering, understanding and interpreting overall and specific social, economic and political environments in which the organisation operates, as well as understanding, dialoguing with and interpreting expectancies of specific organisational stakeholder groups before management decisions are taken.

   From this perspective, listening therefore is a strategic skill for PR practitioners and communication in a continued alternation, when not in a full overlap, between listening and narrative.

   If listening is a strategic skill then it is urgent that both at a university level as well as in ongoing professional education, programmes supply specific competencies to enable professionals to learn how to listen at least as much as to learn how to narrate. Today the latter is dominant while the former is practically not-existent (except for research, where it is usually interpreted as a mostly technical tool).

3. The Accords acknowledge that the consolidated, linear, material, hierarchic and mostly shareholder-oriented organisational governance and management structure, although still very present in every corner of the world, is being increasingly contaminated by twenty-first-century paradigms such as the network society and fuzzy value networks, thus significantly modifying strategic planning processes used to identify and quantify the creation of value, such as the value chain, in large parts materially and linearly oriented. Fuzzy and immaterial value networks instead create value based on the quality of relationships amongst network members and amongst different networks.

4. The Accords acknowledge that every organisational function is increasingly involved and interested in improving skills and competencies in creating, developing and governing stakeholder relationships and therefore those public relations functions that enable, facilitate and supply knowledge and tools in this area of expertise, bring measurable added value to the coherence, enhancement and effectiveness of the organisation's licence to operate.

   The organisation that excels in this strategic contextual function, as well as in the more traditional strategic political function which supports the organisation's leadership in reinforcing reputation and stakeholder relationships, can be defined as a communicative organisation.

5. The Accords acknowledge that public relations brings substantial and measurable added value by supporting the organisation in its:

   (a) sustainability – interpreted as a transformational opportunity for the organisation to align and ensure its very existence with societal and stakeholder expectations;

   (b) governance – interpreted as a definite option for a stakeholder rather than a shareholder governance model that attributes to the board or elected officials the responsibility of defining stakeholder relationship policies on the basis of a situational selection of priorities;

(c) management – interpreted from the perspective that the time of implementation of a decision has become a strong indicator of the decision's quality, and can be significantly supported by a clear understanding of stakeholder and societal expectations before the decision is taken.

These are the three areas of the Accords which highlight the organisational and societal value of public relations.

6. In parallel, the Accords acknowledge that public relations directly contributes to the quality of:

(a) internal communication processes – interpreted as relevant to an ever-changing group of internal and boundary stakeholder groups;

(b) external communication processes – recognising that all forms of organisational capital can gain or suffer by the quality of communication processes between the organisation and its external stakeholders;

(c) the organisation, which is more than ever involved in aligning internal and external communication processes due to the increasing fading of the boundaries between the two.

The implementation

Following the six-month process to their approval through the adoption of the described global and collaborative effort, now comes the time of implementation of the brief, and this is of course at the moment unreportable.

But, there are many possible paths that actors (professionals, students, educators, associations, companies, consultancies) could follow.

Certainly the *least effective* is to simply 'translate' the text of the Accords and artificially integrate them into day-to-day practice.

The actors would certainly ensure more effective results by adopting a process that may look something like this:

(a) read, understand and interpret the contents;

(b) evaluate which may be more applicable to the specific stakeholder groups the specific actor believes to be more relevant to the achievement of the overall objectives of the brief which are, on one hand, to advocate the areas of organisational activities where public relations creates more value and, on the other hand, to improve the overall reputation of public relations vis-à-vis other professions and other management functions;

(c) create a content platform including arguments from the suggested references but also from other more specific references the actor will want to include, if deemed coherent with the overall contents;

(d) having selected the appropriate contents and the relevant stakeholder groups, engage in a direct research effort to establish a base from which to begin an implementation programme and to set specific objectives. This does not necessarily imply a major effort, but a serious one – yes!

For example, limited or no available resources might lead actors to random dialogue or telephone calls with stakeholders. This option may make sense, as long as it is a seriously thought out effort and not lip service or just nice to have. The best option is of course that the more scientifically sound the research effort, the more reliable the results. Yet, a non-implementation with the alibi that there are no resources to research, may well be worse than an effort based on necessarily insufficient research data;

(e) on the basis of the results of this initial research effort and the hypothetical (but realistic) adaptation of the contents, the actor develops and implements a consciously planned public relations programme including direct relationships, indirect output and dissemination via all relevant traditional and digital communication channels to develop relationships with selected stakeholder groups;

(f) towards the end of the two-year period of the exercise, the actor will want to implement a second control and final research effort along the same lines of the base one (as already described) and evaluate and measure the effectiveness of the effort;

(g) most importantly, from the very beginning, the actor will want to register on the Global Alliance dedicated digital space,[29] constantly reporting on implementation activities, reactions, experiences, successes and failures, so that all other actors may reciprocally benefit from their and their peers' efforts.

Task

Even more importantly, every individual reader of this chapter could volunteer to monitor what, if anything, their professional association is doing (or has done) to implement the Accords, volunteer to contribute to the effort, report to the hub on these activities and basically, move on to ensure that the public relations profession proves capable of gaining the reputation and licence to operate as its professionals deserve.

Question

Having read previous chapters, what would you consider to be the main concepts, or even selling points, for professional public relations practice?

REFERENCES

Amabile, T. M. (1996) *Creativity in Context*, Boulder: Westview Press

Antonovsky, A. (1987) *Unraveling the Mystery of Health – how People Manage Stress and Stay Well*, San Francisco: Jossey-Bass Publishers

Baagoe, H. and Hamrefors, S. (2006), *The Launch of 'Free Television'*, Stockholm: Swedish Public Relations Association

Cloninger, C. R., M.S. Dragan and T.R. Przybeck (1993) 'A psychobiological model of temperament and character', *Archives of General Psychiatry* 50: 975–90

Csíkszentmihályi, M. (1990) *Flow: the Psychology of Optimal Experience*, New York: Harper & Row

Hamrefors, S. (2002) *Den uppmärksamma organisationen*, Stockholm: Studentlitteratur

Ingvar, D. H. (1985) 'Memories of the future': an essay on the temporal organization of conscious awareness', *Human Neurobiology* 4: 127–36

Ingvar, D. H. (1991) *Tidspilen – Cerebrala essäer*, Stockholm: Alba

Landkvist, F. and S. Hamrefors (2006) *What is the Right Information to the Right Person at the Right Moment?* Stockholm: Swedish Public Relations Association

Marion, R. (1999) *The Edge of Organization: Chaos and Complexity Theories of Formal Social Systems*, Thousand Oaks, Cal: Sage Publishing

Nordblom, C. and S. Hamrefors (2007) *Communicative Leadership. Development of Middle Managers' Communication Skills at Volvo Group*, Stockholm: Swedish Public Relations Association

Normann, R. and R. Ramírez, (1993) 'From value chain to value constellation: designing interactive strategy', *Harvard Business Review* 71, July/August: 65–77.

Teigland, R. and S. Hamrefors (2005) *The Development of Communication Networks in Knowledge Intensive Companies*, Stockholm: Swedish Public Relations Association

---

[29]www.globalalliancepr.org

Conclusion

As for public relations itself, the thinking for the Accords, discussed in the last chapter, will not stop, and while some might disagree with parts of the contents, they are asked to put their concerns forward to further shape the emerging debate. It is the debate, as well as its findings, which it is hoped will raise awareness of public relations as a serious academic discipline and an important professional practice.

Reading this book might be part of a career development for you or the beginning of a new adventure, but if you are setting forth into the public relations profession it should definitely not be the last book you read. You might be studying for a CIPR award or involved in an undergraduate degree programme at university. Either way, this is the first small step on a tall and exciting ladder that can take you to the top, as a professional practitioner, to the Chartered Award or as an academic to a PhD and beyond. Start with the booklists given at the end of each chapter and take your interests forward through them and by joining the growing number of PR and communication conversations on the web.